Easy
Answers
for Great
Gardens

Easy Answers for Great Gardens

500 Tips, Techniques, & Outlandish Ideas

Marianne Binetti

SASQUATCH BOOKS
SEATTLE

Printed in Canada

Distributed in Canada by Raincoast Books, Ltd.

04 03 02 01 00   5 4 3 2 1

Cover design: Karen Schober

Interior design: Kate Basart

Cover photograph: Kim Zumwalt

Interior illustrations: Deborah Cooper

Copy editor: Kris Fulsaas

Library of Congress Cataloging in Publication Data

Binetti, Marianne, 1956—

      Easy answers for great gardens : 500 tips, techniques, and outlandish ideas / by

      Marianne Binetti.

            p.   cm.

      ISBN 1-57061-213-7 (alk. paper)

      1. Gardening—Miscellanea. I. Title.

      SB453.B534 2000

      635—dc21

Sasquatch Books

615 Second Avenue

Seattle, Washington 98104

(206) 467-4300

www.SasquatchBooks.com

books@SasquatchBooks.com

Dedicated to the gardeners who turn to my column

each week with their questions and suggestions, especially those

generous souls who contributed the tips, shortcuts, and

gardening goofs that appear in this book.

✎

Special thanks to the professors and research scientists

of Washington State University, and to my family

for their perennial support.

Contents

Introduction ix

ONE
Soil, Compost, Mulch, & Fertilizer
The easy answers to a great start 1

TWO
The Garden Setting
The easy answer to selecting, siting, and planting 13

THREE
Gardening in Pots
The easy answer for poor soil or drainage problems 19

FOUR
Annual Plants
The easy answer for fast, cheap color 37

FIVE
Bulbs & Tubers
The easy answer for fresh forms, dazzling color 51

SIX
Perennial Plants
The easy answer for diversity in your garden 65

SEVEN
Roses
The easy answer for color, fragrance, and beauty 87

EIGHT
Super Shrubs
The easy answer for beautiful bones 109

NINE
Trees
The easy answer for shade and structure 123

TEN
Ground Covers
The easy answer to too much space, too many weeds 137

ELEVEN
Vines
The easy answer for onward and upward growth 149

TWELVE
Lawns & Lawn Substitutes
The easy answer for showcasing plants 159

THIRTEEN
Pests & Weeds
The easy answers for winning the pest and weed wars 181

Index 199

Introduction

The easy answer for a great garden is to work smarter, not harder. The more you know, the better you'll grow. That's what *Easy Answers for Great Gardens* is all about— a collection of answers to the most-commonly asked questions about gardening, along with plenty of gardening tips, dirt cheap tips, gardening goofs, and out-landish ideas. *Easy Answers* was written with the help of hundreds of successful gardeners, and its unifying theme is that gardening should be a pleasure for the gardener, not a demand. Plenty of other gardening books offer more involved or time-consuming solutions to gardening problems. This book focuses on only the easy answers for more carefree landscapes.

Of course, the term "carefree gardening" is an oxymoron. If there weren't any maintenance to do in the garden, there would be no gardening. The goal of this book is to cut back on the gardening chores you really don't enjoy doing, be it weeding, watering, amending, spraying, or all of these. There is no room for guilt in the garden. Problems with plants and pests are a fact of life, not a personal failure. The longer a person gardens, the more plants he or she will kill—and learn from. Want to know the important difference between new gardeners and passionate, experienced gardeners? The new gardener discovers a dead plant and is filled with sadness and guilt. The experienced gardener discovers a dead plant and is filled with a bit of glee, because now there is an empty spot to try something new!

Over the past years, I've had the fun of answering thousands of gardening questions in a weekly newspaper column. I don't write these columns alone. Readers send in questions, so they write half the column for me each week. They are also quick to offer better answers if mine aren't so accurate or easy. These same readers respond immediately if a suggestion doesn't work or a shortcut has long-term detrimental effects. Gardeners are a passionate people and if someone doesn't like an answer I give, I hear about it. The nice thing is that a critical letter usually contains a helpful suggestion or another way to solve the problem. Sometimes these debates go on in the column for months, as more readers become involved with the issue or write in with their experiences. Throughout this book, in the side-bars called "Conflict & Controversy," I relate some of the more memorable contro-versies. Gardeners can have strong opinions, but that's part of the fun. Don't worry about which side of the debate you should be on. Remember that you have the right to ignore any gardening advice you don't like.

The questions chosen for the book were those that were asked the most often about the most common plants. Growing the right plant in the right place is the simple solution to avoiding many problems, so you'll find lists recommending certain plants for specific situations and also sidebars called "Easy Answers" that address various landscaping problems. You'll also find "Outlandish Ideas" sidebars, which were added to keep the fun and creativity in gardening. Some are whimsical, others rebellious, all are meant to inspire your creativity and remind you that we don't have to take gardening so seriously.

Sometimes the answers in this book won't be what you want to hear (who wants to be told to throw away a beloved but blight-infested lilac?). And sometimes the answer won't even be right. A proper diagnosis of a sickly plant should involve a house call, a careful interview, and a good guess. Gardening is an art, not a science, and each patch of earth is as unique as the person that tends it. So nobody can really predict what solution will work or know for certain what went wrong just from symptoms described on paper. Like doctors that practice medicine, horticulturists just make educated guesses, and then hope the prescription cures the patient. Sometimes the plant patient simply grows out of it, and many times this happens without any help from the treatment at all—but we consulting horticulturists are quick to take credit anyway. Gardeners consider miraculous recoveries to be payback from Mother Nature for all those times a perfectly healthy plant dies for no apparent reason.

My own two acres of gardens have been my best teacher and a fertile ground for experimentation and the composting of mistakes. But like most of you, running a home, raising a family, and meeting deadlines takes up most of my day. I fit gardening in when I can, which means all my plants must be able to be ignored for weeks at a time. My quest for the perfect garden ended years ago, when fresh out of college with a degree in horticulture and a new home to landscape, I attempted and failed to keep my entire garden beautifully weed- and pest-free, while at the same time trying out every new and interesting plant that hit the nurseries. Mother Nature laughed at my lofty goals of the perfect garden, and I soon realized I'd never win a war against such a powerful woman.

This book is written so that more gardeners can have grand dreams but realistic expectations. Go ahead and grow a rose garden if that's what you want, but have your eyes wide open about the routine maintenance certain roses require. I aim to keep my own garden presentable and ready to meet the public at a moment's notice, but I also want the freedom to continually try (and fail) with new plants and propagation techniques. This is why I use every landscaping tip, trick, and optical illusion described in this book, and am always looking for more. Maintenance for me is often a wild act of desperation performed when I have some free moments, rather than routine dedication to chores, scheduled and accomplished on time.

I am also wary of using too many pesticides and chemicals, being suspicious of products that tell me to cover my skin when applying them and wash my clothing afterward. So instead of telling you to apply a fungicide to control blight or fungal infection, I'll be more likely to suggest you dig out the plant. I don't have the time or inclination to mix up smelly poisons for three straight weeks and give a shrub its chemo treatment, so I figure you don't either. Wasteful? Maybe. But giving an ugly, sickly plant a death with dignity is more practical than taking expensive, heroic measures like repeated sprayings that may not work. I call this "throwing in the trowel" on a problem plant, or the "shovel solution" (or for large plants, "giving them the ax"). It's a quality of life issue—yours, not the plant's.

Plants are not children. When they act up, you can be harsh and even throw them away. There doesn't have to be a lifetime commitment. Remember the great thing about gardening: You get to bury all your mistakes, so dead plants aren't failures, they're just composting opportunities.

Whether you decide to just thumb through this book to laugh at the gardening goofs and outlandish ideas, to use the index to zero in on a pressing problem, to save money with the dirt cheap gardening tips, or to read it all from cover to cover as a garden primer, vow to worry about your garden less and enjoy your garden more. And above all, not to work too hard!

Chapter One
Soil, Compost, Mulch, & Fertilizer
The easy answers to a great start

There are a few basic questions that need to be answered to ensure that more plants live than die under your care. Beginning gardeners or experts trying to cut back on routine maintenance should remember that if you meet the demands of food, water, and shelter, your plants will grow forth and prosper. The trick is figuring out the unique needs of different plants and, if necessary, how to change your environment to meet those needs. ✄ Start with the soil. It's at the roots of every great garden.

SOIL

Q **I just moved into my first home. How do I know if I have good soil?**

A If by good soil you mean that your dirt will let you grow a wide variety of plants, then look for soil, or loam, that is dark in color—like chocolate cake—as opposed to khaki tan, clay gray, clay yellow, or clay red. Unlike clay, good loam drains well after a heavy rain (no small lakes after a storm), and unlike sandy soil, it holds moisture for several days after a good soaking.

Q **Can I just add lots of fertilizer to my lousy soil and grow great plants?**

A I wish. The plant roots need a comfy place to spread out, and so the texture and drainage of your soil is as important as how fertile it is. You can't offer plants a gourmet

Gardening Goof

"When I first moved into our home, I felt so unsure of myself when it came to the landscape that I did nothing—for five years my yard sat ugly and unplanted. Then I just decided to start doing! The more I did, the more I learned, and the more I wanted to know. Now I'm not afraid to try anything and I'm like a junkie for gardening information. I only wish I had dug in and started sooner."

buffet, but no place to settle down comfortably for the night. Soil with good texture is loose and friable, not hard-packed clay or sandy.

Q I intend to plant lots of new trees and shrubs. Do I need a soil test before I plant?

A Nope. The easy answer is to ignore all the soil test hype. If you live in an area with a lot of rain, like the Pacific Northwest, your soil is more likely to have a low pH, which is great for acid-loving plants like rhododendrons, azaleas, and native trees and shrubs. If you live in a dry area such as southern California or Arizona, your soil is more likely to be alkaline, or basic, which appeals to the drought-resistant native plants. Either way, you can add more organic matter to improve your soil, and then plant natives and what you see growing well in your area.

Q What is a soil test, and what if I flunk it?

A A soil test allows you to play mad scientist for an hour by buying a kit from the garden center and then following the instructions on the box. The process is only slightly more complicated than taking a home pregnancy test, but it does not involve any urine and watching the results develop is not nearly as riveting. Most tests tell you the pH, or acidity level, of your soil.

Q Why do I care about acid in my soil?

A The more you know about your soil, the easier it is to choose plants that like to grow in your yard. This makes gardening easier—the whole goal. Some plants, such as rhododendrons, azaleas, and camellias, like an acid soil with a low pH. Acid soil has a pH of 6.9 or lower. Other plants, such as lilacs, most grasses, and vegetables, do better in a more basic or neutral soil with a pH of 7. Most soils fall someplace in the middle of the pH range.

Q What else does the soil test tell me about my soil?

> ## Gardening Tip
>
> "Anyone with rocky soil needs a dry rock streambed snaking its way through the landscape. As your garden grows, so does the streambed. This way you're never more than a stone's throw from a place to get rid of the rocks you encounter when planting. A few larger boulders strategically placed in the bends of the stream will add a realistic look. Plant ornamental grasses and iris alongside the bed, maybe add a curving bridge, and you'll be happy for the rocks in your garden."

A That depends on the test. Some also test for the three major nutrients needed by plants: nitrogen, phosphorus, and potash (potassium). Scientists use a shorthand for these nutrients, calling them N, P, and K, respectively. (For more about these nutrients, see the Fertilizer section later in this chapter.)

COMPOST

Q What one thing can I do to improve my soil?

A Add organic matter—lots and lots of organic matter. Compost, grass clippings, fallen leaves, spent flowers, coffee grounds, manure, and other dead pieces of things that were once living are examples of organic matter. Layering on a foot of organic matter isn't too much to improve some poor soils, but adding a thin frosting just an inch or two deep also does a lot to improve the quality of the soil.

Q Where do I get all this organic matter?

A The easy answer is from your own compost pile. Experienced lazy gardeners just compost all yard waste in a corner of the yard and spread this on top of the soil once the matter has rotted.

Making your own compost to improve your soil can be easy. If you're just starting to build your soil, bring home three bales of peat moss or hay, and several sacks of steer manure. Dig a hole roughly the size of the bag of peat moss or bale of hay and save the soil in a pile. Arrange the peat moss or hay bales around the hole to form three walls. Now collect all your grass clippings, fallen leaves, spent flowers, and dead plants and pile these near your hole. Then build a green and brown lasagna using the soil you saved from digging the hole to layer between the green garden debris and the brown layers of peat moss and steer manure. Cover your pile with a final soil layer when it is several feet high. Keep the pile moist but not wet and just let it rot. In a few months, you'll have compost.

Q Adding all this organic stuff to the soil and making compost seems like a lot of work. Is it really necessary?

A Nope. You could just keep your lousy soil and have fewer choices of plants you can grow. Junipers and Johnny-jump-ups (a species of viola) are two plants I've seen thrive in dry, rocky, hard-packed soil. If you want more options and plant choices, invest a little energy into improving your soil. It is work that really pays off.

Q Do I have to dig all the organic matter into the soil?

A No. Digging is work. The easy answer is to just lay the compost, manure, or soil amendments on top of the soil you want to improve, and let the earthworms do the work. You need to be patient, however, as the worms turn the soil slowly. Organic matter shoveled on top of the soil in the fall should be mixed in by spring.

Q If I want to plant right away, but I have lousy soil and no compost—and no intention of building a compost pile—how do I get the organic matter into the soil?

A You can buy compost, peat moss, and steer manure in bags at a garden center. These are sometimes called soil amendments because you use them to amend the soil. Mix the peat moss and manure together in equal parts (a ratio of 1:1) and then work as much of this as you can afford into the top six inches of the soil—or just add the peat moss and manure mix to the places where you add plants. You can also purchase composted products in bags at garden centers. Whitney Farms compost and Cedar Grove compost are two examples.

Q What can I add to my soil to improve it besides steer manure and peat moss?

A There are a lot more options besides just peat moss and steer manure when you're looking for something organic to beef up the soil. Mushroom compost is a great alternative for roses, vegetables, and flowers but is too strong to use around rhododendrons and azaleas. Alfalfa pellets, often sold in bulk as rabbit food, are another high-nitrogen treat for your soil. You can buy chicken manure, "zoo doo," even bat guano to amend your soil, and they will all make a change for the better. Other soil

Gardening Tip

Although I have energy and endurance, I am a wimp at lifting anything heavy. If you're a wimp as well, ask the garden center to load the heavy soil amendments into your car, and when you arrive home, spread out a tarp and roll the bales of peat moss or bags of manure out of the car and onto the tarp. (So what if they split open?) Now drag the tarp to the lousy soil and roll the bales off. Slit open the plastic bags and encourage the contents to spill out. This avoids any lifting and saves your back.

amendments include the "ghoul brothers" (blood meal and bonemeal) and the "sea sisters" (kelp extract and seaweed). Always read and follow the instructions on the package label when amending the soil.

Q **What if my soil is sandy and dry and won't hold water?**

A The easy answer for changing soil from sandy to spongy is to add lots of organic matter over several years. Meanwhile, grow drought-resistant plants.

Q **What if my soil has a lot of clay and drains poorly?**

A Adding organic matter is the easy answer to loosening up hard clay soil. Both lime and gypsum are other soil additives that are also used to improve clay soils, but don't expect immediate results—it may take several years to loosen the tight particles that make up a clay soil. A new product called Claybusters offers the quickest improvement for hard-packed clay soil. These types of soil additives are sold in bags at garden centers (and compared to fertilizers, they're really cheap!). Meanwhile, grow plants that tolerate poor drainage.

Q **I have a large lot, and improving all my soil sounds like a lot of work. How can I avoid all the time and sweat of improving the soil in a huge yard?**

A Spot composting. Just improve your soil one spot at a time with organic matter and compost whenever and wherever you add a new plant.

Q **What if I don't have compost to add to the holes at planting time?**

A Resort to a shovelful of peat moss and a shovelful of steer manure, mixing this well into the planting hole and loosening all the surrounding soil as much as your muscles can handle.

Q What if my soil is lousy and I don't want to add organic matter or compost, but I still want to grow beautiful flowers and healthy vegetables?

A Gardening in pots or raised beds is the easy answer if you have lousy soil but want to start growing right away. Collect big pots and grow everything in containers of potting soil. Or build raised beds and fill them with wonderful topsoil or compost.

MULCH

Q What is a mulch?

A Mulch is a blanket or covering on top of the soil. It is used around plants to smother weeds, hold in water, regulate temperature, and make the yard look nice. Mulch is also used in pathways to keep the weeds down. The most common mulch in the Northwest is bark chips, but in other parts of the country you could also mulch or cover the bare soil with gravel, cocoa-bean hulls, sawdust, or pine needles. If you mulch around plants with sawdust, beware! Sawdust uses nitrogen as it breaks down, which means that plants mulched with sawdust won't get their share of this important nutrient and could show their distress by turning yellow. Add a high-nitrogen fertilizer or, better yet, mix sawdust with chicken manure if you use it around plants as a mulch.

Q What is the easy answer on which mulch to use around plants?

A Use what is most available. In the Northwest, this means bark chips. You can even have a load of bark delivered right to your yard and spread for you by a lawn maintenance company. Sometimes bark chips that are ground into very fine pieces are called bark dust. These smaller pieces do not block the weeds as well, but the finer bark does look nicer and it breaks down more quickly to improve your soil. You can also purchase bark chips mixed with manure or packed with added nutrients from sewage sludge. Many cities sell their cleaned and recycled sewage waste (called Milorganite) at true bargain prices. Big chunks of bark are best used around established trees and shrubs, where you just want to keep the weeds down. Remember that a layer of newspaper under any mulch deters even more weeds.

Dirt Cheap Tip

"I've given up coffee, but I still stop by the coffeehouse on a regular basis. I swing by to pick up the spent coffee grounds and then make beautiful compost with them. Using coffee in this way makes both me and the plants happy—and it doesn't stain my teeth!"

Weedless Garden Paths

There are some creative ways to mulch your pathways and win the war on weeds. Consider these weed blocks for use as inexpensive garden-path surfaces.

OLD CARPETS AND THROW RUGS: Don't throw them out—throw them down on the ground to smother your worst weeds. Sections of carpet laid between the rows of a vegetable garden or alongside a fence line and covered with a mulch of bark chips or gravel keep the weeds out for many years.

CARDBOARD: Thin cardboard from cereal boxes decomposes quickly, but thick cardboard from packing boxes lasts a long time if laid flat and covered with a pathway material of wood chips.

SAWDUST: If you have access to lots of sawdust, you can use it on top of newspapers in pathways. You won't have to worry about any sawdust robbing plants of nitrogen if you just stick to using sawdust only as a weed-blocking pathway material.

Dirt Cheap Tip

"Here's the easy answer to using up that old Christmas tree. Chop off the branches and lay them over your tender plants after Christmas, and the boughs will offer protection from the winter storms. This looks rather messy, but if you're a procrastinator it gives you another couple of months before you have to worry about brush disposal, and it may even save a few roses or tender perennials from frozen foliage."

Q What is the best mulch for improving my soil?

A Compost is the easy answer. Make lots of compost and spread it all around your plants every year.

Q But what if digging a hole in my soil is hard work? It is full of rocks and stones.

A The easy answer is to build raised beds. Otherwise, get a crowbar for large boulders and a pickax (not a shovel) for smaller stones, and wedge the stones out of the soil where you want to plant. You could always stack the stones to build walls and form raised beds (or create a dry streambed—see the Gardening Tip on page 2). Build up good soil on top of the rocky soil and your digging problems are over.

Use Raised Beds for Planting Without Digging

If you want to avoid digging into your stony, clayey, or hard-packed ground, build raised beds using landscape timbers, rocks, or bricks to form the sides of the beds.

Fill in the bed with topsoil you've purchased, or make your own great soil by mixing one-third peat moss, one-third steer manure, and one-third sandy soil. Add other soil amendments depending on what you want to grow.

Raised beds drain quickly and are the easy answer for low spots or hard-packed clay soil. Raised beds are easier for gardeners who have trouble bending over or kneeling. Raised beds are especially nice for vegetable gardens because the soil is never compacted by foot traffic, so root crops thrive in the soft, loose soil.

Raised planting beds with gently sloping sides are sometimes called "berms" of earth, and give any yard a professionally landscaped look.

FERTILIZER

Q Do I have to use fertilize?

A Nope. There are plenty of plants that do well without fertilizer. The more you mulch or improve your soil, the less you need to fertilize. Also, the deeper you can encourage your plants' roots to grow (by watering less often, but really soaking the soil when you do), the less you need to fertilize. Some plants in some soils will definitely need fertilizer.

Q What plants need fertilizer the most?

A Fast-growing plants with plenty of flowers are the hungriest, so roses, blooming annuals, and perennials need the most fertilizer. If you're willing to garden without these blooming spectacles and to grow only plants that like your soil, you can garden without adding any fertilizer—ever.

Nutrients and Numbers on a Fertilizer Label

Fertilizers you buy must be labeled with the ratios of the three major nutrients, nitrogen (N), phosphorus (P), and potassium (K). If a fertilizer has all three of the major nutrients, it is called a complete fertilizer. There are also six minor nutrients needed by plants, and sometimes these are in fertilizer as well. Minor nutrients include iron, zinc, and calcium. The NPK label tells you not only the nutrient percentage, but also the chemical source of the nutrient.

An easy answer to the fertilizer label mystery is to remember that the first number is nitrogen, which promotes green leaf growth, so on lawn foods the first number is the highest. On plant foods for flowers and fruits, the second and third numbers, phosphorus and potassium, may be higher than or equal to the nitrogen, such as 5-10-10 or 20-20-20.

The higher the numbers on the label, the stronger or more concentrated the fertilizer. A lawn food with nutrients derived from chemicals in a 20-6-12 ratio is more concentrated (and works faster) than a lawn food derived from an organic source of nutrients with a 3-1-1 ratio. However, the organic fertilizer will not burn or overdose the plants as easily and usually breaks down more slowly in the soil, providing a longer-lasting food source.

Q I never want to fertilize and my soil is decent. What should I plant?

A Trees, shrubs, and ground covers can survive in most soils without additional fertilizer if you choose varieties that are native or adaptive to your soil type. You will also have to learn to leave some fallen leaves and other organic debris over the winter to act as a natural mulch and nature's own fertilizer.

Gardening Tip

"I once read that if mushrooms were sprouting up, it could be that some foreign object was rotting beneath the soil, usually a leather glove or chunk of cedar. Well, I was curious about the persistent mushroom patch in our new yard, so I went digging. I found a leather collar still attached to the bones of a dog! Remind gardeners not to bury their pets with collars-or at least to bury them a few feet deep."

A Liquid Diet of Free Fertilizers

Giving your plants soup for supper is a quick and easy way to add nutrients to their drinking water. *Word of warning:* These are not balanced fertilizers (containing all three major nutrients—nitrogen, phosphorus, and potassium), so don't count on them as the only food for hungry plants like flowering annuals, perennials, and roses.

WATER FROM BOILING VEGETABLES: The unsalted water that was used to boil any type of vegetable can be cooled and used to water your plants. Remember, do not add salt to the water.

WATER FROM BOILING EGGS: The calcium in eggshells leaches into the water, supplying nutrients. Many African Violet growers swear by eggshell water to get their violets blooming again. Do not add salt to the water.

MANURE TEA: Your plants will love this tea party. Plunk a pile of horse or cow manure into a bucket of water and cover with a board and a rock—this is to keep the smell in and the flies out. Let the manure and water steep for a few days. Add a scoop of the dark brown liquid to your watering can and then dilute with more water until the solution is the color of weak tea. Use this manure tea for feeding all plants.

POTLUCK COMPOST-BUCKET STEW: Keep a bucket handy for collecting dead flower heads, weeds, and other garden debris. Add a little water and let the mixture sit. The water will turn brown from all the soil particles and rotting plants. Use this nutrient-rich liquid to water your plants.

Gardening Tip

"Here's how I made a great garden area without buying any topsoil. I just put sheets of newspaper on top of my lawn and bordered this with landscape timbers. Then I began layering grass clippings, leaves, and spent flowers in this new bed, building up the layers one foot deep over a summer and capping it all with a mulch of bark in the fall. The newspaper killed the grass below and then it decomposed, so when spring arrived, I dug into nothing but rich, black soil and my garden is looking great!"

Q What is the best type of fertilizer for the lazy gardener?

A There's no easy answer here. It depends on the gardener and the plants. If you want a lot of color, you need the quick action of a water-soluble fertilizer that can be mixed up in a hose-end sprayer or watering can and used on hungry roses, perennials, and annuals. Lots of blooms, lots of fertilizer. If you're satisfied with the natural look, then scattering a slow-release granular fertilizer around the roots of flowering shrubs in the spring should be enough feasting. If you're willing to work harder and not have to invest in commercial fertilizer, start a compost pile and spread finished compost a few inches deep as a mulch on the top of the soil around trees and shrubs. A compost mulch not only feeds the plants, but also blocks out weeds and seals in moisture.

Q How do I apply fertilizer?

A If a little bit is good, a lot is not better! Using too much fertilizer can burn the tips of the plants' foliage and show up as brown or black on the leaves. An overfertilized lawn looks black. Fertilizer burn is most common with concentrated chemical fertilizers, but fresh or "hot" manure also burns plants. It helps to water your plants before you fertilize. Thirsty plants suck up the moisture and fertilizer too quickly. This could cause fertilizer burn, or the plant's version of indigestion.

Chapter Two
The Garden Setting
The easy answer to selecting, siting, and planting

There's a lot more than just the soil and fertilizer to think about when you decide what to plant. Where the plant will be growing; how much sun, shade, and water it will receive; and how much space it will take up are other considerations that can add to the carefree beauty of a garden or create maintenance chaos. ❧ Actually getting the plants into the ground is another consideration, as this is usually the only time in a plant's life that you get a chance to prepare the soil where the roots will be growing and establish a good foundation for future growth. ❧ For a really great garden, put more time and thought into selecting the right plants for the right spot. Get them off to a good start, and you'll have the easy answer to less maintenance.

SELECTING

Q **I don't have a green thumb and don't know much about gardening. What should I plant?**

A The easy answer is to plant what would grow best in your soil and climate. This means you'll have to observe carefully what type of conditions you have (how much sun, moisture, wind, and space), and then grow what likes those conditions. Instead of planting roses just because you like roses, notice that you have shade and moist soil, and grow the ferns, mosses, and native woodland plants that will thrive in this situation.

The quickest way to finding the plants that will like your particular conditions is to visit a nearby nursery with experienced help, tell them your situation, and let them

Dirt Cheap Tip

"Mail in those post-cards found in gardening magazines so you'll start getting free mail-order catalogs sent to your home. The color catalogs are full of plant photographs and make great reference sources when you want to identify a mystery plant or get more growing information about a plant that you like."

recommend their favorite hardy plants. From these local recommendations, you can pick what you like the best.

Another recommendation is to notice what grows well in your neighbor's yard.

Q **There is a corner of our yard where the sprinkler won't reach, and each summer the lawn turns brown. The sun is hot, the soil is dry, and nothing seems to grow there.**

A Hot, dry sites are often the perfect place for a living Persian carpet of drought-resistant ground covers. Sedums, succulents, and thymes thrive even in poor, rocky soil, and the variety of textures and colors makes a lovely accent for any landscape.

Q **I would like some shrubs and flowers in the front of our home, but the western exposure means the hot afternoon sun just beats down and then reflects off the house wall to fry the plants. Any flowering plants for such a hot site?**

A Shrubby potentillas, dwarf barberries, spiraeas, and heat-tolerant flowers such as yarrow, sedum 'Autumn Joy', ivy geraniums, and zinnias are just a few that can handle the heat.

Q **We are gone for weeks at a time in the summer. How can I find out which plants won't need water?**

A Ask at the local nursery about drought-resistant plants. There are plenty of plants that can survive on rainfall alone no matter where you live. Many are natives to the area and naturally adaptive to your climate. You could also consider a drought-resistant lawn substitute, or an automated sprinkler system.

Q **How do I know what plants like sun and what plants like shade?**

A The easy answer is to read the plant label or ask at the nursery. Garden reference books are also quick

Gardening Tip

When you notice a healthy, happy plant in someone's yard or at a park, and would like to consider the same specimen for your own landscape, take note of where the plant is growing. Is it getting morning or afternoon sun? Is it out in an exposed location or in a more protected site close to the house? Is there a mulch around the roots? Try to find out what type of soil it is growing in and how fast it grows. Duplicating the conditions that grow a great-looking plant is the easy answer to giving a plant what it wants.

sources of this information. This sounds simple, but many new gardeners forget that they need this important information before making a decision about where to plant. One generalization (that means there are always exceptions) is that plants with large leaves (rhododendrons, hydrangeas, hostas) need less sun to do well than plants with small leaves (potentilla, herbs, sedums).

Q **What if my garden gets some sun and some shade depending on the time of year?**

A Great. This is the way most plants like it. It is the afternoon sun in the summer that destroys shade-loving plants. If a wall faces north or east and gets only morning sun, you can grow shade-loving plants. If the side of your house faces west or south and is shaded most of the day but gets the late, hot afternoon sun, you will need to plant heat-tolerant plants.

Easy Answers

Weaning Your Plants from Water Worries

❦ Plant the thirsty plants together so you'll have only one spot to water. Azaleas, begonias, lobelia, and fuchsias are the summer bloomers that insist on frequent drinks, so grow them as neighbors and keep a watering can sitting nearby to remind yourself to water often.

❦ Always use a mulch on top of the soil. A mulch not only keeps water trapped in the soil, it also shades the roots so they require less moisture.

❦ Add plenty of organic matter to your soil. It stores moisture when you water, so it is available later. (If adding organic matter to your soil is starting to sound repetitious, this is because it really does cut down on garden maintenance.)

❦ Provide shade from the hot afternoon sun. Shaded plants lose less moisture through evaporation. Use only drought-resistant plants such as sedums and succulents in the hot spots, keeping the cooler locations of the landscape available for thirsty plants.

SITING

(Q) I want to add a flower garden, but don't know where to begin when it comes to choosing the site. Where's the best place to start?

(A) Look for convenient pockets of space close to the house, right off the patio or alongside walkways and driveways. Think of these as "putter zones" where you can start small and slowly add more plants as you improve the soil and learn more about what you would like to grow. These close-by putter zones or small pocket gardens are especially helpful if you have a large yard or are just starting out and don't know where to begin. Keeping the putter-zone garden close to the house and right off a path, porch, or patio means you can meander outdoors in your slippers to check on the growing progress or tend to watering and other maintenance chores just by stepping outside the door.

(Q) What if after I plant I notice there is more sun or shade than I thought and the plants aren't doing well?

(A) Move any plants that don't grow happily. The easy answer to most plant problems is to put the right plant in the right place, so it can lead a healthy and independent life. Many an ugly or spoiled-rotten plant has been transformed into a hard-working specimen just by a simple move. The younger the plant, the easier it is to move, so don't wait.

(Q) What if I move my plant to a new spot and it still doesn't perform or demands a lot of care?

(A) The easy answer is the shovel treatment. Just dig it up and throw it away. Carefree gardening means not putting up with demanding plants. To harden your heart for the shovel treatment, remind yourself that there are plenty of well-behaved, independent-minded plants out there that would be happy to grow in your yard, if only you would get rid of the spoiled brats that you fuss over and adopt the good guys instead. Discovering what plants grow well for you is the lifetime work of the carefree gardener.

Gardening Tip

For smaller pot-bound annual or perennial plants, butterfly those root-balls. This means to split the root mass from the bottom halfway up the middle, and then spread the two sections apart like butterfly wings. Now they'll flutter on out to the surrounding soil and develop a stronger, more independent root system.

Q How can I tell if my plants are getting too much sun? Do plants get such a thing as sunburn?

A Yes! Sunburned plants may have pale or scorched-looking blotches on the leaves, sometimes with brown in the center of the yellow. Move sunburned plants to a more shaded location. Another option for newly planted specimens is to set up a screen or large umbrella for temporary protection from the sun during the afternoon. Over time, many plants (even shade-loving impatiens) will learn to adjust to more sun than they could handle when young or when first planted in the sunny site. Plants, like people, can build up a "tan" to handle more sun over time.

Q My plants grow as tall and leggy as a chorus line. There's lots of space between leaves as plants lean toward the right or flop over with weak stems. My yard is so dark and shady that nothing seems to grow.

A There are plenty of plants that will really think they have it made in your shade. Transplant the spindly, leggy, sun-loving shrubs to a brighter site or they'll never look happy. Choose shade-loving plants that grow luxuriant instead of leggy in those dark corners. Ferns, broad-leaved evergreens, woodland trees and shrubs, hostas, impatiens, begonias, and many others love the shade.

PLANTING

Q We have an older home and most of the plants are messy and overgrown, blocking the windows and spilling onto the pathways. We plan on replacing them with smaller, dwarf shrubs but don't know how close together we should be planting.

A It all depends on the mature size of the shrubs or flowers you will be planting, and how patient you are about waiting for small young plants to fill in. In general, leave open space at least three to four feet wide between shrubs, a foot between perennials, and six inches between annuals. Always consider dwarf, compact, and slow-growing shrubs for up close to the house.

Q How do I know how big a hole to dig when adding a new plant to the garden?

A A really good gardener will dig a hole twice as big as the roots of the new plant. A "good-enough" gardener will dig a hole just a few inches larger than the root spread, but really loosen up the soil in the bottom and sides of the hole.

Releasing the Roots Ruthlessly and with Relish

Plants that have been growing in their pots for too long may be root-bound, and they will not transplant well to the big world without a little help from you in inviting them to spread their roots. Massaging the root balls and gently teasing them apart is nice, but you can make quick and easy work of what is not a delicate task. Use a sharp knife and cut just partway into the root ball of a fibrous rooted plant as you rapidly turn the plant for a quick slice on all four sides. Azaleas, rhododendrons, ferns, and most perennials are examples of plants with a fibrous or dense root system.

Trees, shrubs, and roses with long, woody roots can be root pruned with a sharp ax much more quickly than with pruning shears. Cut off any long roots that are broken or soft and black. Spread apart the woody roots and dig a hole large enough to accommodate them. Releasing the roots is something to do with relish, not reservations.

Q After I add a plant, I see the leaves fold in or curl under, and the plant looks limp, lifeless, and weak.

A Droopy leaves could be a sign of extreme thirst. Dig into the top two inches of soil and see if it is dry below the surface. Always water deeply after planting so the soil is dark and moist all the way to the root zone. If you don't see improvement by the next morning, you may have a plant with a root problem instead of a drinking problem.

Warning: Plants that have been overwatered will have the same limp and lifeless look as those that are underwatered. (Their roots are rotting from too much moisture, so they can't absorb the water that is there.) This is why you need to check the soil with your finger before giving any limp or wilting plant more to drink.

Chapter Three
Gardening in Pots
The easy answer for poor soil or drainage problems

Let your garden go to pots! It's the easy answer for many problems including poor soil, lousy drainage, active kids, and digging dogs. ✿ *Container gardens are a great place for beginners to start setting down roots, because as long as you choose a pot with a drainage hole, use the right soil, and remember to feed and water, you've got an easy answer to successful gardening.* ✿ *Experienced gardeners ready to branch out into more adventurous container plant combinations can experiment with different types of plants in pots and unusual arrangements. See the Outlandish Ideas sidebars in this chapter if you need fresh inspiration for potted plants.* ✿ *You don't have to be an artist to create a wonderful window box or creative color combo for a container. Just think for a moment about the color of your home's exterior or patio furniture, and let some shades of inspiration seep in. Narrow down your color choices by aiming toward either a cool pastel palette— best for the shade—-or hot, vivid colors to brighten a sunny spot.*

Gardening Tip

"I enjoy cooking, and planted herbs in a large half barrel outside my kitchen door, but the mints and oregano were so aggressive that they took over all the space. Now I grow these aggressive herbs in gallon-size pots, and sink the pots into the soil of the half barrel planter. The rest of the barrel has soil for the slower-growing and dwarf herbs."

PLANTS

Q **What can I grow in pots besides just flowers?**

A The easy answer is you can grow anything in a pot that you can grow in the ground—even trees. But you'll need really big containers for really big plants.

Plant a Tea and Teacup Garden

STEP ONE: Hunt through your cupboards or at garage sales for broken teacups and saucers.

STEP TWO: Depending on how many cups and saucers you want to use, choose a window box or bowl-type container. Fill the container with soil.

STEP THREE: Arrange the teacups so that they lie on their sides, and add the saucers sticking up out of the soil. Hide broken or chipped parts of the pottery in the soil. Arrange the cups and saucers so they are partitioning the surface area of the container into different sections.

STEP FOUR: Plant "tea plants" into each section. Lemon balm, chamomile, and mint are some easy-to-grow tea-making plants that spread quickly, so they appreciate the dividing walls made from the cups and saucers to keep them in place.

STEP FIVE: For your tea garden harvests, start with two tablespoons of fresh herbs for each six-ounce cup of tea. Put the herb in a tea ball or just lay it in the bottom of a teapot and add boiling water. Let the herbs steep for about ten minutes. Now enjoy fresh herbal tea as you wander through the garden.

Q I am overwhelmed when I see all the choices. What flowers look best in pots?

A For the easy answer, see the sidebar "Winning Color Combinations for Containers," on page 22. These groupings win the award from garden club groups as the most memorable combinations.

Choose plants with different heights. This is especially important for window boxes. It looks nice to have some tall and spiky flowers near the back, medium full shapes in the middle, and hanging and draping vines in the front. Use this same idea when filling up pots, but keep the height in the center, and the draping vines on the sides.

Q What about choosing colors to mix in a pot?

A Anything goes when creating colorful containers, but to get a coordinated look, use the brightest color or biggest plant as your guide and choose complementing hues for the supporting players. A pink geranium with a tiny bit of lavender in the eye of the petal would suggest a deep purple or lavender petunia partner, and the white in the variegated leaves of the ivy dangling over the sides might inspire white alyssum as an accent flower in the same pot.

Q I want to match the flowers for my container gardens to the style of the container. What are the designer suggestions?

A In more rustic-looking wood window boxes or aged half-barrel planters, grow more casual-looking, sprawling flowers such as petunias, zinnias, and flowers with lots of different colors. A variety of colors and more floppy foliage make flowers appear more casual. In a classic urn-type pot or matching symmetrical window boxes flanking a front door, use more upright, formal flowers. Geraniums, evergreen or ivy topiary, and fibrous begonias are examples of flowers with a more structured, formal flair.

Another tip is to consider the color of the pot. Many wood and clay pots are neutral in color and go well with any plant color, but you may be inspired by the bright colors on a piece of Mexican pottery and fill it with orange and yellow marigolds. Or the soft colors of a recycled metal canister or old cooking pot used as a planter may inspire you to pick up the patina of age with rich shades of purple and gray.

Winning Color Combinations for Containers

Several years ago I took a strictly unscientific poll while researching plant combinations for carefree color. The question posed to several hundred garden club members, experienced and just budding, was this: "Think back over the past years and describe the most memorable flower combinations that you've ever seen planted in a container." These are the unforgettable color combinations nominated as gardeners' favorites.

FLOWER AND COLOR WINNERS FOR A SUNNY SITE:
Bright red geraniums, deep blue lobelia, white petunias; variegated trailing ivy as an accent. This is a patriotic tribute that looks playful and formal at the same time. Try it in window boxes in the front of a formal brick or white house, or in classic terra-cotta containers.

FLOWER AND COLOR WINNERS FOR A SHADY SITE:
Soft pink impatiens, light blue lobelia, white begonias; a touch of green foliage from feathery maidenhair fern or trailing variegated vinca. Cool pastels and white flowers look best in the shade, because they light up the darkness.

ALL-TIME FAVORITE COLOR COMBO: Sky blue and bright yellow is the grand prize winner if you don't know what to plant. Light blue pansies and clear yellow tuberous begonias for the shade; forget-me-nots and yellow tulips in a spring planter; baby blue ageratum and yellow marigolds for the sun. The summer look of bright yellow sunshine against a clear blue sky must be the inspiration that made so many gardeners remember this classic blue-and-yellow color scheme.

Gardening Tip

You can put fragrance where you'll enjoy it the most—right on your deck or patio—if you choose fragrant plants for your outdoor sitting areas. A pot of sweetly scented flowers next to the front door is also a memorable way to welcome guests—because nothing evokes nostalgic memories like a sentimental scent.

Q How many plants should I try to grow in a pot?

A The more the merrier when it comes to creating overflowing color. Just remember that plant-packed containers need more water and fertilizing. Go ahead and crowd lots of plants into a pot. Ignore the spacing suggestions that you would use if the flowers were planted in the ground.

Q Is it okay to grow vegetables and herbs in the same pots as flowers?

A Yes! Mixing edibles and ornamentals is perfectly all right as long as you remember not to use any harmful pesticides on any of the plants. The ruffled leaves of lettuce look especially attractive edging a container garden, or add beans to a teepee or tomatoes to a trellis in a large pot of flowers.

Q What are the best vegetables for growing in a pot on a sunny balcony?

A Small cherry or patio tomatoes make colorful and bountiful container plants, and hanging baskets of everbearing strawberries are also an edible treat. For a drought- and heat-tolerant combo, mix the colorful foliage of sun-loving herbs, such as sage, rosemary, and basil. Remember that herbs do not need as much fertilizer as blooming flowers.

Fragrant Flowers for Containers: Patio Partners with Great Scents

SUMMER LILIES (SUCH AS ORIENTAL LILIES AND THE MADONNA LILY): The huge blooms have an exotic scent. The 'Stargazer' Oriental lily rebloomed for several years in a pot that I left undisturbed on my protected patio. The bulb was planted in the bottom third of a large pot, so each year I was able to add annual flowers to the top layer of soil. Once the lily faded, I snipped off the flowers and let the foliage die back naturally so it could make blooms for the following year.

ENGLISH LAVENDER (*Lavandula angustifolia*): Mix English lavender with other herbs or plants that like sun and dry soil conditions. The stiff, spiky growth form of this aromatic plant makes it perfect for the center of a mixed planting on a sunny patio.

SWEET ALYSSUM (*Lobularia maritima*): This sweet-scented low grower blooms in white, purple, and lavender, and reseeds easily. Use it along the edges of pots. It can also be used peeking out of the pockets of a strawberry jar, an urn-shaped pot with openings in the sides for planting.

FLOWERING TOBACCO (*Nicotiana alata***):** The white form is most fragrant, especially at night. It's tall enough to use in the center of large containers with upright annuals such as geraniums along the sides to keep it from flopping over.

GARDENIA (*Gardenia jasminoides***):** This fragrant favorite can be left outdoors in mild climates; otherwise, overwinter it as a houseplant. It's wonderful as a formal specimen sitting on the patio.

SNAPDRAGONS (*Antirrhinum***):** Their scent is fresh and cinnamon-spicy but not overpowering. Their upright form makes them great for the center of a large container; dwarf forms are good for smaller pots.

FRAGRANT TUBEROUS BEGONIAS: These are new, hybridized hanging plants that have the delectable scent of fresh fruit. Blooming in deep shade with the colors and scents of apricots, lemons, and nectarines, the tubers can be lifted in cold climates and repotted each spring. If your deck or patio is shaded or north facing, this is the flower for you.

HERBS: For quick snips and whiffs of herbal inspiration, plant starts of basil, thyme, fennel, and oregano into a strawberry pot or clay container with well-drained, gritty soil (add sand to potting soil). Keep this pot in a sunny site right outside the kitchen door.

CONTAINERS

Q How big a pot do I need to grow flowers?

A For carefree gardening, stay away from small pots. They dry out too fast and need more fertilizer. Pots at least a foot wide, or that hold one cubic foot of potting soil, are best.

Q What about clay vs. wood or ceramic pots?

A For the least amount of maintenance and longest life of your pots, choose neither wood nor clay pots. Use the lightweight fiberglass, plastic, or resin pots because these don't dry out as fast or crack like clay, and can sit out all winter without rotting like wood. You can find nice-looking, very lightweight resin pots on the market that really do look like clay or cement. If you really want to make an investment in classic garden containers, consider cement, concrete, or iron urns.

Frugal but Stylish Painted Pots

Here's a common dilemma. New home owners spend all their extra money on painting and repairing the new house. Then they are left with little money, but an urge to decorate the outside spaces. They're also left with plenty of empty paint cans.

STEP ONE: Grab three metal paint cans, poke drainage holes in the bottom with a hammer and nail, and cover the outside of each can with white butcher paper or oilcloth, or just remove the paint label and paint the metal cans white.

STEP TWO: Now drip a bit of paint down the sides of this white background using vivid primary colors or the trim colors that you used on your house. Be sure you use a color that you can match flowers to.

STEP THREE: Visit the nursery and buy three types of flowers in the colors that closely match the paint that is dripping down the white paint cans. Plant one type of flower in one color in its matching can. (Don't forget to use potting soil.) Put bright yellow marigolds in a can trimmed with yellow paint spills, red geraniums in the red-trimmed can, and have deep-blue lobelia spilling from the can with blue splattered paint.

Play up the painting theme even more by using a wooden ladder on your deck or patio to display the potted plants on different levels. You can even hang these recycled cans from hooks using the convenient wire handle on the paint can. Use paintbrushes and hand tools as accents to hang from hooks, on a wooden ladder or set them on the steps of an aluminum ladder. You'll have a colorful, casual, and contemporary garden with the honest look of a work in progress.

Using paint-dripped cans and a shiny metal ladder to add height and drama to an outdoor space is also a "metro chic" look for condos and city loft areas—especially for adventurous gardeners who don't take themselves, or climbing any social ladder, seriously.

Harvest from a Kitchen Chair or Plant a Flower Seat

Plant a chair garden to elevate your plants closer to eye level and accent a patio or planting bed.

STEP ONE: Remove the seat from a metal chair, wooden press-back chair, caned chair, or piece of outdoor furniture.

STEP TWO: Use chicken wire or wire mesh to make a sagging seat for the chair. Secure the sides of the mesh to the frame of the chair seat with wire or staples.

STEP THREE: Line the planting area with moss, covering all the wire mechanics on the sides of the chair. You can also wrap the entire chair with moss, with the help of a glue gun and clear fishing line.

STEP FOUR: Fill the moss-lined seat with soil and plants. You could choose just one type of ground cover to make a living chair cushion, or lay sod on top or plant grass seed to make a "Lawn Chair." Tie a pair of scissors to the chair with raffia ribbon to encourage hand mowing. If edible thymes and herbs, such as dwarf oregano and basil, are used, it can be a "Kitchen Chair." Mint plants creep and take over gardens; put your mint in a chair garden to keep it easy to harvest but under control. If the planting area of the seat is shallow, there won't be much room for the roots to grow; choose shallow-rooted, forgiving ground-cover plants such as succulents, thymes, and mosses.

Matching Container Gardens to Your House's Architecture

The type of container you choose determines the style or look of your potted gardens, and it's fun to match the type of pot to the style of your home.

CAPE COD, COUNTRY, OR COTTAGE STYLE HOUSE: Recycled objects such as wagons, wheelbarrows, and baskets make charming containers for casual flowers such as daisies, lobelia, and cosmos.

CLASSIC COLONIAL, BUNGALOW, OR TRADITIONAL BRICK STYLE HOUSE: Rolled-rim terra-cotta pots are the classic containers for any style of home, and look great with the clean lines of a traditional home. Dwarf evergreen shrubs neatly clipped into geometric shapes, or ivy topiaries, are the most formal, but you can use the classic red, white, and blue color scheme or blue and yellow flowers to add more color while staying formal. Urns and other containers that sit up high are also great matches for traditional homes.

CONTEMPORARY, MODERN, OR ANGULAR STYLE HOUSE: Sleek and even shiny pots in vivid colors or plain white add zing to contemporary architecture. Stand chimney flues or cement culvert pipes up on end for a modern-looking pedestal you can fill with soil and plants. For a clean, contemporary look, try growing one kind of flower in one color in one pot. Place next to this a second and third pot with complementary colors of the same flower or a different type of flower. For example, imagine a pot of pink wax begonias, a second pot of lavender petunias, and a third container of deep blue verbena sitting in the corner of a patio. Each planter holds only one type and color of flower, but together the trio makes a colorful composition.

Gardening Tip

"I've had a terrible time keeping my small clay pots watered, but they came with a wall planter that I love, so I have to use the small pots. Then I discovered that if I lined the clay pots with a plastic bag (with drainage holes, of course), the soil would stay moist for days longer, saving me from the chore of daily watering."

Q I'm a scavenger. Can I reuse old pots I find at tag sales?

A Certainly! Don't skimp on the potting soil, but the pot can be old, ugly, recycled, or reclaimed. I've never felt it was necessary to sterilize or disinfect old pots with bleach or heat. Just wash them out well to get rid of any stowaway fungus or bugs.

Q I want to group a collection of pots together on my patio, but want to avoid the disorganized hodgepodge look.

A Group pots in clusters of three or five for a casual look. Line pots up in a row for a more formal look. Space them evenly along the edge of the patio to make an enclosure or serve as outdoor walls to a garden room. Stagger the heights by using overturned pots or crates as pedestals and risers to give your pot collection more depth.

Q I have a lovely decorative urn that I like to use as a planter, but I don't want to plant directly into the urn itself. Can I use a pot within a pot?

A Sure. Use a smaller plastic pot inside a large decorative pot that you would like to protect, and grow your plants in the smaller pot. Use overturned plastic pots or a block of wood inside the large pot to raise the level of the smaller planting pot so it is just below the rim of the decorative urn. Hide the exposed rim of the planting pot with moss or bark mulch. This is especially convenient for spring bulbs or other seasonal flowers that you will be replacing throughout the year. You can easily change the inner pot for seasonal color.

Dirt Cheap Tip

Recycle, reuse, and reinvent the potted garden. Anything that can be drilled for drainage and hold soil is fair game for using as a container garden. Consider these items for interesting pots: a kitchen colander, a child's wagon, a rusty wheelbarrow, chimney flues and cement culvert pipes stood up on end, baskets lined with plastic garbage bags (poke holes with a sharp knife), wooden or bright plastic milk carton storage crates, metal washtubs, large tins from olive oil or industrial-size cans of tomatoes (leave on the colorful labels—great for growing herbs), and metal bike baskets— still attached to the bike and lined with moss.

Recycle Pots for Towers of Flower Power

Recycle old pots by stacking three different sizes of pots and planting in each one.

STEP ONE: Take a large, bowl-type pot, at least sixteen inches wide, and place a plastic four-inch pot inside of it, upside down and off to the side. This four-inch pot will be hidden under soil and used to support the next pot, which will go in at an angle. Fill the bowl with soil, leaving a depression in the middle.

STEP TWO: Set a second, medium-size pot (this one could be broken, cracked, or chipped) partway on its side, so that it leans at an angle on the top of the overturned four-inch support pot. Fill partway with soil.

STEP THREE: Place the third, smallest pot into the soil of the medium-size pot. It can be lying partway on its side or standing upright.

STEP FOUR: Plant this leaning tower of pots with tough perennials and drought-resistant annuals. The smallest pot won't have much room for soil and root growth, so it is important that the last plant on top be drought tolerant. A dwarf ornamental grass or hen and chickens (*Sempervivum*) would work well.

A trio of pots in a tower makes a great way to grow a collection of succulents and thymes for carefree gardening. Use pea gravel as a mulch and don't overwater. Tiny rock-garden plants such as dwarf dianthus, Lewisia, and saxifrage do well in small clay pots that have been set as accents into larger pots. For cascading color, use drought-tolerant foliage plants such as a dwarf licorice, lobelia, and petunias in the large and medium pots, and a geranium in the smallest pot on top.

STEP FIVE: For a rustic finishing touch, use broken pottery or even cracked teacups and chipped plates to fill in and add color to your leaning tower of planted pots. For a less rustic variation on the theme, use three unbroken clay pots, one large, one medium, and one small. Fill the largest pot three-quarters full with soil, and stack the medium pot inside. Use an overturned pot inside the largest pot to support the medium pot, if necessary. Now fill the medium pot three-quarters full with soil and stack the smallest pot inside. You now have a stacked and contemporary-looking "tower" of pots, and can add more soil around the sides and plant flowers in the soil of each one.

STEP SIX: To maintain your tower, do not fertilize or water sedums as you would a container garden of blooming annuals, because you want to keep these plants stunted and dwarfed to appreciate the stacked pots. Many succulents can survive on rainfall alone. Water from the top pot first, as drainage from the top will water the medium pot and then trickle down to the largest pot. After watering the top pot, wait an hour and feel the soil in the bottom pot. If it is moist, you won't need to water the medium or large pot.

Q **I have a collection of cracked, broken, and chipped clay pots that I can't bear to throw away. What ideas will put them to work in my landscape?**

A A garden of ruins is the easy answer here. Lay broken half pots on their side in a garden bed. Plant low-growing flowers or ground covers just inside the cave that is formed by the pot, to give the appearance of a pot tipped over with plants spilling onto the ground. Repeat, using two more pots that range from large to small—it will look like a tower of pots that has toppled over with the garden blooming among the ruins. For more broken pot ideas, see the Outlandish Ideas sidebar "Putting Pot Shards to Use," on page 31.

> ## Gardening Tip
>
> "Wire tomato cages make a great cone-shaped topiary form if they're used upside down with a finial, or decorative accent, on top. Gather together the wire legs of the tomato cage that stick up into the air and poke them into the finial or top piece. Iron finials that are hollow are available at some garden shops; wooden finials used as post toppers or for Victorian trim can be found at lumber stores. I've also used a small clay or decorative flower pot turned upside down with modeling clay in the bottom for a finial. Into sports? A baseball, tennis ball, or golf ball can be drilled with three holes and used as your topiary top knot."

Putting Pot Shards to Use

Here are some unusual ways to recycle broken pots.

❧ Make a pot graveyard. Collect broken pots and pieces of pottery and arrange in a gravel-covered area: Add succulents, low-growing ground covers, or an unusual specimen plant to oversee the collection of retired pottery, smashed pots, and fragments.

❧ Use small broken pieces of pots as pathway material. Put your cracked clay pots in a bag and hit it with a hammer to break them into tiny pieces. Add these to accent your gravel pathways or use to decorate homemade stepping-stones.

❧ Use pot shards (large pieces of broken pottery) as plant labels. Use a waterproof felt-tip marker or grease pencil to write plant names on the pottery pieces, and arrange them so they poke up out of the soil at the base of the plants.

❧ Use chipped and cracked clay pots to lure and trap slugs and bugs. Moist clay pots laid on their sides and hidden behind a plant or shrub will collect the bugs you don't want in the garden. Check the inside of the pots often and dispose of any garden enemies.

SOIL

Q Can I use the soil from my garden beds in my pots?

A No! Potting soils need to be lightweight and drain well or you'll have potted disaster. You can make and amend your own potting soil, but please don't just scoop up dirt from the ground and use this in your pots. Using poor soil in your pots is the quickest route to container gardening failure.

Q What type of potting soil should I use?

A A lightweight mix using peat moss as a base is my personal favorite, but I've also had good luck with organic-based potting soils that contain composted bark along with perlite to lighten it up for air circulation. If I'm growing perennials or potted shrubs, I add some of my own compost to purchased potting soils.

Q So a good potting soil would have perlite? What is perlite?

A Perlite, found in many good brands of potting soil, is the small white chunks that you can squish between your fingers. Perlite is air-filled volcanic rock that helps potting soil have better drainage and air exchange, and keeps it light.

Q Can I make my own potting soil?

A Yes, and making your own is worth it if you have a lot of pots to fill. You do need to make a lot of potting soil to justify the expense of gathering all the materials. If you're just going to plant a few pots, then even a frugal gardener is better off buying potting soil on sale, or asking at a greenhouse if you can buy some of their potting soil in bulk.

Q What if I don't have compost to add to my potting soil?

A At most garden centers, you can purchase compost that is weed free and great for pumping up potting soils. Whitney Farms and Cedar Grove are two companies that sell bagged compost. Compost adds a richness to any potting soil, and can even help cut back on fungal diseases. Add at least a handful of compost to any potted plant for improved vigor. We now know that compost added to the soil, even if you fertilize your potted plants, is like an immunization shot against disease.

Q I hate to waste. Can I reuse my potting soil from year to year?

A Yes, if it is not too full of roots. Mix in fresh potting soil or fresh peat moss and perlite, because over winter the soil will have compacted. Mixing in some fresh soil adds the pockets of air that roots need. Used or recycled potting soils also need fertilizer, because the plants previously growing in them will have sucked out most of the nutrients.

Q Should I add compost to the potting soils for herbs, sedums, and succulents?

A No. These plants need extra-quick draining soil and do better in a lean mix without compost. Add an extra scoop of sand to increase the drainage. These plants also prefer clay pots over water-retentive plastic or lightweight resin containers.

> *Gardening Tip*
>
> **Recipe for Mix-It-Yourself Potting Soil:** Mix until well blended five parts peat moss, five parts perlite, and two parts composted steer manure or good compost. Add one cup granulated organic plant food for each cubic yard of potting soil you make.

Q **I often run out of potting soil before I run out of pots I want to fill with plants. Is there some way I can stretch my potting soil to make it go farther?**

A Yes, it's the gardener's version of watering down the soup. Supplement your purchased potting soil with amendments you might already have. Empty your bag of potting soil into your wheelbarrow or onto a tarp spread on the ground. Now add a few shovelfuls of purchased, composted steer manure, peat moss, fine ground bark, or some screened compost from your garden. Add an extra scoop of sand or perlite if you're growing sun-loving plants that need perfect drainage, and an extra shovelful of leaf mold (half-decayed leaves) if you're growing shade-loving annuals that like their soil moist. Supplementing your potting soil with compost, peat moss, and sand is a good trick if you're running out of potting soil but have just a few more pots to fill and don't want to stop what you're doing to run out to buy more potting soil.

Q **I notice that if I use some of my own compost to supplement potting soil, I have to deal with bugs in my pots of flowers. How can I debug my potting soil?**

A Earwigs, sowbugs, and tiny slugs are a few of the scavengers that feed on composting soil and that can multiply rapidly in a pot and start to nibble on your plants. You can debug your pots with a piece of potato. A cut potato wedge will attract the scavengers at night and can be removed from the pot in the morning and tossed back into the compost pile. It may take several potato lures over the season to keep the stowaways under control, but most of the compost bugs would rather eat decaying plant material than the fresh new growth of your potted plants.

Top-Drawer Idea to Display Blooming or Potted Plants

Everyone needs more storage for garden supplies, but not everyone has the room for a garden shed. Convert a nightstand or chest of drawers into garden storage using these shortcuts. This converted nightstand is best sitting on a covered porch or patio where it is protected from the weather and conveniently puts your most frequently used supplies right outside the door. It also provides a place to put blooming color where it won't be overlooked. You'll wonder how you ever got by without the convenience and character of your new gardening chest.

Gardening Goof

"I have window boxes that I fill with ivy geraniums every year, and the first year they looked spectacular. The second year they did just okay, and the third year they barely bloomed at all, even though I fertilized. Finally I changed the potting soil. The improvement was amazing! Now I replace at least half the soil with fresh potting soil and compost in each window box every spring."

STEP ONE: If the wood surface is in poor shape, you can spray-paint it with enamel or exterior house paint—bright flower colors (yellow, violet, or blue) work especially well to draw attention to this outlandish piece of outdoor furniture, but if you're more subdued, match it to the color of your house. Now's your chance to get creative with stencils or paint. Border the drawer fronts with painted vines, or paint each drawer a different color.

STEP TWO: Secure the lowest drawer that you will want to plant in so it is halfway open, using a nail or screw to keep the drawer partway open.

Add garden-theme novelty knobs to replace old drawer pulls. Nature-inspired knobs are available at home centers in the shape of leaves, twigs, or insects. To make inexpensive garden-theme drawer pulls, visit a craft store for miniature hand tools. Drill a hole through the wooden handle of each tool and insert the screw from the original drawer pull. Or use full-size hand tools with wooden handles that can be drilled in two places and screwed across the front of a large chest of drawers.

STEP THREE: Line the drawers with colorful squares of waterproof oilcloth. You can also use inexpensive waterproof tablecloths cut into sections. Let some of the fabric spill out over the sides of the open bottom drawers that you will be planting.

STEP FOUR: Set potted, blooming plants inside the partway open planting drawer, and hide the pots with moss if you wish. Use the other drawers for storing garden seeds, fertilizer, and hand tools.

STEP FIVE: Use a nail to attach a wooden clothespin to the side of the chest. Clip your garden gloves here so they can dry between wearing. Add additional nails or cup hooks to the side of the chest for hanging hand tools or balls of twine. Set a waterproof place mat on top of the chest and use it for additional storage of pots or as a display surface for more potted plants.

Gardening Goof

I used to recommend using "ghost poo," or those Styrofoam packing peanuts, in the bottom of pots because they serve as lightweight drainage material. Now I've found that they are too hard to collect when it comes time to empty the pot and add the old potting soil to the compost pile. The Styrofoam peanuts not only won't compost, but they blow all over the yard if you spill them. Small overturned or squished plastic pots make a neater drainage material for filling space in the bottom of large pots.

Q I have these huge pots for growing flowers, but it takes a lot of soil to fill them up. If I'm just going to plant annual flowers that die at the end of summer, do I really need to fill the pots all the way with soil?

A No. As long as you provide six to eight inches of soil for the roots of your annuals, you can fill the bottom half of deep pots with drainage material to save on the expense of buying so much soil.

One way to take up space is to recycle the plastic pots that the plants come in by turning them upside down inside your larger pots. Even the six-packs used for bedding plants can be squished and used for drainage fodder in the bottom of a large pot.

Chapter Four
Annual Plants
The easy answer for fast, cheap color

Buying a few marigolds or impatiens and slipping them into pots or planting them into the ground for "color spots" is the way most beginning gardeners start to grow and begin to set roots into this fascinating adventure we call gardening. ❧ Annual plants are also the least expensive way to dip into designing a garden because often you can buy a plastic six-pack of young annuals for less than a dollar. Easy to find for sale at garden centers, nurseries, even grocery store parking lots, popular annuals such as impatiens and petunias sometimes are sold dirt cheap as a loss leader to get you inside the store doors. ❧ If you're already an annual fanatic and know all about the colorful antics and growing demands of annual flowers, skip to later in the chapter and check out the sidebars. ❧ If you're just getting started and want to be able to buy some flowers from the garden center and keep them alive and blooming all summer, then this is a good place for you to begin your gardening lessons.

Gardening Goof

When choosing annual plants, bigger does not always mean better, and a plant in bloom isn't necessarily better than one still in the young foliage stage. One year I planted petunias side by side, and the big, tall, already blooming petunias pouted when planted, but the short, fat, bushy young plants adjusted more quickly and had more blooms all summer long.

SELECTING & SITING

Q I'm a beginning gardener. When I go to buy plants from the garden center, there are two sections of flowers—perennials and annuals. What's the difference?

A The life span. Any plant that dies (when it's not your fault) before the year is over is an annual, as opposed to a perennial plant that returns each spring. An easy way to remember the difference is that *annuals must be planted annually,* or every year.

Annuals are mostly flowering plants, but also plants with really colorful foliage. The most common annuals are flowers such as petunias, marigolds, lobelia, and impatiens. Annuals are plants that live life in the fast lane. They grow fast and bloom fast and are constantly trying to set seed and "sow their wild oats." These playboys of the plant world demand lots of extra food and water to support their intense, party-centered lifestyle.

In warmer climates, some plants that would be considered annuals, such as geraniums, are more like perennials in that they can survive the winter and rebloom for a second summer.

Q **I like to garden, but wouldn't think of bedding down with my flowers. Why are annuals sometimes called bedding plants?**

A They didn't get the name from sharing the sheets, but because flowering annual plants were originally used for "bedding out" or setting into formal groupings to make beds or blocks of color. This was very popular during Victorian times, when labor was cheap and estate gardens grew their own annual flowers from seed in their own greenhouses—tended by their own gardeners—to make intricate flower-bed designs. Today the term "bedding plants" also includes flowering annual plants that would go into pots and hanging baskets.

Q **So if annual flowers live only one season, do perennial flowers live forever?**

A Wouldn't that be nice! Perennials are plants (mostly herbaceous, or nonwoody) that live through the winter and then restart and grow again the following year—unless rain, ice, or pests kill them.

Dirt Cheap Tip

Make your own seed tape for planting evenly spaced rows of annuals or vegetables. Cut strips of paper towels and make a thin paste of flour and water. Dip a paintbrush into the flour paste and pick up a seed, then touch the paper strip; be sure to space the seeds evenly. Dry the strips on the back of a chair or on a rack, and then roll them up and store until spring, when you can plant the seed tape right in the ground.

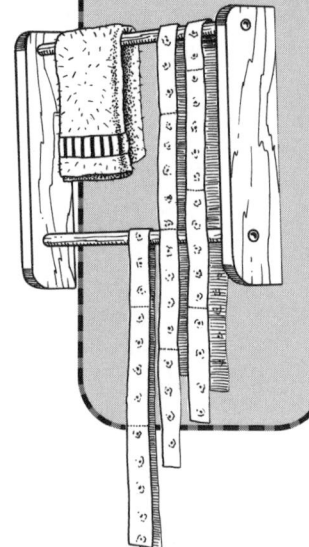

Grow Your Own from Seed, Snips, or Cuttings

Lots of annuals are easy to grow from seeds or cuttings that you save over the winter. Nasturtiums, alyssum, and lobelia are three that may even reseed themselves in your garden.

❧ To collect seed from your poppies or other annuals you'd like to replant, place a brown paper bag over the spent flower and shake the dried seeds into the bag. Label and store in paper envelopes over the winter, and toss on the ground in spring.

❧ Snip and pinch the tops of coleus, impatiens, and licorice plants at the beginning of the growing season. This not only makes them branch out and get bushier, but these pinching crumbs are easy to root in a glass of water or in soft soil. Now you have more plants!

❧ Take cuttings from your geranium plants and root them the easy way in blocks of Oasis or green florists foam. Snip off a top branch about four inches tall, remove the lowest leaves from the stem, and insert into a two-inch square of moist Oasis. Repot into soil when new roots show. You can save your geraniums indoors over the winter, then take cuttings from the winter-weary plants in early spring.

Q Why not always grow perennials so you don't have to keep buying annual flowers each spring?

A Because perennials are more conservative, blooming for a few weeks or so and then conserving their resources to make it through the winter, much like the hard-working but boring ant in Aesop's fable. The more enthusiastic and colorful annuals get all dressed up and party all summer long with continuous blooms and "look at me" personalities. Annuals are the grasshoppers that run out of reserves by winter and freeze to death, but before they go, what a show! Perennials can't match the excitement of annuals for continuous color.

Q When I go to buy flowers, all the rows of plants are overwhelming. How do I know whether I am buying annuals or perennials?

A The easy answer is to just ask. If you shop in a garden center, they usually place all the annuals in one area and the perennials in another. The annuals are often more cold sensitive and available in late spring, while perennials may show up early and be available for planting all summer. Annuals are also cheaper!

Perennials are usually sold one plant per pot, while annuals come in six-packs or plastic containers divided into cells or sections so you get more than one plant for the same price.

Easy Answers

Which Annuals Grow Best Where

Here is a quick guide to figuring out which popular annuals would grow best in which areas of your garden.

LOCATION: Sun, in a pot with potting soil and fertilizer.

EASY FLOWERS: Geraniums, marigolds, alyssum.

LOCATION: Morning sun or shade, in a pot with potting soil (remember to water and feed).

EASY FLOWERS: Impatiens, begonias, lobelia.

LOCATION: In the ground, full sun, good soil (protect from slugs and fertilize).

EASY FLOWERS: Petunias (they spread!), zinnias, snapdragons.

LOCATION: In the ground, morning sun or deep shade, good soil that has been loosened well and amended with peat moss or compost.

EASY FLOWERS: Impatiens, wax begonias, lobelia, pansies.

LOCATION: Poor soil, full sun (loosen and remove rocks, water when really dry).

EASY FLOWERS: Nasturtiums, California poppies, alyssum (can plant from seed).

LOCATION: Poor, dry soil, shade (found under trees with large roots or under roof overhangs).

EASY FLOWERS: None. Use pots in this area to grow shade-loving annual flowers, or work on improving the soil and plant flowering ground covers instead.

CARE

Q Once I plant my annual flowers, how do I keep them happy and blooming all summer?

A Feeding, weeding, watering, and deadheading (removing spent blossoms) are the maintenance demands of annual plants that shower you with blooms all summer long. Since annuals live only one year, they do demand care to keep up the constant and intense bloom cycle that makes them so popular with color-hungry gardeners.

Q How often should I fertilize my annual flowers?

A The easy answer is to fertilize annuals often. If you grow annual flowers in pots and you use a fertilizer that mixes with water, you may need to fertilize as often as every two weeks depending on how much you dilute the fertilizer. The best advice is to read and follow the label directions.

Q But I'm so busy in the summer, I often forget when I fertilized last!

A Slow-release fertilizers are the easy answer for forgetful gardeners. These are plant foods you work into your soil at the beginning of the season and that slowly release nutrients all summer long. Osmocote is the trade name of a slow-release plant food you mix into the soil. It looks like tiny round pearls. You could also use slow-release organic plant foods or improve your soil with so much compost and additives that even the annual flowers won't need additional plant food—now that's a great gardening goal! Another idea? Mark the times to fertilize right on your calendar.

Q There are so many fertilizer choices out there that I'm overwhelmed! What fertilizer do you recommend for my potted annuals?

A For annual flowers in pots, something that you can mix in the water will get to the plants the fastest. A fertilizer with all the major nutrients and micronutrients is best, as potting soils rarely contain much food for the plants. Look for brand names such as Rapid Grow, Miracle-Gro, and Peter's Professional Plant Food, or ask at the greenhouse or nursery where you buy your plants for the name of the fertilizer they use.

Organic vs. Synthetic Fertilizers

If you're new to gardening, you probably don't realize that fertilizers come from two different sources, but that the end result, or what the plant uses and needs, comes out the same. Organic plant foods get their nutrients from things that once were living or are by-products of living things. Organic fertilizers are made from blood meal, cottonseed meal, and other organic materials like manures.

Synthetic or "chemical" fertilizers get these same nutrients from nonliving sources manufactured from nonliving products. Ammonia and urea are examples of chemical sources of nitrogen. Nitrogen is one of the major nutrients needed by plants. In an organic plant food, the nitrogen may come from chicken manure, while the nitrogen from a synthetic/chemical fertilizer might come from ammonium, but to the plant, nitrogen is just nitrogen no matter where it came from.

So what are the folks from the "organic" camp so excited about? Organic plant foods improve the soil over time, making it more able to support plant life without any additional handouts. The nitrogen from the chemical ammonia is quickly used up by the plant (which is why synthetic plant foods show such fast results), while the nitrogen from chicken manure is released more slowly and helps to feed and nourish the millions of tiny organisms that make up the soil and make it alive and fertile. Organic plant foods add lots of other mysterious additives that just help the soil to grow better plants.

Think of synthetic fertilizers as fast food from McDonald's—efficient and filling, even addictive, but not something that is good for you if that's all you eat. Organic fertilizers are like health foods—not as glamorous, no instant gratification, but the building blocks for a long and healthy life.

You can live a balanced life and grow a healthy garden and still use both types of plant foods. Actually, potted annuals live for such a short time that I don't mind that they become chemically dependent on shots of commercial fertilizer for the summer. If it gives 'em a rush and keeps them in the party mood for blooming, I put up with their dependency. But flowers growing directly in the soil—now that's a different story.

Q What type of fertilizer should I use to grow the flowers I put into the ground?

A Annuals or bedding plants in the ground are still big-time feeders. You should spend some time improving the soil by adding manure, compost, and additives such as blood meal and bonemeal, or work granular fertilizer into the soil before you even plant. Or you could fertilize for the first year or so with synthetic or chemical plant foods until you've improved your soil with organics to the point where it is fertile enough to support lots of flowers all on its own.

Reminder: Always water before and after you fertilize so that the plant won't be burned by fertilizer indigestion. This happens when thirsty plants suck in the fertilizer and water too quickly.

Q I have too much area and too many pots to fertilize using a watering can. My hands and shoulders are no longer as strong as they once were. What is the easy answer to fertilizing a large collection of potted flowers?

A The quickest and easiest way is to use a hose-end sprayer that you screw on to the end of your hose. The fertilizer and some water goes into the jar, and the water from the hose mixes with this concentrated fertilizer to feed and water your plants at the same time.

Q I planted a flower garden with geraniums, lobelia, and petunias, and prepared the soil well with lots of granular fertilizer put into the holes before adding the plants. Now the leaves of all the flowers are black on the tips! The geraniums have a dry, brown margin around the foliage. What went wrong?

A I smell fertilizer burn. Too much fertilizer burns the margins of the leaves, and newly planted annuals are the most susceptible to fertilizer burn because they are just getting their root systems settled in. (How would you like to be force-fed a heavy meal after major surgery?) Always follow the label directions about fertilizer, and instead of adding granular fertilizer to the bottom of the planting hole, mix it into the surrounding soil.

The easy answer if you've overfed? Flush the soil with lots of water to dilute the fertilizer. Chances are your plants will recover.

Q How do I keep my flowers looking great all summer? Mine seem to fade and get leggy by August.

A Pinch, deadhead, feed, and water.

Deadheading Keeps Annuals Rockin'

Deadheading is not the same as being a fan of rock and roll. It is a term for removing the spent flowers from annuals so that they won't think the deed of reproducing is done and the party is over, and then go to seed.

Deadheading does the same things to plants that Viagra does to humans. It extends the time that plants stay in a virile or reproductive stage. By deadheading you can keep your marigolds and geraniums blooming recklessly and trying to reproduce until late summer. That's well into their 80s in plant years.

Pinching is a type of light pruning in which you use the pinching fingers to just snip out any long and lanky growth, which keeps your annual flowers compact, bushy, and blooming. Petunias are prime candidates for a good pinch. The pinched "crumbs" from petunias make great cut flowers.

Fertilizing gives annual flowers the energy and enthusiasm to keep up the party pace. Fertilizer, like the energizer bunny, keeps annual plants going and going. Follow the instructions on the label, and don't think that just because a little is good, a lot is better.

Q What if I just can't remember to deadhead and pinch my flowers or don't have the time?

A Choose carefree annuals that shed spent flowers themselves and don't need deadheading. These include wax begonias, impatiens, alyssum, ageratum, nicotiana, and lobelia.

SPECIAL EFFECTS

Q What can I plant in a narrow bed that is only one foot wide and located alongside a pathway, leaving little room for flowers?

A Use low, mounding annuals such as impatiens, fibrous begonias, lobelia, and sweet alyssum. *Bonus:* None of these polite plants need deadheading!

Q I have a retaining wall near the patio that is in full sun, with just a bit of planting space at the top. I'd like to hide and soften the wall with flowers.

A Cascading annual flowers to the rescue! If the soil is really poor, use nasturtiums and portulaca; if it's halfway decent, plant trailing petunias, ivy geraniums, and hanging lobelia. A cover-up and color too!

Return to Victorian Bedding-Out:
Cookie Cutter Annual Gardens

Why not display your annual "bedding" plants in heart-shaped, crescent, or sun-shaped beds? Just outline the shape of the bed on the lawn using string or a hose to get the size that you want, and cut away the sod. Improve and loosen the soil, and choose a color theme to echo the simple cookie-cutter shape.

PINK AND RED SWEETHEART FLOWER BED: Trim this heart-shaped bed with low-growing red impatiens, add pink fibrous begonias to form the middle layer, and in the center display red, white, and pink geraniums.

YELLOW AND ORANGE SUNSHINE FLOWER BED: Cut a circle into the lawn with rays extending out. Use short "Teddy Bear" sunflowers or hot orange African marigolds in the center, and fill the "rays" with the sunset colors from zinnias, calendulas, and dwarf marigolds. Of course, these flowers love to bloom in full sun.

CRESCENT MOON BED OF SILVER AND LAVENDER: A crescent sliver cut from the lawn is an easy way to grow a gray and lavender theme garden. Plants with gray foliage are drought- and insect-resistant, so this garden won't demand all your days and nights. Use the silver foliage of Dusty Miller in the center and lavender ageratum to fill the middle layer, and edge the moon with the bright white of low-growing lobelia or alyssum.

Q I want to grow flowers with a tropical or vacation resort look around my patio. I'm really not the pastel petunia type of gardener. What should I plant?

A You want annual flowers with a tropical punch. Go wild, get the tropical jungle look, and do something different with your container gardens and hanging baskets. Use bright annuals that banish the boredom with hot colors, vivid foliage, and growth that moves in a samba rhythm. (See the sidebar "Tropical Punch in Pots on the Patio" for ideas.)

Easy Answers

Tropical Punch in Pots on the Patio

These annuals have bright colors, bold foliage, and the enthusiastic growth that adds a jungle look.

'TERRACE LIME' SWEET POTATO VINE (*Ipomoea batatas*): Call the color chartreuse or lime green, who needs flowers when the foliage glows this bright? They should sell sunglasses with this one. The large leaves spill over pots and trail from baskets on this heat-tolerant vining annual.

'OUTBACK SUNSET' (*Lysimachia congestiflora*): The foliage is yellow and green, and the bell-shaped golden flowers toll loudly with even more color. The growth habit is trailing but tidy, and the colors as loud as a Hawaiian print shirt.

'PARROT'S BEAK' LOTUS VINE (*Lotus berthelotti*): The silvery gray foliage is a great contrast with the other tropical-looking annuals, but once this draping plant begins to bloom, you can almost hear the squawking from the jungle parrots. The flowers are a bright red-and-orange mix, and this sun-lover blooms heavily if the nights are cool.

Add a Lick of Licorice for Carefree Color Accents

Helichrysum petiolare is a great plant with an awful name. That's why the common name licorice plant has added to its popularity. These furry-leafed, branching-foliage plants are shade tolerant, drought resistant, pest resistant, and disease resistant—and never need deadheading because they don't flower. Wonderful for mixing with bright-colored foliage and flowering plants in baskets or pots, they appreciate a good pinch if they grow out of control, and the pinching "crumbs" root easily in any soft soil.

'LEMON LICORICE': Velvet softness will make you want to cuddle up and pet these lovely golden leaves, but this fast-growing, branching plant wastes no time taking over, so you'll want to pinch while you pet or use it as a ground cover. 'Lemon Licorice' really shines when paired with dark purple or burgundy foliage plants.

'LICORICE SPLASH': More compact and not as wild growing, its foliage is a soft, furry gray with even splashes of creamy white—excellent when paired with warm colors.

'DWARF LICORICE': Solid gray leaves with the lovely velvet look and a very compact growth habit make it a great pot mate.

Q We are renting and don't want to invest a lot of money in permanent plants, but want to screen the neighbor's yard with some pretty flowers—that grow quick!

A Jack had the right idea when he planted the bean stalk, because there is an annual vine called scarlet runner bean that runs, not walks, right up the side of a trellis or string offered as a support system. Vining nasturtium, sweet peas, cardinal climber, and morning glory are other fast-growing annual vines that you can plant from seed. And there are always sunflowers—a row of seeds sown in May will grow into a temporary wall of flowers by August.

Q I work long hours during the day and want to enjoy my flowers when sitting on my patio on summer nights.

A Liven up the nightlife by planting pink, white, and silver annuals. Dusty Miller has silver leaves that reflect the moonlight, and white alyssum is fragrant as well as fabulous looking when moonstruck. Nicotiana, or flowering tobacco, is another annual that comes in a pure white form that scents and brightens the evening air.

Plant Fragrant Annuals for More Sensual Nights

Plant these fragrant flowers right outside a bedroom window. Summer nights with the windows open and a sweet scent wafting through the air . . . need I say more to lure you into planting these scent-ual annual flowers?

DIANTHUS: Also called Sweet William, this is an old-fashioned annual that is also grown as a perennial in mild climates. The flowers bloom in tidy round nosegays just perfect for burying your nose in.

PURPLE PETUNIAS: Not all petunias have a scent, but the blue or purple varieties are the most fragrant.

SNAPDRAGONS: This is another tough flower that may return the following spring. The knee-high snaps are easier to grow because they won't need staking.

SWEET ALYSSUM: This low-growing, self-seeding annual even blooms in gravel that covers hard-packed earth and sprouts in the cracks of sidewalks and patios. I let it grow wild in between the brick pavers of my courtyard so I can enjoy the sweet scent all summer. Like many flowers, the plain white varieties have the most fragrance.

PROBLEMS

Q I bought two dozen marigold plants, planted them outside in the ground, and then woke in horror the next morning to find all 24 plants blackened and curled. What went wrong?

A Overnight damage that severe sounds like frost burn. Cold nights can surprise gardeners in the spring

Gardening Goof

The middle of May is usually the frost-free date in our area, and I eagerly planted colorful coleus in the garden. The next morning they looked like they had melted: the leaves had fallen from the stems. It's not just frost that kills some annuals, but cool night temperatures, which can shock plants that haven't been hardened off or allowed to get used to the cold.

and are especially hard on tender, heat-loving annuals such as coleus, zinnias, and marigolds. Next time, harden off your newly purchased annuals by letting them spend a few nights on a covered porch or patio before introducing them to the cold, cruel world.

Q **How am I supposed to harden off my annual flowers or get them used to the cold outdoors when I don't have a covered porch or patio to use as a halfway house? I usually don't have time to cart around flats of moist and dirty plants each morning and evening in my good work clothes.**

A Use a wagon or wheelbarrow to store your newly purchased tender plants. Wheel them into the garage or shed at night for protection from the cold, and take them out to the sun during the day. After a week they should be tough enough to go into the ground.

Q **My lovely lobelia and impatiens are being eaten alive! Each morning more and more of the plants have missing parts. I do see some slight trails of slime. Is this slugs?**

A Slugs or snails consider soft and succulent new growth (like young annual plants) a gourmet feast, and they will travel clear across barren patios and climb the steps of decks to get to your flowers. Always protect newly planted annuals with slug bait or beer traps or by handpicking the slimy creatures at night. (For more slug help, see Chapter Thirteen, "Pests & Weeds.")

Gardening Tip

Keep some old sheets handy if the evening news predicts a cold front on the night you just finished planting your annual flowers into the ground. Toss the sheets over the tender young things the first few nights and remove the covering in the morning. You can call this your blanket insurance coverage.

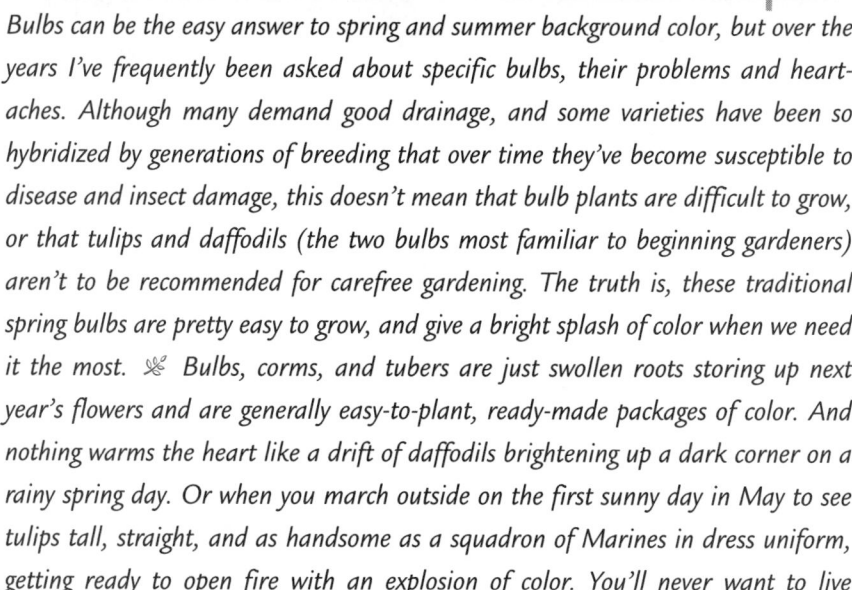

Chapter Five
Bulbs & Tubers
The easy answer for fresh forms, dazzling color

Bulbs can be the easy answer to spring and summer background color, but over the years I've frequently been asked about specific bulbs, their problems and heart-aches. Although many demand good drainage, and some varieties have been so hybridized by generations of breeding that over time they've become susceptible to disease and insect damage, this doesn't mean that bulb plants are difficult to grow, or that tulips and daffodils (the two bulbs most familiar to beginning gardeners) aren't to be recommended for carefree gardening. The truth is, these traditional spring bulbs are pretty easy to grow, and give a bright splash of color when we need it the most. ✺ Bulbs, corms, and tubers are just swollen roots storing up next year's flowers and are generally easy-to-plant, ready-made packages of color. And nothing warms the heart like a drift of daffodils brightening up a dark corner on a rainy spring day. Or when you march outside on the first sunny day in May to see tulips tall, straight, and as handsome as a squadron of Marines in dress uniform, getting ready to open fire with an explosion of color. You'll never want to live another spring without cheerful daffodils and proud tulips socializing in and protecting your garden. ✺ The best part about planting bulbs is that the flower is already formed—all curled up and waiting to sprout forth as soon as the chill of winter (or a fake chilling period in the fridge) unlocks the door of development, letting loose the troops. ✺ For color and cut flowers that last well into the summer, consider tubers such as dahlias, gladiolus, tuberous begonias, and lilies. These may demand more work than tulips and daffodils, but the rewards make them worth it. Lovely, luscious lilies are currently the flowers with which I am most smitten.

Gardening Tip

"I plant my tall gladiolus bulbs in a circle around clumps of Shasta daisy. The glads come up through the daisy blooms and add color without looking so stiff and formal."

SELECTING

Q I bought some bargain-priced tulip bulbs by mail. The bulbs seemed very small, and when spring arrived, they sent up only green leaves and no flowers. How do I avoid this disappointment?

A This is the question I'm asked most often about small bulbs. Buying bulbs at a bargain price is no bargain if they're too young to bloom. Read the fine print before you order. Make sure you're buying bulbs large enough to bloom the first year. When it comes to tulip and daffodil bulbs, size does matter.

Q I planted 100 bulbs that I purchased through a mail-order catalog for only a penny each. They were guaranteed to grow. When spring came, lots of thin green leaves came up, but only five or six flowers. What did I do wrong?

A The easy answer: You didn't spend enough money. Bargain bulbs are often cheap because they are so small, and often too young and immature to make a flower. If you just ignore the bloomless bulbs and let the green leaves die back naturally this spring, they could mature another year in your garden and bloom for you the second spring. They were guaranteed to grow, not to bloom. Sometimes such a company may even advertise "guaranteed to bloom"—meaning not all 100, but at least one bloom. To avoid disappointment and for less work digging and planting, spend that same amount of money on a smaller number of full-size bulbs, or hand-pick the largest bulbs from the open bulb bins at your garden center. You won't have 100 blooming bulbs, but the bulbs you plant will have huge, beautiful blooms for a better return on the energy you invested.

Dirt Cheap Tip

In the mild Pacific Northwest where I garden, you can buy and plant bulbs as late as December (at a major discount) and still enjoy blooms the following spring. You may not get the varieties you want, however, and in open bins, bulb colors and varieties will have been accidentally mixed together so you can't be sure what you're buying. I consider this part of the delight. Plant a dozen red tulips, and one pink blooms after all the rest. A little grace note from Mother Nature, just to remind you she doesn't like us gardeners controlling everything.

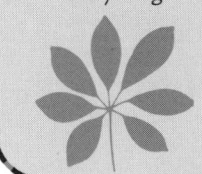

Tulips That Live for Years: Loyal Little Dwarfs

All species tulips, or the *greigii* type, will naturalize or come back in bigger colonies if you can give them the sun and well-drained soil they crave. These tulips actually do better in rocky, summer-dry soil than they do in the rich, moist, fertile soil most other flowers love. They are closer genetically to the wild tulips that thrive in the mountains of Turkey. Some to consider include:

'LILAC WONDER': This tulip has a yellow center and pastel lavender petals on a six- to eight-inch stem.

'TARDA': Plant one bulb, get three or four yellow and white blooms, each on a five-inch stem.

'RED RIDING HOOD': Bright red flowers and a surprise bonus—the leaves have lovely red and green stripes.

'TULIP TORONTO': This multiflowering tulip has purple mottled foliage eight to ten inches high.

Q Does this mean you should never buy bulbs on sale at bargain prices?

A No, don't confuse small, immature bulbs (usually sold in bulk by mail) with sale-priced bulbs you'll find at the end of the season at your local nursery or garden center. The real bargain bulbs are these large, healthy bulbs that go on sale in late autumn just to move them out before winter sets in. The only thing wrong with them is that they're taking up space in a retail store that could be used for selling Christmas wares.

Q What are the bulbs that spread naturally and bloom dependably year after year?

A Grow with the "timesaving triplets"—small, dependable bulbs such as lily-of-the-valley, windflowers (*Anemone blanda*), and species crocus. These three return in larger drifts year after year, are easy to plant because you don't have to dig such deep holes, and together give months of cheerful spring color from early to late spring. As an added bonus (as if all this wasn't enough), the foliage on these three is polite and nonfloppy, and won't make a mess in the landscape that is as obvious as the traditional tulips and daffodils.

Q What are the easiest tulips to grow?

A The easy answer to easy tulips is to think short. Rock garden tulips, species tulips, dwarf tulips, and any tulip less than a foot tall will bloom early in the spring when you're the most hungry for color, and also have shorter leaves that will fade quietly into the background after the blossoms are done. (See the sidebar "Tulips That Live for Years: Loyal Little Dwarfs" on page 53 for names of easy-to-grow tulips.) *Reminder to beginning gardeners:* Leave the foliage from tulips and other bulbs alone after the flowers fade if you want them to make more flowers for next year.

Q In my yard, dark shade from tall trees makes a spring burst of color difficult.

A Plant scilla or wood hyacinths for colonies of bell-shaped flowers in blues, pinks, and whites. These bloom even in deep shade, and scilla should win the award for least-demanding bulbous bloomer.

Q My spring-blooming bulbs provide great short-term color. But what can I plant so I have color accents and cut flowers that continue throughout the summer?

A Spring-blooming bulbs are what readers of my weekly newspaper column write in to ask about the most, but summer-blooming bulbs are the real easy answer to great color accents. Why replant annuals every year or fuss with perennials that need dividing and pruning when you can plant a lily bulb and enjoy fragrant cut flowers for as long as you have your garden? Easy-to-grow summer-blooming bulbs (or tubers, a type of bulb) include dahlias, gladiolus, tuberous begonias, and lilies.

Q Lilies—though tempting—seem too extravagant and demanding for my simple garden. What do you think?

A I, too, used to think that lilies were too stiff and formal to grow in my carefree garden. Their stems were tall and bare and ugly after blooming, and if they weren't staked, their heavy flower heads might fall over in a rainstorm. But they would bloom in partial shade, year after year, and wouldn't demand lots of fertilizer. And their fragrance would waft through the summer air to lure me closer and seal my fate forever as a lily lover. Yes, Lily has won me over. My garden now sprouts forth with different varieties of this regal queen of the bulbs from June until August, and our relationship is going well. Sometimes I do have to set a wire tomato cage around the huge orientals to keep them from flopping over, and the lower-growing

Asiatics need some spring protection from the slugs, but these small acts of maintenance are rewarded with great appreciation when the huge buds break open and the glory of growing lilies fills the summer air.

Q **I'd like to grow dahlias, gladiolus, or begonias for summer color, but they seem like too much work. Are they worth the effort for us lazy gardeners?**

A For many flower lovers, digging and storing winter tender bulbs *is* worth the effort (although there is a easier way—see the sidebar "No-Dig Dahlias" on page 64). Gardeners with a lot of shade will enjoy tuberous begonias and find them worth bringing in and storing each winter, because the bulbs increase in size year after year. Bring on the bulbs and take on the tubers; they can be an easy answer to a more colorful and carefree landscape.

Q **Dry shade under my fir trees makes it difficult for any flower to live, and in winter—although I appreciate the evergreen boughs—I am also hungry for some color!**

A Plant a colony of hardy cyclamen with dainty pink flowers and heart-shaped leaves for a natural woodsy look. The species *Cyclamen coum* blooms in dry shade in winter or very early spring, just when you need flowers the most.

Q **I'm a snowbird and go south for most of the winter and spring, so I miss out on the traditional spring bulb display. I enjoy my home garden the most in summer and fall.**

A Forget about daffodils and tulips; plant summer-blooming lilies and glads, and autumn-blooming crocus (*Colchicum*) and hardy *Cyclamen neapolitanum*. Fall is a fresh new season in the garden, and late-blooming bulbs can make it seem like spring.

Q **The mature blooming shrubs in my garden have low branches, and there's not enough room under the overhang for tall tulip and daffodil bulbs.**

A *Anemone blanda*, or windflowers, hug the ground with daisylike purple and blue blooms, and the foliage is ferny and subtle. These bulbs return in large clumps over the years. Crocus, grape hyacinths, and hardy cyclamen are other options for low growing bulbs.

Q **Can I grow bulbs in pots?**

A Of course! Summer bulbs are especially good for container gardens, as they pop up through other companion flowers in the same pot.

CONTAINERS

Q If I add lilies to a pot, how do I make sure they will come back each year?

A To keep a loyal lily coming back each year, you must make sure she doesn't rot or freeze in the winter. I put the pot under the eaves of the house in the fall so it won't be flooded with winter rains. In our mild climate of the Pacific Northwest, the rain rots these bulbs more often than a hard freeze kills them. You may want to rip out the annuals that share the pot and replace the top six inches of potting soil before adding more flowers in the spring. Don't disturb the bottom few inches of soil where the dormant lily bulb rests.

Outlandish Ideas

Potted Surprises

Blooming spring bulbs in containers are a glorious sight, and can make an impressive welcome at the front door. The problem is that spring bulbs have a short bloom time, and by summer the fading foliage and spent flowers do not a pretty picture make. Here are several ways to have your bulbs and tidy container gardens too.

BURIED ALIVE SURPRISE! Bury a few tulips and daffodils in the bottom of your pot, and then plant a perennial ground cover such as ajuga or thyme on top. The bulbs will push up through the ground cover and look wonderful—but after they bloom, you can replace parts of the ground cover with great-looking, chunky geraniums or large marigolds arranged around the dying stems of bulbs to hide them from view.

POTS WITHIN A POT SURPRISE! Fill a large container with potting soil, but as you near the top, set a six-inch plastic pot into the soil so it is buried just up to its rim but still empty. Now buy potted tulips or daffodils at the garden center or florist that are in the same-size six-inch pot, and set this blooming pot of flowers into the reserved area of the container. Now you can add summer annuals or perennials to the container without digging around the tulip roots. When the last tulip fades away, lift out the bulbs, pot and all, and store in a cool, dry spot. By this time, the garden center will have annuals for sale in six-inch pots so you can easily slip these summer bloomers into the spot vacated by the tulips.

SPRING PICK-ME-UP/DIG-ME-UP. Early blooming bulbs like snowdrop and crocus are much appreciated because their flowers come when winter weather still makes gardening outdoors difficult. There is a way to enjoy the detailed beauty of these spring miracles, even though they don't last long as cut flowers: Don't cut the blooms; dig them up instead. Use a small decorative flower pot and escape outside between winter storms armed with a trowel. Dig up a shallow-rooted crocus or snowdrop and plop it into the pot with its original soil from around the bulb. Don't replace the hole with soil. Now watch the promise of spring unfold indoors for a week or so in the comfort of home. Budded bulbs will bloom earlier inside, forced by the warmth. After the blossoms fade, return the plant—bulb and soil—to its original spot in the garden. It will never know what happened, and will still bloom happily outside next year.

LOYAL LILY SURPRISE! Plant a lily bulb in the center of a large pot that is at least one foot deep. Make sure the lily is at least two thirds of the way down in the pot so that there are several inches of soil below the bulb and a good eight inches of soil covering the bulb. Now plant summer annuals or perennials on top and forget about the buried lily. Each summer, lily will poke up her head and display her fragrant blooms. I've enjoyed the same lily in the same pot without replanting for five years. Sometimes I add petunias and geraniums to the pot, sometimes impatiens and a few perennials. I usually forget about the lily buried under the soil until midsummer when the stem shoots above the heads of the lower-growing plants. Then the fragrant flowers are a lovely surprise.

Q If I plant annuals in the same pot with lilies or other summer bulbs, won't the other flowers hurt the bulbs?

A Not if you use a large enough pot. A container two feet deep is best, so the bulbs can be left undisturbed in the bottom twelve inches of soil. One year I even added an annual vine of purple bells to the pot. When the tall stem of the

'Stargazer' lily shot up, the purple vine grabbed hold for a ride to the sky. When the lily blooms start to fade, I cut them off but leave the stem and leaves alone so they can work on making next summer's bloom. The purple bells of the rhodochiton tolled merrily along, using lily as a support system. Being the strong and regal gal that she is, Lily didn't mind playing the supporting role at all.

PROBLEMS

Q **The first spring after I planted my tulips, they bloomed beautifully. The next spring nothing came up but a few healthy-looking leaves. What did I do wrong?**

A Tulips are not that dependable when it comes to encore performances, for several reasons. Maybe the leaves were pulled off and cleaned up too early last spring before they were allowed to ripen and form next season's flowers. Maybe they weren't planted deep enough, or maybe insects or disease got to the bulbs. Don't spend too much time or energy fretting over the problem—it happens to lots of gardeners with lots of different bulbs. If you love tulip flowers in the spring, plant fresh tulip bulbs each fall.

Q **What is wrong with my tulips? The leaves are distorted and the flowers were tiny and never opened.**

A This sounds like a viral or bacterial infection. Or it could be bulb mites, tiny white insects with four pairs of legs, which form colonies on the bulb itself. You can dig up the sickly bulbs to look for the mites or to feel the bulbs for soft spots that indicate they are disease ridden. The cure? No easy answer here. Do not compost them; dig 'em up and throw them away.

Q **My tulips came up with soft, brown, rotted spots on the leaves and deformed flowers. What should I do?**

A The easy answer to these rotting problems: Dig them up and throw them away. It could be a basal rot or crown rot. Plant only clean, undamaged, firm bulbs.

Q **Rodents keep eating my tulip bulbs! I know because I have tunnels and burrows in this area, and I have even dug in and discovered some half-eaten bulbs. What is the answer?**

A Cage them—the tulip bulbs, not the rodents. Save the plastic crates that strawberries come in and set these in the hole when you plant your tulips. You can even set one strawberry cage upside down over the other with the bulbs caged safely inside. Secure the plastic baskets together with wire. You could also make heavy-duty wire baskets with wire mesh or hardware cloth. Or plant daffodils instead—they're poisonous to most rodents.

(Q) **My daffodils sent up leaves and no flowers the year after blooming beautifully the year before. What happened?**

(A) The foliage was probably cut down too early the spring before. You must let the leaves ripen and turn yellow after the flowers fade because they are making next spring's blossoms.

(Q) **My daffodils sent up leaves that are deformed and yellow with swollen bumps on them. They barely flower at all. What is their problem?**

(A) Sounds like bulb and stem nematodes, a tiny roundworm that attacks bulbs most often when they are in soil that does not drain well. The worms dig into the bulbs themselves but are barely visible to the naked eye. The cure? Dig up the bulbs and the soil around them and throw them away—do not compost.

(Q) **I didn't get around to planting my daffodil bulbs right away, and now they feel soft in places. Are they still good?**

(A) No! They could be infested with the bulb fly, which lays eggs near the base of daffodil leaves and then the larvae make burrows into the bulbs as they sit in storage waiting to be planted. Always buy firm bulbs with no soft spots. The heartbreaking cure for your soft-hearted bulbs? Do not compost them; throw them away.

(Q) **My daffodils that bloomed had weird, distorted flowers and the leaves came up yellow, very strange looking. Any hope?**

(A) This could be bulb mites, tiny insects that thrive in warm and humid conditions and love to infest slightly injured or bruised bulbs. Buy and plant only firm, unblemished bulbs. The cure? Dig up the bulbs and surrounding soil and throw them away—do not compost.

(Q) **The leaves on my daffodils have reddish brown spots. The flowers rot and the foliage becomes streaked.**

(A) This sounds like leaf spot, fire, or scorch—all names for a fungal disease that can be a problem in hot, humid weather. You know the sad but easy answer—dig up the bulbs and throw them away.

Q The flowers of my gladiolus have white streaks and the blooms are not normal looking. What is going on?

A Sounds like the classic symptoms of a thrip invasion. Thrips are tiny insects that infest the corm (bulblike root), the stems, and the flower petals of glads. They are difficult to control even if you use an insecticide because they burrow deep into the tissue. If you've read the previous questions, you know what the dreaded answer is: Dig up the infested corms and throw them away. If they really mean a lot to you, try soaking the corms in a solution of Lysol and water for several hours. Figure one capful of Lysol to one bucket of water. Do this before you store the corms for the winter, and the Lysol could clean you thripless for fresh planting the following spring.

Q My glads came up beautifully in the spring, then the leaves turned yellow and dry and they never did bloom. What did I do wrong?

A Maybe you handled the corms too roughly. It sounds like a bacterial or fungal infection invaded the corms after they were planted. Sometimes this happens when the corms are damaged or bruised, allowing an entrance for these troublemakers. Treat all bulbs with a gentle touch. Meanwhile, dig up and destroy your damaged corms.

Q I was wondering what was happening to my begonia flowers; they seemed to be disappearing without a trace. Then one morning I saw the thief—a squirrel would pluck a flower and scurry away with it in its mouth. How can I keep the squirrel out of the begonias without harming him?

A Put some spice in his life. Red cayenne pepper is the hot tip to retraining the taste of your squirrels and other rodents. Sprinkle the buds and flowers with the pepper, and after a few mouthfuls your squirrel will think nuts are pretty good after all.

Q I planted some dahlia tubers, but once the shoots started to come up, they were nibbled to the ground! I can't see any worms or insects.

> ## Gardening Tip
>
> "The dark or golden pollen from lily blooms stains clothing and tablecloths. Use a dry paintbrush to brush away the drips, or use masking tape to lift the pollen from fabric. The oil from your fingers, or water, could set the stains. Snip out the pollen-bearing anthers from inside the lily flowers to avoid pollen stain worries."

A Dahlias (and hostas, delphiniums, and hundreds of other plants) are very attractive to slugs. Look for shiny trails of slime or set out a saucer of beer and see what stops by for a drink. Now don't despair. Dahlias can be nibbled all spring long and still make it to giant blooming spectacles by late summer. In my garden it happens every year.

A Lazy Gardener's Confession

The Dirty Secret of Daffodil Depth

Daffodils are like tulips and most other bulbs—the deeper you plant into loose, rich soil, the more likely it is that your bulbs will return year after year. The reality is that digging down eight inches or one foot to plant bulbs is a lot of work—especially if you have less-than-perfect soil with rocks, clay, and hardpan.

A dirty depth trick is to dig one large shallow hole two or three inches deep, set the bulbs in pointed end up, and then cover not just with the soil you took out of the hole but also with compost, bark mulch, and any other soil you can rob from another part of the garden. This way the bulbs are buried at least six inches, but you only had to dig down half that far—plus they are under an obvious mound of fresh soil so you'll remember where you put them. Putting 10 or 12 bulbs into one communal hole is fine as long as they aren't touching one another and you don't expect more than one or two years of blossoms out of them. If you have hard winters, you need to plant deeper than three inches or the bulbs could freeze, but here in the Pacific Northwest, where winters are mild, I cheat and plant my bulbs shallow. But I get the job done quickly and I get away with it. Sometimes I dig them up after they bloom and move them to another spot to let the foliage ripen; sometimes I cut off the leaves and stems right to the ground so I won't have to look at the mess, and then plant new bulbs in the fall; and sometimes I just let the daffodils ripen on their own and they surprise me by blooming beautifully the second and third year—even though they were planted only three inches deep.

> ### Gardening Tip
>
> "I use rebar as stakes for my dahlias. I paint the bars green during the winter and reuse these strong and durable stakes year after year. You'll find rebar for sale inexpensively at hardware stores and building centers."

CARE

Q If I planted daffodils in an area of my garden and they developed an insect or disease problem, how long before I can safely plant fresh daffodils in the same spot?

A Sorry, there's no easy answer. Some fungal spores and insects can be present for years, waiting to infect your next batch of bulbs. To be safe, for at least five years I would plant new bulbs in a container of fresh potting soil to avoid contamination. Above all, improve your drainage by raising the beds and adding sand and organic matter.

Q When is the best time to fertilize bulbs?

A Most bulbs don't need a lot of fertilizer, but they appreciate the extra nutrients most just before the flowers open and again when the flowers have faded and the foliage is turning yellow. This is when the plant is sending nutrients down to next year's developing flower.

Q What type of fertilizer do bulbs need?

A A liquid or water-soluble plant food works well because the nutrients can be absorbed by the foliage and get to work quickly, but traditionalists use bonemeal in the soil at planting time for an organic boost to the swollen roots.

Q Can I plant my Easter lily after it is done blooming?

A I wish you would! Easter lilies make great garden plants and will return year after year with summer blooms. The bulbs won't continue to bloom at Easter, however—they wait until summer when grown outside. The tip to remember is to plant Easter lily bulbs deep. After you've enjoyed the plant indoors, remove the faded flowers and cut off the top half of the stem. Now carefully remove the plant from the pot and plant it a few inches deeper than it was originally growing. (Yes, I know you're always supposed to plant at the same depth it had been growing, but sometimes you get to break the rules.) The Easter lily may surprise you and send up another flower shoot in the fall, but after that it will bloom each summer with the other lilies of the garden. Be prepared for it to grow much taller than when purchased. The ideal spot would get morning sun but afternoon shade. A few chunky perennials near the base of the lily help hide the bare stem after it blooms; hostas and daylilies do the job. Like most bulbs, your Easter lily needs well-drained soil and will really appreciate it if you'll loosen the soil well to a depth of one foot.

Are Returning Tulips Myth or Fact?

One spring I was asked about a way to hide the ugly tulip foliage that followed the blooms, slowly ripening and dying. This person was disappointed by how few tulip flowers returned to bloom the second year. She wanted large, late-blooming tulips, not the short, early, species tulips that return more dependably (see the sidebar "Tulips That Live for Years: Loyal Little Dwarfs," on page 53). I suggested she just cut off the leaves and stems after the flowers bloomed and treat the tulips as annuals, planting fresh bulbs each fall.

The following week, an indignant reader of my newspaper column wrote this: "How could you say that tulips don't return each year? In my garden a few Darwin tulips have grown over the years to great colonies, with 50 or more blooms. I haven't done anything to them except that I planted in very good, well-drained soil 8 to 12 inches deep, and I put a spoonful of bonemeal in the bottom of each planting hole. I also planted a species tulip that is shocking pink with bright yellow centers ('Persian Pearl'), and from 6 bulbs planted ten years ago, I now have more than 100 blooming tulips—and I've never replanted! What I can't figure out is how I get tulips popping up in places I've never planted them before. Must be the squirrels moving them around for me in the fall."

He is indeed correct. Some tulips, especially the species and rock garden varieties, will return and spread easily if you have wonderful, loose, quick-draining soil and can plant them a foot deep. Most of us have soil that is less than perfect, and digging a hole one foot deep is a test of determination and strength because of the rocks, clay, or hardpan just a few inches down. Most of us also wish for those wonderfully cooperative squirrels that must tiptoe through his tulip beds, politely planting the small offset baby bulbs to surprise him in new locations each spring.

Gardening Tip

"Bulbs are the easiest way to let my young children help me in the garden. Seeds are too small for them to handle and young plants are too tender, but I can let the little ones handle trowels and bulbs, and they can't really hurt too much. I make a game of it by telling them we are putting the baby bulbs to sleep for the winter, so they need a nice warm hole to sleep in and then we cover them up with a blanket of soil."

No-Dig Dahlias

Where I live in the Pacific Northwest, it is recommended that dahlias and other tender bulbs such as glads and begonias be dug up and stored in a frost-free area over the winter. I am ready to confess that my dahlias have not been dug up for eight years, and I don't intend to dig them up in the future. Instead, I just throw an old section of oilcloth from a picnic tablecloth over the dahlia bed sometime in October after I cut off the frostbitten stems and leaves. To keep the waterproof canvas from blowing away, I pile on some dirt or bark or even lay a few fallen evergreen boughs on top. My dahlias grow in a raised bed out near the vegetables, so I don't have to look at this arrangement much, but if I did, I would just spread a bag of bark over the tablecloth. That's all. I'm done with winter storage. In the spring I remove the covering. In June the dahlia shoots finally mature past the slug fodder stage, and in August bright orange blooms welcome the autumn season.

I learned it is the wet soil more than the cold weather that kills off so-called tender bulbs, and if you can keep the winter rain from falling on your tender bulbs and corms, they can survive some freezing weather. I must admit that my dahlias are growing in a raised bed. The raised bed makes for better drainage, and a bulb would rather die (literally) than have wet feet. Sometimes I don't get around to covering them at all and they still come back and bloom. Before the dahlia fanciers go berserk over this no-dig method of storing dahlias, I must also confess that I have only one variety of dahlia, a sturdy orange fellow that looks great in fall arrangements. Some of the more unusual dahlias may not be as tough as my carefree orange dahlias that return each year.

Chapter Six

Perennial Plants
The easy answer for diversity in your garden

Perennials are the easy answer for wide diversity and often hardy durability in the landscape, but they should not be considered maintenance-free plants (although some are pretty easy to ignore). ✤ *The explosion in the popularity of perennials over the years has happened in part because busy gardeners have been told these wonder plants will fill their gardens with flowers year after year and not need the maintenance of annuals, which must be replanted each spring. In reality most perennial plants flower best in great soil, may need staking or pruning, and often disappoint beginning gardeners because they may flower for only a few weeks instead of several months the way annuals do. Perennials can return in larger clumps each spring, but only if the winter rains, freezing weather, or garden pests don't do them in.* ✤ *Perennials are the easy answer for mature, experienced, and patient gardeners, or for gardeners willing to do some research and plant the right types of perennials for their specific growing conditions.*

SELECTING

Q What is a perennial plant?

A Any plant that survives the winter to come back and grow again in the spring is considered a perennial. The most familiar perennials are the popular flowering plants like daylilies, peonies, and iris. Annual plants, if you remember, are those that die each winter and must be replanted annually.

Q Aren't things like shrubs and trees perennials since they come back year after year?

A Technically yes—but among gardeners, the term "perennials" refers to herbaceous or nonwoody plants that come back year after year.

Q So a herbaceous perennial has nothing to do with herbs?

A Nope, but that's a common mistake. Herbs are sometimes perennials and sometimes annuals, depending on your climate and how hardy the herbs are.

Q Is it true that some plants are perennials or come back year after year in mild climates, but in a colder climate, that same plant is an annual and dies in the winter?

A That's right. A lavender plant may be a perennial in San Francisco and an annual in Spokane. To further confuse the issue, a lavender plant may be considered an herb in many nurseries, because it is used for flavorings or medicinal use, but a landscape plant in other nurseries, because it is also used for hedges and landscaping shrub borders.

Q If I want a perennial flower garden that returns each year, can I mix in annuals and other flowers?

A Of course. Mixing in self-seeding annuals such as pansies or alyssum gives you flowers that return each year the way a perennial would, even though these plants return from seeds dropped on the ground, not because the mother plant survived the winter.

Q What is the easy answer for choosing perennial flowers?

A There is no easy answer, because this depends on your soil and exposure. In most cases, for lazy gardeners with average to poor soil and a tendency to neglect their gardens, the easy answer is to use self-sowing perennials that reseed themselves (you won't have to divide them), and long-living perennials such as hostas, peonies, and daylilies, which can go for years without demanding division and renewal.

Dirt Cheap Tip

"Before I started landscaping my first yard, I had gotten into the caffeine habit, stopping by my favorite coffee shop whenever I needed a boost of energy. Then I noticed the nursery next to the java joint. I began to wander while I sipped my double tall, wondering how I could afford all those beautiful plants. Then it hit me: The answer was in my coffee cup. I could have bought a perennial plant in a four-inch pot instead of a cup of coffee! From then on, I bought perennials, one at a time, whenever I needed a lift. Who needs caffeine when you can garden for a high?"

Reseeding Perennials for the Lazy Gardener

Self-seeding perennials are a boon because, although the plants may survive the winter to bloom a second year, their real advantage is the talent they have for self-seeding or planting their own offspring each fall, with fresh new plants sprouting each spring. This means you can toss out any older plants that have grown leggy, diseased, or ugly and know there'll be children along to take their place.

To enjoy the benefits of these carefree wonders, practice the laid-back gardening philosophy and do not fertilize much, water too often, or weed constantly. Above all else, let the faded flowers stay on the plants near the end of summer so they can make seeds, spill the seeds onto the soil, and sprout next summer's flowers. Loose soil without a deep mulch makes the best seedbed. Of course some of these enthusiastic seedlings will sprout where you never thought of planting flowers, such as in the cracks of walkways and behind shrubbery, but the young seedlings are all easy to transplant to a more suitable position or to cull from an undesirable area.

Warning: The two reseeding perennials that follow are sometimes hard to find at nurseries. You may have to order from a catalog or visit a nursery that specializes in perennial plants.

ROSE CAMPION (*Lychnis coronaria*): These tall, gray-leafed plants have striking magenta flowers that the Victorians loved, but soon fell out of fashion when later garden writers started the myth that magenta or hot pink clashed with other flower colors and should be banished from the garden. (Frankly, it would be best for us laid-back gardeners if such color snob purists were banished from the garden.) Lychnis has furry, soft leaves, and so it is slug resistant, deer resistant, drought resistant, and very tolerant of poor, rocky soils. It blooms happily year after year in the dry, poor soil under a cedar grove in my yard. To make the color snobs happy, there are also white and light pink forms of lychnis, but I have not found these as quick to reseed as the bold and brilliant magenta variety.

FEVERFEW (*Chrysanthemum parthenium*): A member of the chrysanthemum family, feverfew has foliage that is a delicious lime green and flowers that are like miniature white daisies with yellow centers. Feverfew is usually tall and narrow-growing like lychnis (flowers bloom at the top of one-foot stems), and these two make a great duo for summer color. The name feverfew comes from the herbal use of this plant, still said to bring down a fever and relieve headaches. Feverfew does fine in partial shade or full sun, and it does prefer more organic matter in the soil than the rock-tolerant lychnis. Add faded feverfew blossoms to your compost pile, and you'll be sprouting plenty of new plants if you spread the compost as a mulch in the spring.

Q I don't know what perennials to start with. What are some easy perennials that would also be easy to find for sale at the local nursery?

A In the perennial kingdom of carefree plants, daylilies are the reigning kings, peonies the regal queens, and a hosta plant, because it loves the shade, could be called the prince of darkness. (For the dirt on how they grow, see the sidebar "Growing Carefree Perennials: Daylilies, Peonies, and Hostas," below.)

Q I am looking for some very specific perennial varieties for a color theme garden I am planning. The local nurseries don't carry the perennials I want, or the best plants are sold before I can get down there. Help!

A The easy answer for finding very specific perennial plants is to order by mail or off the Internet. This is often the only way to get rare or unusual perennials without traveling long distances. Try to buy from the companies closest to where you live, for shorter shipping times and plants more attuned to your climate. (See the sidebar "Garden Resources" on page 71 for ideas.)

Growing Carefree Perennials: Daylilies, Peonies, and Hostas

DAYLILIES (Hemerocallis): These have long, straplike leaves and bell-shaped flowers that bloom in shades of mostly yellow and orange. The flowers live only for a day (hence the name), but there are many of them clustered at the end of a stalk. Daylilies tolerate poor soil, but bloom better in good soil. They take full or partial sun, and if you give them a two-inch layer of mulch, they'll forgive you when you forget to water. There are tons of daylily varieties. Some daylilies are tidy dwarfs, some are evergreen, some bloom all summer, and some are closely related to the tough, tawny daylilies (*Hemerocallis fulva*) that have escaped gardens to grow wild and that can survive almost anything.

PEONIES (*Paeonia*): Peonies have great foliage and huge flowers, and this makes them good for the center of a flower border or for planting in front of messy plants that you want to hide. (A clump of daffodils done blooming is an example of a messy plant.) Peonies bloom in partial shade, but won't flower if they are planted too deep, so don't pile mulch on top. Peonies can live for generations, and are perfectly happy staying in the same spot year after year without being divided. Depend on peonies for late spring color and tidy summer foliage.

HOSTAS: With their big, broad leaves and rather skimpy stalks of flowers, hostas like the shade. Some have blue foliage (these tolerate more sun), some green and white foliage (these light up dark, shady corners), and some golden and green leaves (great with companion plants that are purple or red). Hostas are easy to grow in pots, and this helps to keep the slugs away—their biggest pest. When your hosta clump gets too big, take an ax, make like Lizzy Borden, and chop up the mother plant. The severed sections can be given away or moved around the garden. Hostas are so tough they seem to handle ax surgery any time of year—as long as they are kept cool and moist as they recover.

SITING

Q What do I need to do to my soil to grow perennials?

A Wrong question. For a more carefree landscape and happy, well-adjusted plants, it is better to ask, "What perennials (or any type of plant) will grow well in my soil?"

Q Okay, what perennials will grow well in my soil?

A In general, if you have pretty good soil or garden loam—loose, rich, and quick-draining—you can grow lots and lots of different perennials. To narrow down your selection, get a perennial-buying catalog so you can study the photographs and read over the growing (and glowing) descriptions. These well-photographed catalogs are like having a free perennial encyclopedia.

If you have soil that is less than perfect, or problem areas, then pay attention to tough perennial plants that actually prefer extremes. Remember, not every plant demands loose, well-drained, and fertile soil to thrive.

Q What perennials can I grow in my poor, dry, rocky soil, which gets a lot of sun but very little water?

A Sedums and succulents are the easy answer if you're looking for drought-resistant perennials. Sedum 'Autumn Joy' stands stiff and majestic with late summer and fall blooms, while *Sedum acre* (gold moss sedum and sedum 'Coral Carpet') are weed-blocking ground covers. Planted in either random or organized patterns, a collection of succulents and sedums intermixed with boulders and gravel adds a texture to the garden floor that can be enhanced with taller-growing perennials such as yarrow, lychnis, and artemesias—plants that also tolerate poor soil fertility.

Easy Answers

Plants for Narrow, Shady Beds

My garden has a long line of hostas and ferns along the shaded north side of the house. It started out as a collection of shade-loving perennials, but over the years the hostas and ferns have dominated, and who am I to argue? This bed is beautiful and carefree all summer. I filled the 30-foot-long bed in just a couple of years by dividing up one contented hosta from the bed whenever I had the shovel handy, and plunking the newly severed hunk of hosta into the ground a few feet away from the mother plant. Then I did the same thing with a chunk of maidenhair fern I had transplanted from the woods. One hosta and one fern became the bounteous hosta-and-fern combo that echoes all the way down the side of the house. This carefree bed is still providing starts for any visitors who dare to admire these two tough, dependable, and prolific perennials, made for shady beds.

Thoughtful (or pessimistic) gardeners might wonder what that long bed looks like in the winter. After all, hostas and ferns die back to the ground five months of the year. Well, in the winter it looks bare. Even worse, with the limp, yellow hosta leaves rotting in the rain, the bed is a mess in late fall. I don't mind because, being located at the back of the house, it isn't seen much by winter visitors. And during the winter when I'm inside looking out, I don't look straight down to see what is right beneath the windows. Instead, I look outward toward the more distant landscape—the place where trees, shrubs, and perennials with early spring and fall interest are planted.

Garden Resources

Here are some of my favorite sources for specific or unusual perennials:

✻ Etera, 14113 Riverbend Road, Mt. Vernon, WA 98273; www.etera.com; 888-840-4024. This grower has a patented system for growing one-year-old plants and then shipping them to consumers and retail outlets in coconut-fiber pots. The pots can then be planted directly into the ground; this produces plants that ship easily all over the country and then, once planted, grow fast! The full-color catalog and web site are wonderful sources of information on perennials.

✻ General Gardening Internet Site, Garden Escape, www.gardens.com. An interactive site with a monthly magazine, on-line shopping, garden chat rooms, and a great horticultural search engine, this is also the spot to check on perennial hardiness in your area, using their growing-zone maps.

✻ *Northwest Gardener's Resource Directory,* by Stephanie Feeney. This unique catalog of nurseries, plant sales, societies, and foundations introduces you to the whereabouts of small specialty nurseries and perennial foundations, and puts you in touch with the folks in the Pacific Northwest who can track down not just perennials but any plant!

✻ White Flower Farm, P.O. Box 50, Litchfield, CT 06759-0050; www.whiteflowerfarm.com; 1-800-503-9624. Each year this mail-order company puts out a beautiful catalog that makes an excellent resource directory with photos and growing and design information. Get on the mailing list and with the turn of each page you'll be inspired to plant more and more perennials.

Q What perennials will grow in the low damp spot of my garden? I think I have drowned more plants than Noah's flood. I don't want to spend the time or money to construct a drainage system or to raise the level of the soil with fill dirt.

A Use tough but lovely plants that adore the dampness. Grow tall and spiky Siberian iris for spring color. The ferny foliage and rocketlike blooms of astilbe and red blossoms of cardinal flower brighten the summer, and fragrant sweet woodruff (*Galium odoratum*) is an evergreen perennial that acts as a ground cover. Let a late spring carpet of self-seeding candelabra primroses light up the area, and you can look at dampness as an asset, not an eyesore.

Q What perennials will grow in the woodland shade of tall trees and large shrubs? I have been using a bark mulch in the area for years, but want something that will take over and fill the space under the rhododendrons, hydrangeas, and azaleas so I won't have to mulch and weed as often.

A Use spreading, shade-loving perennials that enjoy the highly organic soil that results after years of spreading a bark mulch. Hardy geraniums (these are not the large flowering geraniums you see so often growing in pots, but true geraniums) and members of the Lamium family—'White Nancy', 'Pink Pewter', or 'Beacon Silver'— will carpet the ground if the soil is a bit shaded from the shrubs. These shallow-rooted plants are easy to rip up if they get too close to the shrubs, and they'll make a pretty petticoat under the skirts of your bushes. They also have an aggressive nature that crowds out the weeds.

Q What will grow in the dry shade beneath trees or against the dark side of the house where the roof overhang keeps the rain from watering the plants?

A Dry shade is a challenge, but you can still have perennial plants. For height use the upright stalks of strawberry foxgloves or use the native foxgloves you find growing alongside a country road. The late summer- and fall-blooming anemones also thrive in dry shade, as do lower-growing geum, dianthus, and platycodon 'Sentimental Blue' bellflowers. Also explore the possibilities of using woodland plants and sword ferns as ground covers in dry-shade areas. Dry and dark doesn't have to mean dismal.

Q I have pretty decent soil and a sunny location. My problem is deciding how to arrange the perennials. I don't want to end up with a mishmash that looks like a bunch of wildflowers and weeds.

A Plant in groups, or "drifts," as the English landscapers like to say. Just drift right into the garden center and force yourself to buy at least three of any one type of perennial—or, if you're patient as well as frugal, buy just one and then in a few years you can dig and divide that one so that you can have a cluster of identical perennials. Even if you have a small garden, repeat the same plant two or three times in the garden. Repetition can replace chaos and confusion in a design.

Q What perennials do you recommend for a small garden? I have a tiny lot with just a bit of a bed for flowers.

A Perennials that stay small and don't spread quickly won't wear out their welcome in a small garden. Look for coreopsis, scabosia, heuchera, columbine, sedum 'Autumn Joy', dwarf hosta, and saxifrages.

Tough Perennials for Shade and for Sun

PERENNIALS FOR SHADE	HEIGHT
Lady's-mantle (*Alchemilla mollis*)	Low
Astilbe	Medium
Bleeding heart (*Dicentra spectabilis*)	Tall, medium, or low (*depending on variety*)
Foxglove (*Digitalis*)	Tall
Lenten rose (*Helleborus*)	Medium
Hostas	Medium or low (*depending on variety*)
Dead nettle (*Lamium*) 'White Nancy'	Low
Primroses	Low
Lungwort (*Pulmonaria saccharata*)	Medium
Ferns	Medium

PERENNIALS FOR DRY SOIL AND FULL SUN	HEIGHT
Coreopsis	Medium
Purple coneflower (*Echinacea purpurea*)	Tall
Catnip (*Nepeta cataria*)	Low
Euphorbias	Medium
Lavender (*Lavendula angustifolia*)	Medium
Lamb's ears (*Stachys byzantina*)	Low
Sedum 'Coral Carpet'	Low
Sedum 'Autumn Joy'	Medium
Thyme (*Thymus*)	Low

Q What perennials do you recommend for my huge flower bed that runs alongside the driveway? It is in full sun with great soil.

A Big enthusiastic perennials such as rudbeckia daisy 'Goldsturm', phlox, chrysanthemums, yarrow, asters, Shasta daisy, and Japanese anemone will spread happily through your king-size beds.

A Perennial Garden in a Pot and a Pillar

Who needs the work of double digging, mulching, and weeding a perennial bed when you can just pot up all those problems? Use large half-barrel-size containers with several types of perennials as your focal point, and group smaller pots with single perennial specimens around this central tub of plants. Don't be shy about staggering the levels of your potted garden by using stumps, overturned pots, or even crates to elevate the pots.

For a really dramatic flair, use a cement culvert pipe stuck up on end and placed behind your potted garden so that it looks like a hollow cement column. (A length of rebar pounded into the ground inside the pipe will keep it from tipping over.) Now fill the first few feet of the drainage-pipe-turned-garden-pillar with drainage material such as crushed plastic pots, and save room for at least a foot of potting soil. Go wild with perennial plants that have large, draping leaves and vining plants that will spill over the cement sides of the planted pillar. Ornamental grasses also do well and look outlandish growing from the top of sleek columns or plant pillars. Here are some suggested plants:

POTTED PERENNIALS FOR THE SHADE: Use 'Palace Purple' heuchera or small-leafed or dwarf varieties of hosta as midsize plants; lamiums as edging plants; *Vinca minor* or variegated, small-leafed ivy to spill over the sides; and tradescantia or spiderwort as a tall, spiky plant in the center of the pot.

POTTED PERENNIALS FOR THE SUN: Use dracaenas or phormiums as tall, spiky foliage for the center of the pot (both are rather tender perennials, so protect from winter freeze); dwarf grasses such as blue fescue; long-blooming scabiosa (dwarf pincushion flower); and sedum and thymes spilling over the sides.

Q Can I grow perennials in pots?

A Of course. You can grow any plant in a container. The bigger your pot, the longer the perennials can grow without replanting. Most will survive a year or two in a pot that holds one cubic foot of soil.

Q What are the best perennials for growing in pots?

A Choose compact or tidy perennials with great-looking foliage, because perennials do not bloom continuously all summer like annual flowers, so you will be looking at the foliage far longer than you will be looking at the flowers. Don't be afraid to mix a few annuals in with the potted perennials for added blooms. Bacopa and sweet alyssum are two annuals with a fine texture that goes well with potted perennials.

CARE

Q What can I do to make the perennial plants that I grow easier to maintain?

A The easy answer to easy perennials is to improve your soil before you plant. Add lots of organic matter (compost and soil amendments) to the soil so you won't have to weed, water, or fertilize as often.

If your perennial garden is in a windy or exposed site, add a fence or wall to frame the garden and offer protection from the weather. Lay stepping-stones through the area if the beds are wider than a few feet, for easier access when you do routine maintenance, and choose a nonliving focal point (bench, birdbath, or sundial) that fits your garden style so that your perennial garden has a focus even during the winter months.

Q What am I supposed to do with my perennials in the winter? Do I need to cut them back or clean them up?

A The easy answer is to clean up the perennial foliage that is soft and mushy (peonies, daylilies), but leave alone the plants that turn dry and crispy (astilbe, hardy fuchsias). It certainly makes your winter garden look tidier if in the fall you cut back any perennials that are past their prime. Leaving the faded foliage helps to protect some plants from cold weather by snagging fallen leaves and debris, which act as an extra layer of insulation. In spring you can cut back all the winter-weary perennial foliage to get the garden ready for a flush of new growth.

Keeping Weeds Out of Your Perennial Garden

MULCH: Cover the ground with bark chips or compost after pulling all visible weeds. Lay down a newspaper block beneath the mulch if there is a lot of space between plants.

PLANT THICKLY: The less bare earth, the less room for weeds to get a toehold.

IMPROVE THE SOIL: Most weeds thrive in places where blooming plants have a difficult time growing. As you continue to add compost to your soil, the perennials will grow faster and stronger and crowd out the weeds. (Really, this is true.)

Reminder: It is okay to add the weeds you pull to the compost pile. Yes, you are adding weed seeds and then spreading them back onto the garden, but many seeds die when the compost heats up, many weeds are pulled before they flower and get a chance to make seeds, and many weeds don't get a chance to sprout because the perennials spread out and shade the soil (many weed seeds need sunlight to germinate).

Q What do I do about weeds growing in my perennials? I have some grassy weeds that are growing right up through the center of my perennial plants. They appeared after I spread manure all over the beds.

A You'll have to hand-pull the grass or hoe it out with a pointed hoe. Manure is great for improving the soil, but if it hasn't been allowed to heat up and compost, it will sprout with the seeds of pasture grass.

Q Can I cut off the old fern fronds that are brown and dry, and what time of year should this be done?

A You can cut back the old fern fronds any time of year, but it is easiest to do the job in the spring before the new growth is fully extended and not in the way of the old brown fronds. Remind yourself at tax time on April 15 to take on this taxing job. A pair of kitchen scissors works better than pruning shears for removing old sword fern fronds.

"Each June I ruth-lessly prune back my sedum 'Autumn Joy' plants with the hedging shears so they are only a few inches tall. Then I gather the pruned-off tip growth, strip off the lowest set of leaves, and poke the freshly cut stems into any patch of soft earth— even into my pots of annuals. These pruning crumb cuttings almost always root, and by fall I have bushier mother plants and new plants blooming from the cuttings. I have so many of these easy-care, drought-resistant perennials now that I've started giving them away to all the neighbors who admire my late-summer display."

Q My creeping phlox is creeping all over, growing out of my rockery and into my lawn. When do I prune this rock garden plant?

A The easy answer to any pruning question is to do the pruning right after blooming. A light shearing every year not only keeps the plants under control, but encourages a second set of blooms as well. You can also take new starts of these rock garden plants by reaching into the clump and pulling out the thin, loose sections in the center. Replant into soft earth.

Q I have an underground spring (or broken water pipe, I'm not sure which), and I've planted primroses in the moist soil with great results. Now I would like to move some of these happy plants to another shaded section of the garden. What time of year do I divide primroses?

A The best approach is to sneak up on any perennials and perform the surgery of division when they are resting quietly. This means when they are done blooming or when they are dormant and showing no signs of active growth, in very early spring or late summer.

Q How do I know when my perennials are overcrowded and need dividing?

A When you see that the center of the clump is starting to die out, or the plants are no longer blooming as well as they once did. Some perennials, like daylilies and hostas, can go years and years without division or never need it; others, like asters and astilbe, need dividing every other year or they grow woody and lazy.

Spare the ax, the shovel, and the spade on these perennials, which should not be divided: candytuft (*Iberis*), dianthus (pinks), bleeding heart (*Dicentra*), baby's breath (*Gypsophila*), and poppy balloon flower (*Platycodon*).

Replanting Perennial Divisions for Busy Gardeners

The truth is, if you have to divide your perennial plants because they have grown too large, they must like your garden. The lazy gardening oath is to plant more of what grows well and get rid of the plants that struggle. This means you should keep dividing and replanting any perennial that is happy to reproduce, so that your garden is filled with happy, healthy plants. This also means that when you divide the happy plants, you can try them in different locations to find out where else they would be happy to grow, or just keep filling your bed with repetitious drifts of the same perennial. Then you won't have to do much to change the soil when you add the young upstarts.

I sometimes ignore good horticultural practices and rip out a hunk of happy perennial, take a few steps, and stick it into the ground. If it grows, great—I'll have a bigger drift of happy perennial. If it dies because I didn't take the time to improve the soil or keep it watered while new roots were forming, I haven't lost much because I still have the happy mother plant—ready to donate more hunks of herself when the season changes or I find a new spot in which to try her offspring.

Turning your back on the rules and moving pieces of plants whenever it is convenient for you may not be what is best for the plant, but it does teach them an important lesson—adjust or perish. They won't be coddled, so only the strong survive.

Q I am so disappointed with my perennials because they only bloom for a few weeks. I thought I would have flowers all summer the way my geraniums, marigolds, and petunias keep blooming. Is there anything I can do to extend the bloom season?

A Yes. Some perennials such as creeping phlox will rebloom if you shear them back as the last flowers fade. Others, like foxgloves and delphiniums, will send up side shoots if you cut back the main blooming stem. You could also choose perennials with long bloom periods.

Longer-Blooming Perennials

These are plants that repeat, reshoot, or reseed.

LADY'S-MANTLE (*Alchemilla mollis*): The lime-green, rounded leaves on this neat and compact plant are often decorated with dewdrops that dazzle like diamonds. The low-growth habit makes this lady perfect for edging shaded beds. The foamy yellow flowers bloom late in the spring but hang on for months, and although she's prolific, this lady's no tramp about scattering her seed. New plants appear politely around the base of the mother plant or pop up shyly just a few feet away.

CORYDALIS: Soft, ferny foliage and complex yellow blooms appear around April and then hang around until October or the first hard frost. Corydalis will reseed politely, especially in cool, damp soil—it loves shade and moisture. You don't ever need to deadhead or remove the spent blossoms on this one. If corydalis likes your garden, it's there to stay, with lots of seedlings popping up in the most surprising places.

SCABIOSA: Also called pincushion flower or butterfly flower, this plant has foliage that makes tidy clumps from which round pink or blue flowers emerge on sturdy stems. The show starts in May and continues until August if you remember to cut back the spent blooms every few weeks.

TICKSEED (*Coreopsis grandiflora*): Fine, threadlike foliage and cheerful yellow, daisylike blooms do especially well in a sunny site. Protect coreopsis from slugs in early spring and you'll enjoy blooms from May until August. Shear it back if things get out of control and you'll have renewed and refreshed growth full of more flower buds.

FORGET-ME-NOT (*Myosotis*): In a shaded or moist spot, these self-seeding woodland plants form a haze of baby blue blossoms that flower from March until June. When they're finally done singing the blues, rip out the faded plants and toss them wherever you want more forget-me-nots to grow—behind the garbage cans, in the roadside ditches, or around the base of your mailbox. You'll forget where you threw the old plants, but they'll remind you each spring with clouds of blue heaven.

SWEET WILLIAM (*Dianthus barbatus*): This old-fashioned, white-edged red or pink flower blooms in round clusters, looking very much like circles of nosegays. It is low enough to use in the front of the border, providing early and midsummer color in sun or partial shade.

Q When I divide perennials, do I cut, tear, or break apart the clumps?

A This depends on the root system of the perennial. In all cases, you can discard the center or oldest part of the perennial if the roots look dried up or the oldest part is not blooming.

A thick, solid, or matted root system like a hosta, daylily, phlox, or centaurea can be divided with an ax or knife. Just slice out a hunk from the sides and replant.

A shallow-rooted system like a primrose or heuchera can be divided by digging up the clump and pulling apart the root clumps with your fingers where you can see obvious joints or breaks.

A spreading root system like iris can be cut or broken apart where you see the natural breaks in the roots, and a spreading root system from ground cover perennials such as lamium, creeping phlox, and vinca can be divided almost any time by breaking or cutting off sections of the top growth.

Deep tap-rooted perennials like lupine and baby's breath should not be divided. They are best increased by seed or root cuttings.

Q What about replanting?

A Replant as soon as possible in loose soil. If you're a good, hard-working gardener, you will have improved the soil with compost or manure and loosened it to a depth of at least six inches so the new roots can spread out easily. Carefree gardeners just dig a hole in an empty spot and add the new plant section. If it lives, great; if not, there's more where that came from.

PROBLEMS

Q What perennials have the most problems? I want to avoid any perennials that are going to get pests and diseases.

A This is not really a fair question, since the most popular perennials are those planted the most often, and so the odds are that these are the plants most gardeners report problems about. I rarely hear complaints about some really difficult-to-grow perennials, because few gardeners grow them. However, if it's gossip and ruining of reputations you're after, read on for some of the most-asked questions about problems with perennials.

Q I ordered some perennials from a catalog and they arrived very small. After one year, only a few bloomed. Should I rip them out or did I get ripped off?

A Give them some more time. Often, good companies send very young plants through the mail because these youngsters handle the trauma of transplanting better than mature plants ready to bloom. Sometimes they are so young that they need another year before they graduate to blooming size. Sometimes they are biennial plants. This means they take two years to grow to blooming size.

Q I love my bright purple aster plants for their fall blooms, but as they flower, the plants tend to open up in the middle and flop around. They also get some sort of black growth on their lower leaves and start to die near the end of the season.

A Asters flop as they age because, like many perennials, the center dies out. The black you see at the end of the season is most likely leaf blight brought on from the autumn rains. Most asters like a dry location.

Asters are one perennial that needs dividing often. Rip off the side shoots in spring and replant, tossing out the center dead section. (Asters multiply rapidly, so be ready to give lots of aster plants away, or plan on a long aster border.) You can also prune asters in the early summer, much as you would chrysanthemums to keep them more compact and to stagger the blooms.

Q My Jacob's ladder (*Polemonium caeruleum*) was tall and well budded when all of a sudden it just toppled over after a rain. It was just getting ready to bloom and I could scream!

A Screaming at your perennials won't make them better behaved, but if it makes you feel better, go ahead. Jacob's ladder often needs a scaffold or a support system, or it never makes it to the top rung of display in full bloom. You can usually save toppled plants by corralling them with a circle of sticks and pulling them upright, using twine to cage them inside.

Staggered Blooms:
Stair-Stepping the Pruning Cuts

If you want the same plant to bloom in different weeks of the summer, you can stagger the blooms by trimming back sections of the clump on different dates. This trick works best on late-summer bloomers such as sedum 'Autumn Joy', hardy asters, and chrysanthemums.

Cut the front of the plant last so it will bloom last and hide the faded flowers that are behind. A good rule is to cut the back third of the clump to within six inches of the ground in May, cut the middle of the clump back to eight inches in June, and cut the front section of the clump in July. Now you'll have tall, medium, and low sections budded up in late summer for staggered bloom times.

Q I love the bright yellow flowers of basket-of-gold (*Aurinia*) I see blooming in the spring, but when I try to plant this perennial in my garden, it turns soft and dies. I buy big, healthy plants, put them in the sun, and water often.

A Basket-of-gold is a type of rock garden plant, and this means it needs perfect drainage, like that found in a raised bed or rockery. Rock garden plants most often die from "wet feet," the gardener's term for poor drainage.

Q How do I keep my chrysanthemums from growing so large and leggy?

A Cut them back with the hedge shears to six-inch stumps in late spring when they grow to a foot tall. Prune them back several times if necessary up until the Fourth of July and then let them go. You may end up cutting them back three times before they bloom, but the short bushy mums will be full of flowers. You can also stagger the mums (see the sidebar "Staggered Blooms: Stair-Stepping the Pruning Cuts" above).

Q The leaves of my columbine plant have little silvery-white lines all over them. What do I do?

A The easy answer is to do nothing at all. These lines are the tunnels of the columbine leaf miner, and the larvae will soon emerge as a fly and be gone. The plant won't be bothered by a slight infestation, but if they bother you, then pull off the leaves as soon as you notice signs of infection in early spring. Loosen the soil around the plants in the fall to expose any leaf miner eggs to the winter cold.

Q Why do my daylilies have lots of leaves and no blooms?

A Daylilies that aren't blooming could be in too much shade, they may need dividing, or the soil may be so depleted that the starving daylilies don't have enough energy to flower. Some daylilies, like the old-fashioned tawny daylily, can adapt to lots of shade and still bloom; others need more sun to set flowers.

Q What can I do about my delphiniums having brittle stems and breaking in the wind and rain?

A Delphiniums are heavy feeders, and when you give them enough manure and fertilizer to get them to bloom, they grow so fast that the stems become brittle. Try feeding them smaller amounts but more often. Also, instead of using one stake to support these plants, surround them with three stakes and then make a corral from twine so the stalks can't move in the wind. If this sounds like a lot of work, remember that delphiniums are rather finicky plants, but their very showy flowers are worth the extra work to many gardeners.

Q I purchased a foxglove plant because I heard they would tolerate some shade and rather poor soil, but the plant just got bigger, not taller, and never showed signs of blooming. After one year, it looks like a big lettuce plant. Is something wrong with it?

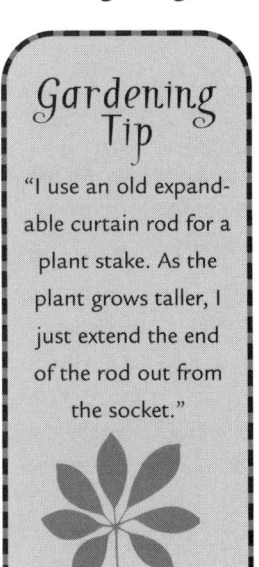

Gardening Tip

"I use an old expandable curtain rod for a plant stake. As the plant grows taller, I just extend the end of the rod out from the socket."

A Stand back and be ready to be dazzled: your foxglove will bloom after two years because it is what is called a biennial plant. After flowering, if you cut back the main flowering spike, side shoots will bloom. Lay the spent flowering stalk in the garden where you'd like new foxglove plants to grow. Foxgloves reseed easily and are slug- and shade-tolerant, so their flowering spires are worth the two-year wait.

Q I planted some succulents that are called hen and chickens in my poor, rocky soil because I thought they were hard to kill. But after one of the biggest "hens" bloomed, it died! What went wrong?

A Nothing. These thick-leafed succulents (*Sempervivum*) die soon after blooming, but they usually send forth so many starts, or chickens, that the empty spot will soon be chick-full of new plants.

Delphinium Confessions: A Perennial I Love to Hate

Yes. I have a personal grudge against delphiniums. These are the tall, striking, very blue or purple flowers you often see looking stately and breathtakingly beautiful in English garden photos. I covet the delphiniums that seem so easy to grow in my neighbor's garden. I just can't grow them myself, so I gossip maliciously about them behind their backs:

Delphiniums are heavy feeders, needing rich soil that drains well but that is very fertile.

Delphiniums are slug and snail magnets, attracting these slimy pests from miles around.

Delphiniums need full sun and careful staking when young or they flop over on their bellies when they bloom.

My garden is mostly shaded, cool, and full of slugs. I confess I am improving my soil and scouting out the sunny spots with a secret goal of still trying to coax a delphinium to bloom—just to say I met the challenge. I have stopped recommending delphiniums to gardeners because I really resent not doing well myself with these beautiful blue perennials.

Q I love my hollyhocks, but each summer they become covered with what looks like brown freckles. Then they curl up and the leaves go dry. Please help.

A Hollyhocks are elegant and old-fashioned—and always blighted with rust. The brown pustules start on the back side of the lowest leaves, then move on out to consume the plants. There's no easy answer here. Try to keep the leaves dry, grow them in full sun, then try to ignore the problem. Cut hollyhock plants back to the ground as soon as the rust is uglier than the flowers are beautiful. Even if you apply a smelly fungicide every few weeks, you won't be free of rust on the hollyhocks, so call them freckles and learn to live with it.

Q My bearded iris no longer blooms. The leaves look healthy enough, but the roots are crowded.

A You need to divide bearded iris every three or four years to keep them blooming. Wait until after the blooming season or in the fall, and then lift the thick rhizomes or roots. Cut out and discard the old, weak, and wrinkled-looking sections, cutting off and replanting the thick, plump, lighter-colored roots. Improve and amend the soil before you replant. Iris like lots of fertilizer if you expect lots of blooms. Do not plant iris too deeply, but just barely cover the tops with fresh soil.

Q After my bearded iris bloom, should I cut off the tall stem?

A Yes, removing the stem but not the leaves is a good idea because sometimes insects get into the iris plants by first penetrating the juicy stem.

Q My bearded iris have leaves with brown dead spots. The problem is growing continually worse.

A You could have a bacterial or fungal infection on the foliage, encouraged by cool, rainy weather. Remove any infected leaves by pulling them from the base. Be sure you plant the iris in well-drained soil with good air circulation and lots of sun. There is no easy answer or super spray that will get rid of the problem, but the Siberian iris is more resistant to these leaf blights than the bearded iris.

Q After my oriental poppies bloom, the leaves turn yellow and look sick. What is the problem?

A Probably nothing. Poppy leaves just look ugly after they bloom. They yellow and die by midsummer, but come back green in the fall. Plant a perennial with nice-looking foliage in front of the poppies to screen the mess from view. A peony or hosta plant can be enlisted into screening a poppy past its prime.

Q Why have my peonies stopped blooming? They did fine for many years, and now I get healthy foliage and no blooms.

A The easy answer is they're planted too deep. Even if you planted them at the correct depth to begin with, over the years soil or mulch may have covered their tops. Scrape away the soil in early spring so that the roots are just barely covered.

Q What can I do to make my peony stems stand up stronger and hold their huge, spectacular flowers up out of the ground?

A Cage the weak and floppy stems by slipping wire tomato cages over the plants when they begin to grow in the spring. You can also try gently shaking the water from the blooms after a rainstorm, or cutting the flowers when they are just breaking from the bud stage and then enjoying them indoors. Cut peony flowers in the morning when they are most full of moisture.

Primrose Paths: Forget Prim and Proper, Plant the Tough Stuff

Be picky about the primulas you plant in your garden if slugs are a problem. The hardy, species primroses are more slug resistant than the soft-leafed but large-flowered and brightly flowered polyantha primroses that are sold everywhere in early spring.

The tough primroses that spread through the moist area in my garden are the yellow cowslips (*Primula veris*) and the low-growing Wanda (*Primula juliae*), deep violet with a yellow eye. Wanda is one of the survivors from my great-grandmother's garden that thrived despite the fact that the garden was untended and ignored for many years.

If you have a really damp or soggy spot in the garden, you can enjoy the reseeding splendor of the two-foot-tall candelabra primroses (*Primula japonica*), with whorls of flower clusters that rise one on top of the other like formally pruned topiary. These primroses have a thicker, tough leaf that makes them less attractive to the slugs and weevils that destroy the primroses with more tender foilage.

Q What can I do about the ants that crawl all over and eat my peonies?

A Ignore them. They are not eating your peonies, they are feeding on the sticky sap that the buds ooze forth. Ants also milk aphids that they set to pasture on peonies, so check for aphids and then wash or pinch them off while the peonies are still in the bud stage.

Q Why do my peony leaves turn black? Some years, the buds turn black and the stems turn black.

A In cool, moist weather peonies are susceptible to botrytis blight. They are also prone to other fungal infections during wet weather. Quickly remove any leaves or buds at the first sign of blackness. Remove any flowers with brown spots as well. Avoid mulching your peonies with manure in the fall or with any other mulch that could hold the dampness near the plants. Give them plenty of room and good air circulation. Fungicide sprays are not very effective on peony fungal infections, so don't waste your time spraying. Instead, practice good fall and spring cleanup of the area to control the infection.

Chapter Seven
Roses
The easy answer for color, fragrance, and beauty

Answers about rose growing in a book for carefree gardening is not the mismatch you might imagine. Roses have gotten a bad reputation among carefree gardeners as high-maintenance plants, and sadly, most of the dirt is shockingly true! They can be demanding plants, hogging water, fertilizer, pruning, and all the attention of the gardener, and then still show up with yellowed leaves and sporadic, aphid-infested blooms. Consider any such bad behavior your punishment for not planting the right type of roses in the right location. ✻ If you make the right variety choices, roses can also be the most benevolent, hard-working contributors of color to the garden—with no more care required than a spring trim and an extra shot of fertilizer.

Gardening Tip

"Here's an easy tip to remember when choosing carefree roses: Think pink without a stink. Pink roses with no fragrance are more likely to have a genetic link to a natural resistance to disease. It just runs in the family."

SELECTING

Q What are the most disease-resistant and easiest-to-care-for roses?

A The easy answer is roses that were bred for low maintenance, not flower size or color. Newer introductions such as the landscape roses Flower Carpet roses and Dream Roses come in several colors, but were developed to have carefree personalities and disease-resistant natures.

There are also a few very disease-resistant hybrid tea roses (see the sidebar "Six Classic, Easy-to-Grow Roses," on page 88), and the hardy species and old-fashioned roses, including *Rosa rugosa,* a repeat bloomer with fragrance. Shop for roses that are easy-care first, and consider the color, size, and fragrance second. Remind yourself that beauty is only petal deep, but disease resistance, easy pruning demands, and vigor are at the root of carefree gardening. There is nothing beautiful about a sickly rose.

Six Classic, Easy-to-Grow Roses

Following are six disease-resistant, easy-to-grow roses that are grouped so that you can remember their names—or at least so the name may ring a bell when you're trying to decide which rose to adopt. Make a mental picture of a queen, with peace and love in her heart. Now think peaceful ('Peace' and 'Pink Peace') and loving thoughts ('Love', 'Honor', and 'Cherish') guided by a dependable queen ('Queen Elizabeth'). Six rose plants are a good number for a small but formal rose garden, and these provide a variety of colors with enough buds to fill a summer's worth of vases.

'PEACE': Extra-large blooms of yellow, pink, and coral

'PINK PEACE': Large blooms, pink version of the above rose

'QUEEN ELIZABETH': Tall, shrubby plant with medium-pink flowers

'LOVE': Red petals backed in silvery white

'HONOR': Pure white blooms with long, pointed buds

'CHERISH': Rose pink flowers on shrubby plants

Q I'm looking for roses, but when I go to the nursery, I'm overwhelmed with the choices. How do I find roses that are disease-resistant, easy to grow, and that will look great in a rose garden?

A The truth is, carefree gardeners may not remember to carry around a long list of disease-resistant roses and refer to it before purchasing rose plants at a plant sale or finding roses in bloom at a nursery. Without the names of some tough roses at the tip of your tongue, you could feel swayed by the colors, fragrance, and bud shape of just any old rose—which, once adopted, could grow into your garden's problem child or, worse yet, a disease magnet.

There are some varieties of hybrid tea roses, which are the most commonly sold type of rose, that are disease-resistant and easy to find. They are described in the sidebar "Six Classic, Easy-to-Grow Roses," and are the easy answer to your question.

Q Are all hardy roses on their own roots also disease resistant?

A Not always, but since they are closer genetically to the very tough wild roses, cold-hardy roses are often disease resistant as well.

Considering Rose Adoption? Interview for Prospective Rose Parents

Before adding hybrid tea roses to the landscape, check your commitment level and home environment with the following questions.

✤ Do you have enough room and the proper home environment to raise a healthy and well-adjusted rose? Roses need five to six hours of full sun a day and good air circulation. They do best when planted at least four feet away from trees, buildings, and shrubbery.

✤ Can you provide a safe, nurturing environment for the developing root system? Roses have roots that rot easily in wet soil. A raised bed with organic matter, compost, alfalfa pellets, or manure added is perfect.

✤ Can you provide consistent, proper discipline with the pruning shears at the right time of year? Tender-hearted rose growers who refuse to hack off hybrid tea growth in early spring will raise spoiled and out-of-control roses. Be firm and consistent. You're cutting back the roses for their own good. Remember the three Ds—remove dead, diseased, and damaged wood—as well as pruning for an open, vase-shaped rose and shortening all canes to 18 inches or less.

✤ Will you commit to proper pruning when harvesting your hybrid tea roses in the summer? Prune properly in the summer by removing spent blossoms and following that stem down to a five-leaflet node or joint. Snip just above this joint to get a long stem and encourage new summer growth.

✤ Do you have the time, energy, and commitment to provide proper nourishment? The healthiest roses enjoy natural, home-cooked compost and manure, but if you're the type who takes feeding shortcuts and are hooked on the convenience of fast food and chemical fertilizers, then your roses will still prosper, but over time the vigor of the roses will suffer as they age.

✤ Are you willing to provide health insurance in the form of frequent visual checkups for yellowing leaves, which may signal diseases and aphid invasions that can be nipped in the bud? Letting small health problems go unchecked on your roses could lead to major medical expenses—even spraying with pesticides and fungicides. Responsible rose growers can keep spraying to a minimum with regular checkups.

🌿 Are you willing to admit defeat and give problem roses a death with dignity instead of letting them suffer a long and ugly decline? Diseased, bug-infested roses are not only a blight in the garden and painful to look at, but they can contribute to the decline of other roses and plants, as insect eggs and disease spores reproduce and are spread throughout the yard. There's no need to take heroic or hospice measures with an ugly rose. Put it out of its misery, then move on. If you find yourself failing to produce healthy, well-adjusted rose plants, then think really hard before adopting any more roses.

Q **Why do hybrid tea roses die more often in the winter? Is this just the rose growers' plan to make you buy new roses every few years?**

A Blame winter loss on grafting, not greed. A graft is when a fancy rose cannot grow on its own weak roots, so it is grafted or attached to the roots of a hardy wild rose. This is called the rootstock, and it does fine in the winter weather, but the spot where the roots and top are joined by the graft is a weak spot. Sometimes new growth shoots up from below the rootstock union and grows into a renegade rose— usually a muddy red color with a wild growth habit. Sometimes the top half of the rose dies at the point of the graft, due to a fickle fall with warm weather or late fertilizing that does not prepare the rose for the first hard freeze. Roses grown on their own roots, without a graft, don't have this problem.

Q **So why does anyone grow those hybrid tea roses if they demand so much care and are prone to so many disease and insect problems?**

A The beauty, the color, the fragrance, the romance of a long-stemmed rose that you grew yourself, shown off in a bud vase. Also because many gardeners enjoy the challenge.

Q **When I go to buy a rose, how can I tell whether it is a disease-prone hybrid tea rose (the hard kind) or the easy-to-grow shrub or old-fashioned roses?**

A The easy answer is to read the fine print and description on the label or box, which tells you the type or class of rose. Sometimes just initials are used to describe the rose type: HT for hybrid tea, FL for floribunda, CL for climber, and so on. Also, if there is a photo of the rose in bloom, look for pictures that show lots of small rose blossoms all over the plant. This means the rose is more likely a disease-resistant floribunda or multiflora rose. Hybrid tea roses show a close-up photo of just one bloom.

Flunked the Adoption Interview? Adopt a Wild Child

If you failed the test for tea rose adoption (see the sidebar "Considering Rose Adoption? Interview for Prospective Rose Parents," on page 89), try offering a home to a wild child. Consider the almost indestructible *Rosa rugosa*. It's so hardy and tough it even survives near the ocean in dry, sandy soil. Unlike most species roses, *Rosa rugosa* blooms from May until September instead of just a heavy flush of blooms in June. Red *rugosa,* more pink than red, has the largest blooms of all the *rugosa* varieties, up to five inches wide.

Red *Rosa rugosa* is extremely resistant to both black spot and mildew, has a lovely fragrance, and, as a surprise bonus, adds fall color to the landscape with changing foliage and really big, red hips. (Unlike fashion designers, rose growers find big hips quite attractive. The hip is the swollen seedpod that remains after the petals fall.) Even the foliage is interesting, with crinkled or pleated leaves that always look thick and healthy.

So what's the downside? This rose, like all species roses, needs lots of room because it grows at least five feet wide and even taller than that. The multitude of blooms are scattered all over the sprawling plant and don't last long in a vase, but since they don't bloom on long stems, you wouldn't be tempted to cut them any-way. Like a true wild child, if given space and tolerance for its unique and inde-pendent personality, red *Rosa rugosa* can become a much-beloved and dependable addition to the family. Use it as a hedge along the perimeter of your garden, or as a background for showing off other plants.

Q Are multiflora, shrub roses, and old-fashioned roses always more disease-resistant and easier to grow than the hybrid tea roses?

A No! There's no easy answer for this one, because some hybrid tea roses are wonderfully tough and resistant to disease, while I have met and received letters from gardeners who found so-called "hardy" roses to be cold tolerant but regular mildew magnets and prone to black spot. Check the list of recommended roses for carefree gardeners on page 88.

Ranking the Different Types of Roses

For the best roses, look for five stars on the "Lazy Gardening Meter." (*Warning:* I've made up these ratings based on my own experience and research—you won't really find the star rankings on the rose labels.)

☆ **HT: HYBRID TEA ROSES:** They are called hybrids because they have been bred from different parents. All this interbreeding makes them more prone to disease than roses closer genetically to their wild ancestors. 'Peace' is a classic hybrid tea rose.

☆☆☆☆ **FL: FLORIBUNDA ROSES:** These have lots more flowers, carried in clusters, but smaller blooms than hybrid teas. Some floribundas have very tiny flowers, as many as 30 blooms on one stem. 'The Fairy' is a hardy pink floribunda with a draping, graceful form.

☆☆ **GR: GRANDIFLORA:** These roses are usually taller (five to eight feet), with more blooms, often in clusters. 'Queen Elizabeth' is a well-known, easy-to-grow grandiflora that mixes well with hybrid tea roses and is often considered to be one. Many grandiflora roses are sold with the hybrid tea roses because there is so little difference in appearance and growth habit.

☆☆☆ **CL: CLIMBERS:** Climbers have long, flexible canes. Some are "sports," or genetic deviants of hybrid teas, and have large flowers (like 'Climbing Peace'), while others are from the floribunda family with many smaller flowers. Most climbers bloom better if their canes or branches are bent horizontally over a fence or arch.

☆☆☆☆ **SR: SHRUB ROSES:** This is a catchall class for all the rose varieties that grow rather bushy and do well in the landscape as flowering shrubs. Some grow as tall as ten feet, some as low as four feet, with all sizes of flowers. 'Simplicity' is a good example of a shrub rose, bred for ease of maintenance and a compact, bushy form.

☆☆☆☆ **OLD GARDEN ROSES:** These are all the favorites that used to be grown before the hybrid tea rose came on the scene in the mid-1800s. These are usually tough and disease resistant, some with romantic blooms and heavy fragrance. Their history and ancestry can be pretty complex, but they are generally gentle giants, hardy and disease-resistant. They are not as disease-resistant as the true old roses, but tougher than the hybrid teas.

★★★★★ SPECIES ROSES: Also called wild roses, these are the original roses that breeders started with to build up the huge flowers and repeat blooms we enjoy now. Tough, almost disease-free, and enthusiastic growers, species roses are perfect for lazy gardeners with room for sprawling thickets of roses. I've never heard of anyone killing a species rose, although some people rip them out when they grow too large. But I don't feel that growing enthusiasm should be held against any plant, so these earn the top award.

TREE ROSES: A propagator's project, these are tea roses or shrub roses grafted onto a straight stem, which has been grafted onto a hardy rootstock. I call these plant pets because they need almost daily care and attention as well as winter protection. Perhaps I resent the fact that I invested a lot of money in tree roses over the years because I love the look of them planted in pots on my front porch, but could never get more than a few years of life out of the fussy things. I award them no stars on the Lazy Gardening Meter.

★★★ MINIATURE ROSES: These have tiny flowers on very low plants, said to be easy to grow. Some varieties have been bred from wild, natural mini-roses with good disease resistance. These are darling plants that most people have no trouble growing.

Q If I find a rose for sale that is not on the list, does that mean it will get diseases and is hard to grow?

A Not necessarily. It could be a brand-new, improved rose, a really old rose variety, or an unusual rose that has not made it on the carefree list because not enough gardeners have grown it and reported on its attitude. Do your own research, ask at the nursery whether anyone has had any experience with the rose in question. If you're a gambler, go ahead and give any rose a try—you could win the low-maintenance lottery.

Q Where can I find the easy-to-grow roses for sale?

A Many nurseries have a variety of roses for sale besides the hybrid teas, and mail-order catalogs are another source of easy-care roses. Roses can be shipped in the mail bare root (without soil) when they are dormant and so, unlike some other plants, they do not suffer as much stress when ordered from a catalog.

Life's a Bed of Roses

Recycle the head- and footboard of a metal bedstead to protect your island rose garden from kids, balls, and pets. Stand the headboard and footboard up by slipping their feet into flowerpots sunk into the ground and filled with gravel. Fill the space between the head- and footboard with a "blanket" of roses.

A child's junior bed works well, because these are often made from metal and painted bright colors. Recycling an outgrown bedstead in the garden is a novel way to get children started with their own rose garden flower bed, and teach them that gardening, like life, can be a bed of roses.

Q When is the best time to buy roses for the yard?

A Late winter or early spring is prime rose-buying time. This is when the roses can be shipped or purchased from the nursery bare root without any soil and planted into the garden before they wake up from winter dormancy and figure out they've been moved.

Q Can't I buy roses in the spring and summer to add to my garden? I want to see them in bloom before I make my choice.

A Yes, roses that did not sell in early winter are often potted up and grown as container plants all summer and sold at your local nursery. Because they are in a pot, they are easy to transplant without disturbing the roots, so potted roses can be added to the garden any time the ground is not frozen. It is just easier on the rose if the delicate transplant operation is done under the anesthetic of winter dormancy.

Q Are there any fragrant roses with good disease resistance?

A Yes, but not many. 'Double Delight' is a red and white hybrid tea rose. 'Fragrant Cloud' has coral orange blooms on a bushy plant. 'Mr. Lincoln' is a dark red hybrid tea with long stems.

Q I want to discourage neighborhood kids and pets from wandering into the yard, but don't want to put up a fence.

A Plant hedge roses or shrub roses, for color as well as thorns. Sometimes called landscaping roses, these are for hedge plantings where you have lots of room. 'Simplicity' has pink blooms, is tall (to five feet) but narrow, so only needs a bed three feet wide, and is a continuous, heavy bloomer. 'Bonica' is pink, disease-resistant, shrubby to four feet wide, and as tall. *Rosa rugosa* comes in several colors—red (really a dark pink) has the largest blooms and most fragrance; it is very carefree but needs lots of room (five to six feet tall and just as wide). 'Iceberg' is a white floribunda with a sweet scent and large flowers for a floribunda on a tall, upright plant. 'Betty Prior' has rose-pink, dogwoodlike blossoms, with the energy and enthusiasm of a wild rose but a more boxy and shrublike shape.

SITING

Q I stare at an eyesore, a large expanse of empty ground on a slight slope, which I view from above from an overlooking deck I use in the summer. Can I have roses here?

A Yes. Terrace the slope and improve the soil if necessary, and then plant ground-cover roses or climbing roses. Allow them to sprawl on the ground, and they will spread and creep, tumbling down and covering the hillside with beautiful summer color. Flower Carpet is a patented series of roses that comes in several colors, including pinks and a white. Flower Carpet roses are always sold in pink plastic pots instead of bare-root since they are practically evergreen in mild climates and rarely go dormant. They have small blooms all summer and into fall, with a growth habit more arching and fountain-shaped than ground-hugging. *Rosa rugosa* 'Red Max Graf' is a vigorous, long-reaching ground cover that tolerates some shade and poor soil.

Q I need summer color alongside a sunny driveway and patio but don't want to block my vision by growing taller roses.

A Choose low-growing and compact floribunda or polyantha roses, low shrub roses that are easy to prune with the hedge shears and that have a continuous display of flowers all summer long. Dream Roses are a new group of roses that are a dream to grow and come in orange, yellow, and pink. 'Sunsprite' has lots of small but brilliant yellow flowers, blooming all summer on a shrubby rose less than three feet tall. 'Europeana' has deep red, velvety blooms on a low-growing shrubby, plant.

Q A raised bed or low wall near my patio or deck or near the entrance to the house needs graceful, draping summer color. Could I use roses instead of annuals or ground covers?

A Great idea. Forget about those leggy petunias or invasive ivy. For summerlong color year after year without replanting, grow hardy, draping floribunda roses. 'The Fairy' is a compact, pink floribunda that tolerates some shade and has bunches of flowers that hang in clusters from pendulous branches.

Q I have a graceful arch and white picket fence, but still need the accent of roses to add to the storybook charm of a country landscape.

A Nothing says charm like a rose blooming over an entryway and rambling along a fence. Why not live in the rose-covered cottage of your dreams? 'Cécile Brunner' has dainty pink blooms that cover the plant once in early summer, but last for weeks. 'New Dawn' has large, light pink blooms; it is hardy and can also be grown as a shrub. 'Blaze' has bright red blooms that are slightly scented; blooms are more numerous on these climbers if the canes are trained to grow horizontally along the fence or arch.

Q I have a narrow bed next to the house, with a pathway alongside; I want to use a trellis to train a rose up the wall, but don't want to get snagged by rose thorns when walking or working with the rose.

A Plant a thornless or practically thornless rose if getting stuck makes you bristle. 'Zephirine Drouhin' is an old-fashioned Bourbon rose; blooms are medium pink, it is thornless, and it is a fragrant repeat bloomer with some shade tolerance.

Q I have a rather shaded and cool yard. What roses will bloom in the shade?

A Pink roses and roses with few petals do okay in cool, partly shaded locations. There is a red ground-cover rose called 'Scarlet Meidiland' that tolerates some shade; a low pink floribunda called 'The Fairy'; and many of the *Rosa rugosa* varieties that also bloom with half a day of sun. Remember, for best disease resistance and more blooms, roses prefer five to six hours of full sun. If you want bouquets of summer blooms in a shaded garden, the easy answer may be to grow hydrangeas instead.

Q My rose garden looks so bare in the winter. Is there a ground cover I can grow at the base of my roses?

A I grow woolly thyme and Scotch and Iris moss around the feet of my hybrid tea roses without any problems. Remember how important good air circulation is for roses, and don't plant any tall ground covers or plants that compete for food and water. Ground-hugging, shallow-rooted ground covers are best or, for summer color, plant low annual flowers such alyssum or petunias. You will need to fertilize and water even more if you have two layers of flowers growing in one bed.

Q I want to mix my roses with perennials to hide the ugly, thorny stems of the rose plants. What are good companion perennials with roses?

A Perennials that have good foliage and hide the naked lower legs of upright roses make good bedfellows with hybrid tea roses. Peonies and daylilies are both easy-to-grow perennials that perform this service well.

CARE

Q In my grandmother's garden, there's a wonderful old rose that I would love to get a start of. Do I dig into the roots and chop off a section?

A It's not that easy. Rose plants are not like daylilies or hostas that can be hacked up and distributed about the garden. They demand a more civilized approach to reproduction. Wait until late summer or fall and then ask permission (from the owner of the rose, if possible) to remove an entire branch or long stem to take home and cut into sections for rooting. You can also bend a branch to the ground and old roses will often root themselves.

Warning: Some roses are patented and protected from propagation unless you pay a fee to the patent holder (although this law isn't enforced too strenuously against home gardeners). Old-fashioned roses usually don't have a patent to worry about.

Q I have all kinds of roses—big ones, little ones, climbing ones. When should I prune my roses?

A The easy answer is in the spring. Depending on your climate, this could be as early as President's Day in February, or as late as Easter, sometime in April. A good rule of thumb is to prune before the new leaves unfold but after the last big freeze or killing frost. If you forget to prune (and carefree gardeners often forget seasonal chores), do it later in the season when you remember, but then, don't prune severely. Just remove the three Ds—dead, diseased, or damaged canes—and shorten the very longest branches by about one-third.

Q Do all roses need yearly pruning?

A No! If you hate to prune or forget to prune, choose the roses that do fine without an annual pruning: rambling *Rosa rugosa*, shrub roses, ground-cover roses, established healthy climbers. Hybrid tea roses are the demanding snobs that look unkempt if they don't get a good haircut each spring.

Gardening Tip

"I don't look at the calendar to know when to prune my roses, I just wait for my forsythia to bloom. When this early spring-blooming shrub is full of yellow flowers, I know it's time to sharpen my shears and shorten the roses."

How to Rustle a Rose or Save Grandma's Living Heirlooms

Old-fashioned or "gone wild" roses grown by homestead families are some of the toughest and most disease-resistant roses you can find. The trouble is, often you can't find them for sale any longer at the nurseries. The tough pink rambler that fills the vacant lot has no name and no history. The bright yellow shrub rose that scents the air in Grandma's garden was there when she moved in 50 years ago, and nobody knows its name. Then there are the roses gone wild in historic cemeteries. These were planted by grieving pioneers over the graves of departed loved ones, a planting tradition now forbidden in modern cemeteries. Roses like these need to be saved, shared, and spread all over yards that belong to carefree gardeners. Here's how to get a piece of the action:

STEP ONE: In the fall or late summer, cut a section from a healthy stem so that it is two feet long and thick as a pencil.

STEP TWO: Wrap this branch in a wet towel or moist newspaper until you get it home.

STEP THREE: Remove all flowers and foliage and cut the now-naked stem into sections about eight inches long. *Note:* Make an angled cut above each top bud on these sections, and a straight cut just below the bottom bud. This will remind you that the bottom end with the straight cut is the end that goes into the soil.

STEP FOUR: Dig and prepare the soil where you want the new rose to grow, by adding a trowel full of peat moss and a trowel full of sand to the area when you loosen up the soil. If you have freezing winters, grow the cuttings in pots that can be stored in a freeze-free location.

STEP FIVE: Insert a pencil into the soil and wiggle it around to make a bigger hole. Now insert the bottom of the cutting into this hole so that at least one bud or node is below ground, and one is above, and firm around the sides. The roses should root readily in moist potting soil or soft earth.

Hints for the paranoid, or tips if your cuttings don't take: Dip each cutting into a powdered rooting hormone, available at garden centers, to encourage quicker roots. Place a bit of sand in the bottom of the hole to discourage root rot. Do neither and have the cuttings root just fine.

By the following spring, you should have new rose plants rooted and showing signs of leafing out from the buds on the stem. At this point, be sure not to let the soil dry out, but do not fertilize just yet. When you see two full sets of new foliage on the cuttings, they can handle a bit of fertilizer diluted to half strength. Now they are strong enough to transplant or share.

Be patient with the roses you rustle. It may take three years before your new rose is large and mature enough to handle sexual reproduction and start blooming.

Q How far back am I supposed to cut my hybrid tea roses?

A That depends. If you want lots of flowers and don't care that they will be smaller, then don't cut back the canes very hard, making them one-third shorter than they were originally. For most hybrid tea roses, this would be to about three feet. If you want huge blooms on long stems or need to get rid of a lot of disease-infested canes, cut your hybrid tea roses back severely, to within one foot of the ground.

Q How far back should I cut my shrub roses or ground-cover roses?

A Trim them as far back as you want. If they are taking up too much space or looking wild, you can prune these roses to within inches of the ground. If you want early flowers and bigger plants, just tidy up any wild long branches and take out the thin branches in the center. Always remove the three Ds: dead, diseased, and damaged branches.

Q This wild branch that is longer and has smooth bark keeps popping up from the base of my rose plant. Every time I prune it off, it comes back. What can I do?

A You have a described a rose sucker. Get to the source of the problem now to prevent years of continued cutting. Suckers grow from the rootstock of roses that have been grafted, mainly hybrid tea roses, and so you must get down on your hands and knees and dig into the ground to find the source of the sucker. It may be popping up from a root, so cut the root off just before the sucker. (Don't worry, the rose has other roots that can support it for awhile.) The sucker may be coming from the trunk below the graft line, and in this case you should grab hold of the sucker close to the base and give it a sharp jerk. This will remove the bud or growth point from the stem so the sucker won't come back—hopefully. They aren't called suckers for nothing. If you ignore the sucker, it could take over and cannibalize the rose, growing into a floppy, muddy red bloomer that soon will be the ugliest rose in the garden.

Are Roses Royal Snobs or Contented Commoners?

The best analogy I can make as to why some roses are such demanding snobs is by comparing them to the British royal family. Traditionally, royalty and roses are much loved for the romance, majesty, and beauty they bring. But like the royal families of England, roses have been interbred for generations, producing some gorgeous specimens that are less rooted in independent survival and more susceptible to disease, weakness, and certain afflictions.

In rose breeding, the quest for bigger, brighter, more fragrant blooms has brought us such flashy and disease-prone roses as 'Green Ice' and 'Sterling Silver'. If you love and lovingly care for these beautiful but spoiled hybrid tea roses, the fact that I call them demanding will upset you every bit as much as it would upset the Brits to tell them that their royal monarchs are spoiled and demand a lot of bowing, money, and service in return for the regal glory and pomp they give back to the commonwealth. For millions of gardeners and loyal subjects, giving roses the royal treatment is worth the price of their grand performance. The pride and beauty of growing a classic, long-stemmed rose has more than just snob appeal. It's a glorious tradition.

Now, getting back to the roots of the rose question, there are plenty of roses that thrive without the spraying and pruning demands made by those beautiful but snobby hybrid tea roses. These more independent, working-class roses are often grown on their own hardy rootstocks, with a vigor much like that of the rugged, hard-working common folks who trace their lineage to tough peasant stock. These tough roses have not been weakened by generations of inbreeding, a practice in royal families as well as the rose family that sometimes produces generations of weak and disease susceptible offspring.

To be fair, there are some hybrid tea or large-flowered roses that bloom with beauty, have a solid, dependable disposition, and can be considered almost care-free if given some support. Consider 'Queen Elizabeth'—the rose or the monarch. Here is a regal specimen who holds her head high despite the squirreling scandals and conflicts that tarnish her relations. She may not bloom in the most fashionable color (ho-hum medium-pink blooms) or intoxicate with heavy perfume, but 'Queen Elizabeth' continues to perform her duties year after year, ignoring the spotlight and scandals that befall her more dramatic kin. She may not be as independent and carefree as the wild roses, shrub roses, or landscape roses, but she is consistent, a classic rose worth keeping in the garden despite the weakness in her bloodlines.

There is also a gorgeous new rose called 'Princess Diana' but tragically like its namesake, this rose is weaker and more vulnerable than the 'Queen Elizabeth'. The 'Princess Diana' rose seems destined to be enjoyed for a short time in the garden, then die young, due in part to her weakness for constant support and continued attention. (Like many hybrid tea roses, 'Princess Di' is also subject to an eating disorder.) Some roses can make it on their own and, like some people, there are other roses with weak backgrounds or improper upbringings that must be coddled, supported, and fussed over—and even then they may whine and disappoint. These dazzling but dependent plants are the reason that roses have gotten a bad name among carefree gardeners.

In my own garden, I grow a dozen or so roses permanently and test five or six new varieties each year. I usually kill five or six new varieties each year, because I refuse to spray or feed routinely, and plant the test roses where they will really be put to the test—some near trees, some in partial shade, away from the careful care that I bestow on the permanent roses that have earned my respect. 'Princess Di' did not survive a year in my garden; although her beauty is to be admired, her dependency is to be disdained—-and that eating disorder of hers I would never put up with. (Constant fertilizing is not my idea of carefree gardening.) 'Queen Elizabeth' has a place of honor, however; even though her blooms are conservative, her disposition is noble and her predictability a comfort.

Most of the roses that pass the test in my garden and that I then recommend do not have the royal pedigrees of interbreeding as do hybrid tea roses. I prefer the roses with a bit of the wild in their bloodlines, roses on their own rootstocks with a fiery independence that makes them less regal in appearance, but more resistant to disease and climate restraints. The flowers on these roses are more numerous but smaller, the growth habit more shrubby or floppy, more rambling

Gardening Tip

"The best investment I ever made for my rose plants was a moisture meter. These look like metal sticks with a gauge on top that, when inserted into the ground, tell you how wet the soil is. With all the mulch I keep around my rose plants, it was hard to tell if the soil was dry six inches below the surface. The moisture meter also tells me instantly if my potted plants or roses need water."

than upright, but more vigorous.

I also prefer to mix these more casual roses into the landscape with shrubs, perennials, and annuals. I still keep my hybrid teas together in a small rose garden so they can be easily tended all at the same time when they need pruning, feeding, and bug plucking, but rose growing is most carefree when roses are treated like the hard-working blooming shrubs they were originally meant to be—not the royal snobs of the garden world.

Q How often should I water my roses? I want to set my sprinkler system so they are watered automatically.

A There is no easy answer to watering any plant. The weather and soil make this so variable. My best guess is to water twice a week during the dry months, soaking the soil to a depth of at least 12 inches. Roses are very thirsty plants, but if you need to restrict their water in the summer, they will just slip into dormancy and stop blooming.

Q What! How can you suggest that it is okay for roses to be watered by a sprinkler system! Don't you know that getting the leaves wet will cause diseases?

A Yes, I've read many times that getting the leaves of the roses wet will cause diseases. But many professional rose growers use overhead sprinkler watering anyway. My own sprinkler system comes on early on summer mornings, so the leaves are dry by nightfall and the roses remain disease free. Although wet foliage sets up a home for the fungus among us, sprinkling the leaves also washes off young fungal spores before they can set up a home. Thirsty roses suffer more than roses that are watered in the morning with overhead sprinklers, although using a soaker hose at the roots is best.

Q I would like to use those soaker hoses around my roses to cut back on my watering chores. Is there a mulch I can use to cover the ugly hoses?

A Soaker hoses are a wonderful way to water roses, and can be covered with a bark mulch to seal in the moisture, insulate against heat and cold, and block out weed growth.

Gardening Tip

"While I work in the yard I set the end of the hose, running slowly, around the base of each rose plant. Every half hour or so I move the hose to a different rose. This way the ground gets soaked but the foliage stays dry."

Q What is the best fertilizer for roses?

A I wish I knew! It seems like every rose expert has a different opinion, swearing by everything from rabbit pellets to Epsom salts. I've decided roses must like a varied diet because the more different types of fertilizers you use, the better they seem to like it. A 5-10-10 fertilizer is the classic rose food, promoting many blooms, but if it's not organic it won't improve your soil—a great soil means you won't be obligated to feed your roses so often.

Organic fertilizers are best for lazy gardeners as well as the roses because they last a long time and your roses won't suffer as much should you fall behind on your feeding schedule. Manure tea, compost tea, mushroom compost, banana peels, coffee grounds, rabbit food—I've tried them all and the roses seem to appreciate every bit of organic fertilizer I throw at them. They also show remarkable growth after I use the premixed, granular organic fertilizers sold in tubs or bags. Just remember that roses are heavy feeders. Feed them.

Q When is the best time to fertilize roses?

A The easy answer is to think of three feedings a year, like this: one to get ready (early spring, to get them ready right after you prune), two to get set (when you see the buds are set), and three to go (after the first flush of blooms goes away). Roses are heavy feeders, so fatten them up for tons of blooms. If you're forgetful, try a slow-release fertilizer that you apply once in early spring. It won't work as well as three separate feedings, but it'll be better than nothing.

Q Is it true that I shouldn't fertilize my roses in late summer?

A True! This is actually good news for us lazy gardeners, as by mid-August there is no more pressure or guilt about getting out there to fertilize the roses. Just relax and enjoy the show. Fertilizing late in the season encourages tender new growth that won't be mature and hardened before the first fall frost.

> ### Gardening Tip
>
> Here's an organic blend you mix yourself to feed to your roses: Mix one cup composted steer manure, one cup bonemeal, one cup blood meal, and one cup alfalfa pellets (rabbit food). Work it into the soil each spring after you prune the roses. *Warning:* Dogs are attracted to the blood meal, so bury this under a mulch to keep them from sniffing about.

Q What about winter protection of my roses?

A The easy answer is to mulch and go. I don't recommend any heroic measures. Carefree gardeners should remember this: If a rose isn't hardy enough to survive the winter where you live, maybe you shouldn't be growing that rose. Let nature take her course. There are plenty of hardy roses that thrive in winters of -20°F below. They are called (now this is easy to remember) "Hardy Roses." These include Explorer Roses from Canada, made from a cross with the reliable *Rosa rugosa*. There are also hardy shrub roses and the very hardy Old-Fashioned Roses. Many of these cold-hardy roses bloom only once a year, but they're worth it.

If you're worried about an especially hard winter damaging your rose collection, add an extra layer of bark mulch in the fall and mound it slightly around the canes. Otherwise, if winter kills a rose, it was a wimp anyway, and didn't deserve to grow in your garden. (Of course this flip attitude is the rationale that gets me over the grief of losing any plant.) If you're going for the romance and beauty of roses, don't be blind to the fact that these relationships don't last forever, and when you lose a rose, that leaves an empty spot for trying something new.

PROBLEMS

Q What are the yellow leaves with black spots that are ruining my rose plants?

A Your roses are suffering from black spot, a common fungal infection that thrives in moist, warm-weather conditions. You can help control the problem by plucking off the lower, infected leaves as soon as you notice the first signs of yellow. By planting roses in full sun with good air circulation and growing only disease-resistant roses, the carefree gardener can often tolerate this problem without resorting to all the work of mixing and applying a fungicide spray.

Gardening Goof

I continued to feed my roses late one summer, hitting them with liquid plant food every time I fertilized my potted annuals. I knew I shouldn't give in to their demands for more food so late in the summer, but the well-budded plants held the promise of a million more roses. In October a hard frost hit and the tender, fertilized rose shoots turned black and ugly. I buried several plants the following spring. Moral of the story: Don't fertilize roses two months before the first expected frost. Roses need to toughen up in late summer to better survive the winter.

If you grow roses as a challenging hobby and are willing to invest the time and money in spraying equipment, there are fungicides available at garden centers that can help prevent and control black spot. Follow label directions. If your roses still get black spot and become unsightly eyesores, consider this care-free gardening, never-fail cure: Dig them up and throw them away, or offer the plants to a rose lover with more time and energy. Roses aren't for every garden or every gardener.

(Q) **What is the white fuzzy growth on the leaves of my roses?**

(A) The same stuff that turns your bathroom tiles black. Mildews thrive in warm, moist environments, and some rose varieties are more resistant to this invader than others. Remove infected leaves, try to increase air circulation, and if your rose is still a mildew magnet, give it the shovel treatment—this means you dig it up and throw it away.

(Q) **Weird leaves sometimes appear on my rose plant. I've seen twisted yellow leaves, rolled leaves, and curled leaves. What should I do?**

(A) The easy answer is to pull them off. Aphids can twist leaves, worms can roll them, and diseases curl and misshape leaves. Visiting your roses often and removing any funny business is the best way for carefree gardeners to avoid the hassle of spraying.

(Q) **Something is putting splotches of light green and white on the leaves of my rose plant. Over the years, more and more leaves are becoming blotched and distorted. White veins and yellow rings, lines, and squiggles appear on the leaves with no signs of insects.**

(A) Sounds like rose mosaic virus. This disease will not spread to other roses or contaminate the soil, but it will weaken and kill roses over time. It is usually introduced when roses are grafted onto infected rootstocks. The cure? Dig up the rose and throw it away.

(Q) **There is a gnarly and thick growth at the base of my rose plant that I think may be affecting the health of my rose—it was once lovely but now always looks sick no matter what I do.**

> ## Gardening Tip
>
> "I don't bother with buying fungicides for my roses, I make my own fungicide spray. Here's how: Get a one-gallon pump sprayer. Into this put one tablespoon of baking soda plus one tablespoon of horticultural oil. Mix it up and spray on the top and undersides of the rose leaves. You can also make this solution without the light oil, but it won't stick to the leaves as long."

A The gall of this disease—called rose crown gall—is that it shows up as distorted, tumorous growths at the base of the plant and slowly kills the rose. The cure? Dig up the rose and throw it away.

Q My rose has several problems. The lower leaves turn yellow with black spots, the newer growth has the soft white fuzz of mildew, and aphids are all over. I'm not sure which problem to work on first.

A Your rose sounds pathetic. It would need a fungicide, insecticide, and improved air circulation to clean up its act. You could try to move it to a better location where it gets more sun and air circulation and improve the soil. Is it really worth it? Unless this is a very special rose, the easy answer may be to dig up the rose and throw it away.

Q Tiny green bugs are all over the new tip growth of my roses. Some are light orange or brown and they don't fly away. They have oval, soft bodies and very skinny legs.

A This is the very disgusting invasion of the aphid army, and the troops build up quickly by making happy noises as they mate and reproduce. This encourages more aphids to stop by for the wild orgy going on, and almost overnight your once-clean rosebuds can be crawling with aphid on top of aphid.

Easy Answers

Rose Diseases? Learn to Live with Them

Sometimes it's most practical to accept the fact that your roses will get black spot, mildew, and rust. These diseases often won't kill the rose, so if the plant can learn to live with the problem, maybe you should too.

In my garden, I position a very fragrant and lovely red and white bicolored rose called 'Scentimental' in the back of my perennial bed. By August the black spot has defoliated the bottom half of the four-foot-tall rose, but I don't even notice. The naked knees of the plant are hidden effectively behind a dwarf rhododendron and a grouping of dwarf daylilies. I can barely see the blossoms by the time summer is at its peak, but I can smell them from five feet away. If you want to give up on spraying fungicides but still want the scent and blooms of roses, learn to live with ugly spotted foliage by hiding the worst of your worries behind other screening plants.

Q  **I don't want to spray my roses. Any easy answer?**

A Yes—easy, but messy. The cure: Use your two pinching fingers to come down hard on the amorous aphid army and then leave the squished and mangled bodies on the plant as a repellent to other aphids thinking about moving in. Insects do communicate, and it must be the screams of terror and pain from mangled aphids that keep all other aphids away from the area if you pinch the first aphid to arrive. You wouldn't want to check into a resort hotel if there were dead bodies all over the place, would you?

Pinching to death colonies of aphids rather than washing them off with soap and water or using an insecticide also seems to encourage the ladybugs and other aphid eaters. Instead of removing the food source for these beneficial insects, you're setting up a buffet table and ringing the dinner bell. Pinching aphids does take persistence, and you'll need to keep checking and pinching all summer long, as new colonies move in that haven't yet heard about the torture treatment they'll receive.

Chapter Eight

Super Shrubs
The easy answer for beautiful bones

Not every landscape has room for more trees, but even the tiniest garden can be improved with outstanding shrubs. 🌿 *To many gardeners, shrubbery means the boxy, overgrown masses that demand constant trimming. It doesn't have to be that way. Shrubs can add early spring color and late fall drama while screening bad views and enhancing great ones. They can frame your house and serve as focal points, growing in soil so wet it could be called swampy or so dry it cracks in the sun. There is such a variety of shrubs to choose from that they can solve just about any problem in the garden.* 🌿 *Flowering shrubs are the ones most loved, and gardeners will go to great depths digging in new soil so they can grow rhododendrons or lilacs like the ones they remember from their childhood or fell in love with at a show garden. There's nothing wrong with altering your landscape's environment if you really want to grow a special shrub, but let's not beat around the bush—there are plenty that grow great no matter what your soil and weather conditions.* 🌿 *The biggest complaints I hear about shrubs are that they grow too large (mostly evergreen) or don't bloom (mostly lilacs and rhododendrons).*

SELECTING & SITING

Q **I want to plant some shrubs under my windows and up close to the house. They'll get full sun (or part sun) and my soil isn't the greatest. I don't really have time to prune these plants or worry about water and fertilizer for them. I just want something evergreen, neat, and tidy.**

A Dwarf conifers are the easy answer! Dwarf Hinoki false cypress (*Chamaecyparis obtusa* 'Nana') or the low-growing 'Blue Star' juniper are two that are easy to find at any nursery, tolerate most soils, and grow in a polite and compact manner. You can ask at nurseries for more fine examples of dwarf evergreens, and you'll be impressed at the variety of foliage color and shapes.

When choosing trees and shrubs, you need to tell yourself the truth about how much maintenance you'll be willing to do and how big an area you have for the mature size, not the next-year size, of the shrub or tree you are considering. I'll admit you won't get dazzling blooms or a fine fragrance from compact conifers, but for many years you won't have to worry about pruning these slow growers, and they won't sulk or need a plant sitter when you go on vacation.

Q **We have a low spot in the back yard that collects water in the winter. Several shrubs have already drowned trying to grow there. What would survive in such poorly drained soil?**

A There's no need to put life jackets on the following drown-proof shrubs:

REDTWIG DOGWOOD (*Cornus stolonifera*): Not to be confused with the pink or Kousa dogwoods, which would drown in wet soils, this is a shrubby, wild-looking dogwood with brilliant red stems that stand out in winter landscapes.

BIGLEAF HYDRANGEA (*Hydrangea macrophylla*): In a water-logged bed of dead plants, this is sometimes the only shrub to survive the flood. It has big balls of blue flowers all summer.

RAINBOW BUSH (*Leucothoe fontanesiana* 'Rainbow'): Evergreen leaves spotted with many colors make this shade lover a great choice for dark areas with damp soil.

FLOWERING QUINCE (*Chaenomeles*): Early spring blooms of orange make this shrub a welcome sight at the end of winter. It has some shade tolerance as well.

PUSSY WILLOWS OR OSIER WILLOWS (*Salix*): Like all of the willow family, these are thirsty plants that will suck up any extra water that drains their way.

Hint: Don't stop with just a single shrub. Notice pleasant shrub combinations and imitate these happy couples and family groupings in your own landscape.

Q **Please come up with a magic solution for my dry and sunny hillside. I've killed many plants in this hostile territory and would like something that will survive.**

A All plants need some water until they get established after the first summer, but once they survive the crucial first year, these should adapt well to a sunny hillside: Rockrose (*Cistus corbariensis*) has summer flowers that are a lovely bonus, but its foliage can look ratty in the winter. Yucca's spiky foliage makes this plant look like it belongs in a desert—it makes an exclamation point in any landscape. Junipers come in many types, but low-growing varieties look best covering a hill. Cotoneaster also has many varieties, but 'Lowfast' is a favorite because it does what its name implies—grows low and fast in poor soil and is drought tolerant.

Great Shrub Combinations: Imitate Professional Plantings in Your Area

If you want to get a quick feel for which shrubs do well in your climate, take a look at what's growing around the banks, hospitals, post offices, and other buildings that have been professionally landscaped. Considering a shrub for the dark north side of the house? Look at shrubs on the dark north side of buildings. Need something low for a hot and sunny area? Look at the low shrubs on the south or west side of buildings.

If you see something you like, snip a section off (ask permission first) and take it to your local nursery or garden center for identification. Ask about any problems it may have.

Q I would like to grow an evergreen shrub in a dark, protected area in my entry. I do not care for needle-leaf plants and I would like something a bit more dramatic than a rhododendron, azalea, or common camellia. I love the tropical look, but do not have the patience to overwinter any tender plants. Although usually mild, sometimes our winter temperatures dip below 20 degrees.

A *Fatsia japonica* or Japanese aralia is a tough, shade-loving evergreen with bold, dramatic foliage that can adapt to most soils and is even happy for years growing in a pot. Wash leaves often to keep it free of mites, and if foliage begins to yellow add a fertilizer with iron. A protected spot near the house is perfect, as cold winds and freezing weather can blacken the leaves.

Q I have ripped out my overgrown junipers and the roof-high rhododendrons that were blocking my windows, but now I need some plants around the foundation of the house. What should I plant that will stay low and evergreen?

A Dwarf conifers are the easy answer mentioned earlier, but for more color, look for slow-growing or dwarf plants with colorful foliage. Winter creeper euonymus is one of my favorites because it comes in an emerald green and also a yellow-leafed form, and can be grown as a casual creeping ground cover, or kept trimmed into a formal hedge.

Burning Bush: For Hot Hillsides and Sizzling Color

A mild-mannered, nicely shaped, but otherwise insignificant green shrub most of the year, once fall comes, *Euonymus alata* 'Compacta' is one hot-looking plant. The leaves turn a red so brilliant they look on fire—and this isn't even the best part. This dwarf burning bush is not only adaptable and drought tolerant, it also is not bothered by insects or disease, and its shape is naturally rounded and well formed. Give it room (even the dwarf variety can get six feet wide and as tall), and give it sun in a well-drained spot. It will warm your heart every fall.

Plant the red-berried cotoneaster under the feet of the burning bush for evergreen ground cover with matching fall color. If you need a tall companion, add a tough and terrific ginkgo tree. Its fan-shaped leaves will turn brilliant yellow just when the burning bush starts to glow bright red.

Q I love flowers but have a lot of shade in my yard. I also have very little time to garden and so I know I want flowers from shrubs instead of perennials or annuals. Please help.

A For easy color made in the shade, the following shrubs do best with some filtered light or at least a few hours of sunlight a day. Most need extra water in the summer if they have to compete with tree roots for moisture. In addition to these, there are several types of daphne that tolerate some shade and bloom sweetly anyway.

BIGLEAF HYDRANGEA (*Hydrangea macrophylla*): This is the shrub that makes the most dependable and biggest splash of color in a shady garden, tossing up huge balls of blue or pink petals and scoring even more beautiful yardage as fall turns into winter and the flower heads dry on the bush.

SHRUB FUCHSIA (*Fuchsia magellanica*): Although this hardy shrub fuchsia may die back in the winter, it will rebloom and grow to 20 feet in a cool but protected location.

RHODODENDRONS AND AZALEAS: These won't produce many flowers in deep shade, but in light shade they will bloom happily. An early pink bloomer called 'Christmas Cheer' flowers even in deep shade—in my garden, about a month after Christmas.

CAMELLIA (*Camillia*): From winter blooms to autumn flowers, camellia is an evergreen that has a wide range of flower forms and bloom times to choose from.

LILY-OF-THE-VALLEY SHRUB (*Pieris japonica*): In early spring, fragrant flowers hang like grape clusters from the branches of this shrub.

Outlandish Ideas

Instant Topiary—or Not Topiary

Evergreen shrubs trimmed into spirals and poodle-tail balls are expensive to buy and time-consuming to maintain. They are also more prone to infestations of mites because constant shearing of the new growth makes for dense inner growth. But here's an easy answer if you want the topiary look in a formal setting or moved indoors for a week or so as a Christmas tree to decorate.

- Visit a nursery and buy a columnar-shaped, naturally tall and narrow evergreen in a gallon-size pot. *Thuja occidentalis* 'Emerald Green' and the upright green columnar juniper *Juniperus chinensis* 'Hetz's Columnaris' work well because they are often sold as inexpensive hedge shrubs and are easy to find.

- Next tie a string to the tip-top of the shrub and wrap the string around the plant in a spiral, making sure the string is evenly spaced. This string is your guide to cutting into the shrub to make a tidy spiral design.

- Use clippers to remove all the foliage under the string to the bare stem of the shrub. Next clip and smooth the rough edges of any side growth.

- Now set your trimmed evergreen into a larger fancy urn or decorative pot, placing gravel or an overturned pot in the bottom to put your spiraled evergreen at the correct level inside the larger pot. This little boost from the bottom also keeps the roots from sitting in drainage water. There is no need to transplant the topiary into a larger container, since the idea is to slow the growth by keeping the plant rootbound. Some flat river stones or moss on top of the inner pot will keep the rim of the smaller plastic pot hidden.

- Keep your newly trimmed spiral out of full sun (its newly exposed bark could get sunburned) and don't allow the soil to dry completely. A trim with the shears twice a year should keep your spiral topiary in good shape. These spiral shrubs are perfect for displaying a string of white lights at the holidays.

Fragrance Without Fuss: Fragrant Shrubs Instead of Lilacs

DAPHNE (many kinds): Some are low and compact, others more upright; they need good drainage or you'll have problems.

MOCK ORANGE (*Philadelphus virginalis* 'Minnesota Snowflake'): Full sun and good air circulation are all this old-fashioned favorite needs to scent the garden with white blossoms in late spring.

SARCOCOCCA (sometimes called sweet box): This evergreen comes in dwarf and taller forms and thrives in shade; the flowers are tiny but emit a welcome vanilla scent in late winter. Grow it near the front door, and visitors will think you're baking cookies.

FRAGRANT SNOWBALL (*Viburnum carlcephalum*): Long-lasting, waxy white blossoms bloom in fragrant clusters on this adaptable shrub, which also offers fall leaf color.

SUMMER LILAC (*Buddleia davidii*): Fast growth each spring supports wands of flowers on arching branches, with a light fragrance that draws butterflies from miles around. This lilac needs well-drained soil—but that's about all—and is resistant to most insects and diseases even if soil is rocky and poor. Cut it back hard each spring or fall to keep it tidy.

Q I want an evergreen shrub that is easy to grow but not the same old rhododendrons I see in my neighbors' yards. I want a shrub that will bloom in the shade and grow just as big as I want it to get, and then stop growing so I won't have to worry about pruning. Oh yes—I also want it to smell good.

A I can offer an easy answer—except for the part about it growing just as big as you want and then stopping. The *Pieris japonica*, sometimes called the Lily-of-the-Valley Shrub, is an easy-care evergreen with spring flowers (they're even fragrant) and shiny evergreen leaves. It comes in several different varieties, including one with brilliant new growth of deep red called 'Forest Flame'. These lovely shrubs are easy to find at nurseries but not as commonly planted as their cousins, the often-overused rhododendrons and azaleas.

Pieris japonica is a great shrub for growing on the north or east side of the house where it will be protected from the hot afternoon sun and drying winds. Like rhododendrons, it loves cool, moist soil with lots of organic matter—dig some fine bark chips or peat moss into the hole when you plant, and it'll be happy for years.

Unfortunately, *Pieris japonica* isn't a magic shrub and it won't stop growing once it gets to be the size you want. However, there is a tiny dwarf *Pieris* called 'Pygmaea'.

All *Pieris japonicas* are easy to prune. The graceful but upright growth form of this shrub makes it a fine plant to use near the front door or in the narrow space between two windows. Because of its year-round good looks and compact root system, this is the perfect shrub to grow in a large pot near a protected entry.

Easy Answers

More Colorful and Low Shrubs to Use Up Close to the House

Don't stop with this list! Your local nursery can show you more of the new varieties that keep coming out to meet the demand for slower-growing, dwarf plants. New homes keep getting bigger, yards continue to shrink (it's that third garage that hogs a huge chunk of yard space), and dwarf varieties of many shrubs continue to be developed. Most nurseries now carry dwarf nandinas or heavenly bamboos, dwarf spiraeas, dwarf sweet box, dwarf heathers, dwarf cotoneaster, and dwarf junipers.

DWARF NANDINA: Also called heavenly bamboo because of its small salmon-and-green leaves and graceful texture, this shrub is not related to bamboo and does not spread by underground roots like bamboo.

'CRIMSON PYGMY' BARBERRY: Purple leaves stand out on this compact plant.

LITTLE LEAF BOXWOOD (*Buxus microphylla*): A small, shiny evergreen.

DWARF CHINESE HOLLY (*Ilex cornuta* 'Rotunda'): This compact shrub has foliage a darker green than boxwood and is more resistant to disease.

KURUME AZALEAS (such as Hino-crimson): This is a whole family of low-growing azaleas.

Yak, 'PJM', and 'Dora': These Three Are Healthy Rhododendrons

Plant these terrific triplets for fuss-free rhododendrons. They will ward off the weevils and shoulder the wind and cold.

YAK (*R. yakushimanum* species): This is not a furry animal from Tibet, but a furry rhodie from Tibet. The furry growth under the leaves is what helps make this species of rhododendron resistant to weevils and tolerant of the cold. It has a nice compact growth habit. The Yaks and their hybrids come in several colors, most with bell-shaped blooms.

'PJM': Its small lavender blooms pop out in very early spring, and this ironclad rhodie seems to laugh at both severely cold and extremely hot weather. The leaves are small and have a touch of purple, which makes this a great background shrub for yellow and lime-green plants. Even weevils won't bother to nibble on 'PJM'.

'DORA AMATEIS': Compact and cute, with white flowers and resistance to weevils, this is one great rhododendron for tidy landscapes. Did I also mention its blooms are fragrant? 'Dora' is a ground-hugging little doll that can win the heart of any gardener.

CARE & PROBLEMS

Q When do I prune my hydrangea? It bloomed beautifully this year after a few years of only a few small flowers. I was pruning it wrong before, so now I am afraid to do anything. The hydrangea is growing too large for its space, but I know if I prune severely, I won't have any blooms next summer.

A The easy answer is to prune summer-blooming shrubs such as hydrangea in the fall (buddleia, potentilla, and hibiscus are other summer bloomers that like fall haircuts). Trim back the branches of your hydrangea that bloomed last summer. These should be easy to identify because the dried flower heads should still be hanging on. You should be able to see the difference between the old wood—light in color—and the new darker wood. Hydrangeas bloom on two-year-old wood, so don't cut back every branch all the way to the ground. Instead, shorten these just a bit, so a few buds of new wood are left. The oldest and thickest branches can be cut back to the ground.

The idea is to keep half the plant in one-year-old branches and half in two-year-old canes. This way you will have plenty of blooms each summer instead of alternating years of feast and famine. Always remove the weak, crossing, and damaged branches by cutting close to the source where they branch.

Q **How and when do I prune my lilac? It is quite old and growing too large. I was also wondering how to start new lilacs from this old shrub.**

A You can prune spring-blooming shrubs such as lilacs, viburnums, and spiraea after they are done blooming. Unlike old people, old lilacs can be revitalized by harsh treatment and a severe pruning. If you are willing to wait three years for blooms, cut the lilac down to a one-foot-tall group of stumps and the plant will start all over. To start a new plant, just remove some of the side shoots already at the base of the shrub by giving them a quick twist where they join to the main plant. Try to gather these young shoots before you prune and plant them out in a different location or give them away.

Q **When can I prune my rhododendron?**

A Anytime you want is the easy answer, but to insure that you don't cut off any flower buds, prune right after the plant finishes blooming. You could also snap off the new growth or light green "candles" each summer to control the size in a more gentle manner.

Q **Do I have to remove all the spent flowers from my huge rhododendrons?**

A Nope. The easy answer is to let nature do her thing and just ignore the mess until the spent flowers dry and fall on their own. However, if you want maximum blooms and growth, and a tidy shrub, snip off all the faded flower clusters.

Growing Happy Rhododendrons and Azaleas

❀ They crave highly organic soil. Add two shovelfuls of organic matter such as peat moss, compost, or bark dust into their hole at planting time.

❀ They are heavy drinkers. Give extra water during summer droughts. These are thirsty plants.

❀ They are acid-loving plants. Do not spread lime, wood ashes, or mushroom compost near the roots.

Q **When is the best time to transplant my overgrown rhododendron?**

A The easy answer is whenever the weather is cool. Think of rhododendrons, azaleas, and camellias as plants on wheels. They are easy to move in any season because they have such a compact and fibrous root system. Just water before, after, and during the adjustment period for the first year while the plant gets settled in its new home.

Don't forget how much these shrubs love organic matter in the soil, and treat them to some peat moss and fine bark chips mixed into the planting hole.

Q **When is the best time to prune my hedge?**

A The easy answer is when you see new growth. For evergreens this is in the spring, for privet and barberry hedges this is in the summer, and for boxwood and Japanese holly, this is anytime in the growing season, because these classic hedge plants grow slowly over a long period.

Q **How often do I have to prune my boxwood and privet hedge?**

A As often as you want. For a more formal look, shear back the new growth once a month or so (formal hedges are high-maintenance monsters), but for a more casual (and healthier) hedge, trim once or twice a year. Or go natural, and let them freely express the shape Mother Nature intended.

Hedging Your Bets on Maintenance: Mixing It Up

The easy answer to less hedge maintenance is to stop thinking of hedges as long lines of green shrubbery that need to be sheared and shaped every few months. A more beautiful and practical way to grow a wall or screen is to mix together flowering, evergreen, and deciduous shrubs in a casual pattern that imitates nature. There are several reasons why the mixed-up hedge makes perfect sense:

🌿 A mixed hedge can have something different blooming at different times of the year. Forsythia flowers in spring, while Rose of Sharon does her thing in August. You shouldn't have to choose; enjoy them both.

🌿 A mixed hedge can have a variation in height, putting the tall stuff right where you need it. A columnar 'Pyramidalis' arborvitae can be lined up to block your view of a telephone pole, but next to that a lower-growing *Viburnum davidii* can be positioned so you can see over it to enjoy the view of your neighbor's flowers.

🌿 A mixed hedge requires less rigorous pruning.

🌿 A mixed hedge can hide your mistakes. As plants grow too large or die in a mixed hedge planting, they can be removed. It won't look like soldiers have deserted the ranks the way it would if you suddenly lost a plant from a uniform hedge.

Gardening Tip

"When it comes time to clean up the dead flowers on my rhododendron, I spread a big sheet under the bush and use a small bamboo rake to claw off the old blossoms. They fall onto the sheet, which I fold up and empty into the compost pile."

Q My lilac bush has brown and black spots on the leaves and the flowers never really bloomed, but turned limp and black.

A This sounds like the symptoms of bacterial or fungal blight, a common affliction of lilacs during moist, mild weather. Prune off any diseased leaves below the point of infection and clean up the leaves in the fall to prevent overwintering spores. Spraying a fungicide every few weeks during wet weather in the spring may help the problem, but it won't solve it. If after several springs your lilac doesn't beat the blight and bloom beautifully, give it the ax and replace it with a more blight-resistant flowering shrub—a butterfly bush, perhaps?

Q My lilac shrub has a thin white powder on the new leaves. It seemed to bloom okay, but the powder appears each summer and makes the leaves fall off.

A You have powdery mildew on your lilac, and the easy answer is to just ignore this fungus and enjoy the blooms in the spring. Good fall cleanup helps stop overwintering of the mildew, and it usually won't kill the shrub. The traditional answer to powdery mildew treatment is to spray with a smelly wettable sulfur spray once or twice at weekly intervals—not something I think is worth doing year after year.

Q The leaves of my lilac roll up and I find a green worm inside. The leaves turn brown and die after they begin to roll. I also see strands or webs holding the rolled leaves together. Please help.

A The leaf rollers have found your lilac, and they need to be tended to each spring until they give up and go away. If your lilac is small and the damage is minor, just squish the rolled leaves as soon as you notice them. You'll have the satisfaction of knowing you're killing the worm inside before it has a chance to mate and lay more eggs. If there are too many rolled leaves to squish, you can prune them all off and get them quickly into a plastic bag. The traditional treatment is to spray with Bt (*Bacillus thuringiensis*) two or three times at three- to five-day intervals—but that's not a very easy answer.

Q I have a hedge of green shrubs called 'Pyramidalis' arborvitae. The problem is, at the end of summer the inner leaves turn brown and fall off. Does this mean it needs more water?

A Not necessarily. The easy answer is it's simply shedding old leaves, or "flagging," and there's no need to worry. If the shrubs continue to put on new growth and lose only a small portion of the older leaves in late summer, you can just call it a sign of maturity.

Gardening Tip

"To keep the narrow-leaf evergreens in any hedge from turning brown after they are pruned, just shear them when they are wet. This trick works on spruce, hemlock, and fir."

Garden Accents:
Fill in Those Missing Links

Garden accents include nonliving objects such as birdbaths, sundials, and outdoor artwork, and these are the things that give your garden personality and pizzazz. They are also the easy answer for solving many landscape problems.

❧ Did death do a number on several plants in your uniform hedge planting? Don't risk planting another shrub in the death zone. Use a lattice screen or fence section to fill in, and place a sundial on a pillar in front instead of more plants.

❧ Missing the middle shrub in your trio of plants that filled the space under your tall Japanese maple? You won't find one to match the other two in the grouping, so get a birdbath to add bulk in the empty spot instead.

❧ Did a hedging tree topple over, leaving nothing but a stump? Add instant height by placing a tall post where the tree once stood, and then secure a collection of birdhouses or a weather vane to the post.

Q My photinia hedge lost a lot of leaves in the winter and now the foliage is getting spots all over. I have noticed this happening every spring, but this year it seems worse. What should I get to spray on the plant?

A Nothing. Leaf spot on photinia is very common, and the latest recommendation is to wait it out and let the tree handle the problem. Fungicide sprays don't seem to make a difference. Leaf spot is caused by damp weather conditions, which is why the symptoms seem to disappear in the summer. If you really can't live with a spotted specimen, consider replacing your photinia with an evergreen hedge of arborvitae or cedar.

Q What is eating notches out of the leaves of my rhododendrons? It started as small bites out of the leaf margins, but over the years it has gotten worse and now the leaves are so full of ragged edges they look tattered.

A The wily root weevil is the most common leaf notcher of rhododendrons. This is a black beetlelike insect that comes out at night and crawls from the soil up the

trunk of the rhododendrons to feed on the leaves. The easy answer to control this pest is to only plant weevil-resistant rhododendrons (see the sidebar "Yak, 'PJM', and 'Dora': These Three Are healthy Rhododendrons," on page 116). If you want to save an established rhodie from weevil attacks, use a sticky black goo called "Tanglefoot" around the base of the shrub, and you'll catch the weevils as they try to cross the goo and become mired. Prune lower branches that touch the ground so weevils will have to use the trunk as their main highway.

Another way to clean up weevils is to spread a drop cloth under the infected plant at night and then gently brush the rhodie with a broom. Weevils play dead when attacked, and this reflex makes the weevils release their grip on the rhododendron leaves.

Chapter Nine

Trees

The easy answer for shade and structure

Trees are often called the bones of the garden because they make up the frame or skeleton of the landscape. It's time this skeleton came out of the closet because I make no bones about the fact that many gardeners like myself make lots of fractured mistakes when it comes to choosing trees. The problem is that trees grow big and are often expensive. This means not only that you will have to live with your mistakes, but also that they'll be pretty hard to hide. (All of the above is also true of most shrubs. For easy answers for successful shrubs, see Chapter Eight, "Super Shrubs.") The reason most of us need more support for our oversized bones is because we just can't believe how big the cute or skinny little tree will become, and if there is a long-term problem, we can't bring ourselves to get rid of the expensive victim. Sometimes the plant tags that are supposed to tell you the mature size of a plant are deceiving. In a mild climate like the Pacific Northwest, plants can grow twice as wide as the label suggests. When a tag says a tree will grow to 15 feet, that doesn't mean it will stop growing at 15 feet; that means it may reach 15 feet in ten years—and after that, the sky (literally) is the limit. Carefully choosing and planting the bones of your garden is the easy answer to a strong skeleton, but most gardeners never get that opportunity. They inherit a yard that comes with an out-of-kilter backbone of mature trees, or a few staggered shrubs lined up like broken ribs. Maybe the bones in your own garden are a bit out of alignment, maybe they're weakened and diseased. The important point to remember about the bones in the garden is that they are replaceable. You don't have to live with the problem trees and demanding shrubs in your own yard—even if you did put them there yourself.

SELECTING & SITING

Q We live on top of a hill with lots of wind and sun, and the soil is very rocky and dry. What trees will survive these hostile conditions?

A Many trees will adapt to high, dry land, but almost all will need some extra water that crucial first year. For evergreens, look for Austrian black pine and Colorado spruce; for small trees, the Tatarian dogwood (*Cornus alba*) and the smoke tree (*Cotinus coggygria*), which does great in poor soils; for a spreading tree to shade the lawn or patio, go with the Japanese pagoda tree (*Sophora japonica*).

Q We have lots of large fir trees around our property, but I would like to add some smaller trees. What trees can compete with the big tree roots and tolerate the shade?

A You're looking for understory trees, the shade lovers that know how to live in harmony with the giants of the forest. The best for woodland gardens are vine maples, Japanese maples, Korean dogwood (*Cornus kousa*), serviceberry, redbud, and the lovely blooming Japanese snowbell (*Styrax japonicum*).

If you want to add some more evergreens under your tall firs, go with western red cedar and western hemlock, two shade lovers that will grow into huge sun blockers when they mature a generation from now.

Easy Answers

Finding a Budget for Nursery Trees: Living Gifts from the Nursery

Birthdays, anniversaries, holidays, and remembrances are all gift-giving occasions that are the perfect opportunity to improve your bones—the bones in your garden, that is. Giving gifts from the nursery can be an easy learning experience even if the tree or shrub is not for your own yard. Walking around and considering the different plants, asking the nursery personnel their opinion, and hearing about the pros and cons of plants you find attractive forces even the most reluctant gardener to take more notice of trees and shrubs in the landscape.

Gardening Tip

Keep the following rather rude trees away from septic tanks and drainfields. They block ditches and clog drainways with their aggressive root systems. They are: birch, willow, and red maples.

Flowering Cherry: Rotting Skeletons in Your Closet?

Gardening Tip

"We have been given many plants and trees over the years, and we just fell into the habit of calling the trees by the name of the person we think of. The hydrangea bush that my sister shared a start of we dubbed "Aunt Mary," and we call her each summer to compare bloom times. The pine tree given us as a memorial plant when my dad died we call "Grandpa," and although our younger kids weren't around to know him, they do know the Grandpa tree and love to hear his story."

What I recommend here always gets me into trouble but, as always, I invite you to simply ignore any advice you don't like.

The easy answer to choosing trees and shrubs is not to plant any flowering trees that need spraying to keep them healthy and not to choose shrubs that are prone to insect and disease problems. This means I no longer recommend planting the superpopular and much-loved flowering cherry. So let the conflict and controversy begin.

There are many types of flowering cherry trees, from the pendant clusters and vase-shaped form of the 'Kwanzan' cherry (*Prunus serrulata* 'Kwanzan') to the grafted weeping flowering cherry (*Prunus serrulata* 'Pendula'), and they are wonderful trees if they are grown in full sun with fast-draining, well-aerated soil. But the truth is, I get more questions about sickly flowering cherry trees than all other tree problems combined—although pink dogwoods are close behind with their own set of woes.

Cherry trees are prone to root rot in soil that contains clay or has other drainage problems, and there is no cure for this problem other than planting in raised beds. Cherry tree foliage is also very attractive to insects, and so they suffer from aphids, worms, and tent caterpillars more than other flowering trees. To add to the drama and trauma, these trees do not like to be pruned, so cutting out damaged or diseased branches upsets the already struggling tree. A deformed and misshapen cherry tree that slowly declines in an ugly death is tolerated far too long in the yards of many gardeners.

Smearing the reputation about the much-loved cherry trees upsets not only gardeners but entire communities. This is the same tree that cities schedule festivals around, and it is the flowering cherry that adorns the grounds of our nation's capitol. The easy answer to most of the cherry tree problems is to choose other flowering trees that won't need to have branches pruned back from blight, or colonies of tent caterpillars sprayed. Cherry trees have been suffering from fungal infections, viral infections, bacterial cankers, aphids . . . no wonder there is a legend about George Washington cutting down his father's cherry tree. In his private life, President Washington was quite the gardener, and I'm sure he was doing his dad a favor by ridding him of a disease-ridden and demanding tree.

Saying unkind things and pointing out the faults about flowering cherry trees and pink dogwoods is like pointing out structural damage and wood rot on everybody's favorite historic building. It may not be what the public wants to hear, but somebody has to say it.

Q We had a problem in our last home with tree roots from our cherry tree poking up in our lawn. We don't want to make this same mistake. What trees besides cherries have surface roots?

A Trees with shallow, snakelike roots that can crack patios and rise like boa constrictors from the lawn are silver maples, poplars, 'Kwanzan' cherry, willows, elm, and ash. Now in all fairness, it is often our own poor watering practices that draw the roots upward. Less frequent but deep watering encourages tree roots to grow down deep where they belong. To keep roots deep, restrict your lawn watering to once a week during dry weather, but water slowly and allow the moisture to seep in to a depth of 18 inches.

Q I need a narrow or columnar tree for alongside my driveway or parking strip next to the sidewalk.

A The easy answer is to plant trees that grow tall and narrow naturally, such as 'Columnare' red maple, 'Columnare' Norway maple, and 'Columnaris' hornbeam. Ask at the nursery for other trees with columnar or narrow growth habits.

Q I need a tree to block out the neighbor's satellite dish, RV, and dog kennel.

A The easy answer is a broad evergreen tree such as deodar or Himalayan cedar (*Cedrus deodara*) or quick-growing Port Orford cedar (*Chamaecyparis lawsoniana*).

Kousa Dogwood: A Dogwood for Disease Resistance

Pink dogwoods (*Cornus florida*) are almost as popular as pink flowering cherry trees, and the sight of a healthy pink dogwood barking out the blooms on a sunny day in May is enough to make any winter-weary gardener decide to devote the garden to dogwoods. You may be one of the lucky gardeners for whom anthracnose has not hit the neighborhood or leaf blight made an appearance. If the pink dogwood trees in your neighborhood are healthy and fungus free, then I may be barking up the wrong tree when I warn you of the pink dogwood blues.

For the past 20 years dogwoods have been suffering from an increase in cankers, anthracnose, and twig dieback that some blame on a change in climate. Healthy, mature trees seem to escape these dangers, but new homeowners investing in their first flowering tree often turn loyally to the traditional pink dogwood and, according to many of the people who read my weekly newspaper column and write in, are routinely disappointed.

Even if pink dogwoods have been muzzled by diseases, you don't have to give up on the entire family of dogwoods. The lovely *Cornus kousa*, sometimes called the Chinese or Korean dogwood or the gardener's best friend, is more resistant to disease and now easy to find at nurseries. *Cornus kousa* is sometimes called the tree for four seasons because it offers starry white blossoms in early summer, fall leaf color, and red winter fruit. In spring the new foliage is breathtakingly beautiful.

Q **I need a foolproof tree that will never need spraying and has drought resistance, good fall color, and interesting foliage.**

A *Ginkgo biloba* is the easy answer. This tree has been around since the dinosaurs. It makes a carefree street or lawn tree, and although this tree doesn't look like much when young, it turns into a long-lived beauty in a few years. The leaves are fan-shaped like those on a maidenhair fern, so it is sometimes called the maidenhair tree. Plant only male trees, as the females have messy fruit. How do you tell a male from a female tree? You don't peek under the leaves, you ask at the nursery.

Q What do you suggest as a colorful accent tree that will stand out against all the green in my landscape?

A The easy answer is to plant trees with purple foliage, such as purple smoke tree, purple leaf plum, or red leaf Japanese maples.

Q We have property that drains poorly and is wet most of the winter. We have already killed several expensive trees. What trees do you recommend for wet soil?

A Trees that adapt well to waterlogged soils include birch, alder, redtwig dogwood (*Cornus stolonifera,* not the pink dogwood), and also any of the willows or aspens.

Messy Magnolias and the Quest for a Rainless Spring

Magnolia trees, sometimes called tulip trees because of their huge pink and white blossoms, are an impressive sight and one that makes gardeners forget what this tree looks like the rest of the year. It must be said that the saucer magnolia has rather pale green leaves and an awkward shape, but it is only after the buds open that the real mess begins. Ever seen a magnolia blossom after a rain shower? The petals quickly turn brown and start to rot; petals shed, turn dark and mushy on the ground, and encourage a feeding frenzy for generations of earwigs and sow bugs. This type of behavior is perfectly acceptable if the flowering tree has some other great attractions such as wonderful winter bark, glorious fall color, or even a cute figure, but the magnolia has none of these. I've decided that until we can have a guarantee of no rain while the magnolias are blooming, I no longer will recommend these prima donna trees. The South can keep her magnolias, which are like a Southern belle who refuses to do anything useful except look beautiful for a very short time. Here in the Pacific Northwest, those fine fat petals just melt away in the rain.

Gardening Tip

"I've learned to prune in stages, taking out just a little bit every few months and then observing what the plant does and how it looks before pruning off more. This way I don't get as sore, and don't have too many pruning crumbs to fit into the garden dumpster."

Proper Placement is the Practical Solution for Disease-Resistant Trees

Follow these tips to have a happy dogwood:

🌿 Filtered sunlight is best. Hot sun can weaken these woodland trees.

🌿 Plant a bit on the high side—on top of a slight mound or raised bed is a good idea. Good root aeration and drainage cut down on soil fungi problems.

🌿 Good air circulation around the roots and branches is a must. Don't grow thick or tight ground covers over the roots of your dogwood, and don't place it in a protected corner with no air circulation.

🌿 Add compost to the soil. Everything—from potted plants to ground cover shrubs—has more resistance to fungal infection if there is some compost mixed into the soil at planting time.

CARE

Q Will it hurt to remove a branch or two from my weeping Japanese maple in the summer? I know I should have done this pruning job when the plant was leafless, but now the new growth is blocking the path.

A Removing a few of the lowest branches from a tree or shrub can be done any time of the year. Follow the branch all the way to the trunk and make a clean cut with sharp shears. *Remember:* You can also remove any dead, damaged, or diseased branches from plants whenever you happen to notice them.

Q What about staking newly planted trees?

A The easy answer to tree staking is to let the tree stand alone, and offer verbal support instead. Mother Nature knows best. New research proves that not staking a young tree can actually make it grow stronger. Blowing about in the wind while it's young forces the tree to develop a superior root system that makes it less likely to suffer storm damage in the future. You may still need to stake young trees for the first year or two if a windy location means they'll be blown to the ground, but routine staking is no longer recommended.

Pruning

Pruning trees makes even experienced gardeners doubt their decisions, so the easy answer to better pruning is to educate yourself with a good book or to take one of the many pruning classes offered at nurseries. Most trees and shrubs need no pruning except for the three Ds (dead, diseased, and damaged material) if you gave proper thought to their placement and mature size when you planted them.

The most-asked pruning question is when to do the job, and the easy answer is to prune whenever the shears are sharp. Another way to put that is not to put off pruning just because you don't know if your timing is perfect. The tree will adapt to your schedule.

WHEN: Whenever. There are experts who claim each of the four seasons is the best time to prune trees. For flowering shrubs, pruning after blooming is the general rule.

WHAT: Take out the three Ds—dead, diseased, and damaged wood.

WHY: Prune to thin or tidy the tree or shrub, to remove crossing branches, and to control size.

WHO CAN HELP GUIDE YOU: Hire a professional the first time and ask to watch. And/or get a good pruning book (such as *Pruning Simplified,* by Lewis Hill), take a pruning class, or ask at a nursery.

HOW: Pruning plants for more beauty is an art form. Don't rush it, and don't do the job when you're angry.

RESOURCE: PlantAmnesty, an organization dedicated to "ending the senseless torture and mutilation of trees and shrubs," puts out a lively and informative newsletter for professionals and homeowners who get into trouble by either overpruning or underpruning. Contact them at PlantAmnesty, 906 NW 87th Street, Seattle, WA 98117.

Gardening Tip

"I use bird netting under my tree in the fall. I lay the netting on the ground and wait for all the leaves to fall. Then I just gather up my net of leaves and drag it to the compost pile. Sure beats raking."

Avoiding Maintenance Mistakes: Look Before You Plant

LOOK AROUND: Don't plant a tree within 25 feet of your house.

LOOK UP: Don't put a tree beneath power lines.

THINK DOWN: Don't put a thirsty tree near drainfields or septic systems.

LOOK AT THE FOILAGE: Trees with large leaves like maples will drop leaves that need to be raked from the lawn each fall.

LOOK AT THE FRUIT: Even nonedible fruiting trees may make a mess on patios or driveways.

Q I have a pine tree that is growing too large for its space. I've heard I should remove all the new growth to keep it compact. Is this true?

A Yes. Removing all the new growth or pointed candles from a pine tree or a mugho pine shrub in early summer will keep the plant more compact and bushy. It is not as severe as lopping off entire branches.

Dogwoods and magnolias can also be kept under control this way. Waiting until June means the new growth is easy to distinguish and can then be lopped off with shears, or the candles can be pinched out with your fingertips. Dogwoods and magnolias will still bloom the following spring if you shear off the new growth in early summer. They also will be fuller and more compact.

Q How much should I fertilize my trees?

A The easy answer to fertilizing trees: Just Forget It.

When it comes to fertilizing trees, we often do more harm than good. Trees have such extensive root systems that they can often get all the nutrients they need from the soil. Extra nitrogen is the one nutrient that may be in short supply for young trees, but if your young tree is within ten feet of a lawn, it's probably stealing nitrogen from your high-nitro lawn food and getting all the green food it can use.

Remember that plants that are overfed grow fast with soft and succulent growth that is more tender to weather damage and more attractive to insects. Make your trees lean, mean, and independent.

Contorted Filbert: High Maintenance Can Be a Labor of Love

Sometimes a high-maintenance tree or shrub that demands frequent pruning or even spraying to keep it looking good is worth the effort.

In my own garden a contorted filbert (*Corylus avellana* 'Contorta') grows in front of the library window where I work, and I really love this comical tree—as much as some visitors abhor it. It's nicknamed the "politician's tree" because it grows so twisted and crooked. Its bare branches provide an artistic curtain that doesn't block the light from the window in the winter, but later the foliage screens out the summer heat. Winter catkins hang pendulously and then bloom right outside the window with tiny carmine blossoms. For some reason this small tree attracts all sorts of wildlife, and it can be downright entertaining (if not distracting) to watch the chickadees, hummingbirds, and small green frogs that visit the gnarled branches and sit for awhile on the nearby window ledge. The summer foliage is also as twisted and strange-looking as the rest of the tree, and visitors have been known to ask, "What's killing that tree?"

If the unusual appearance isn't enough, my contorted filbert is grafted onto a rootstock that continually shoots out suckers of new growth that need to be pruned off from the base of the tree. There is no easy answer to controlling these suckers, other than vigilant pruning. But when you have a plant that you love, all the extra maintenance seems worth it. Perhaps it is a flowering cherry you must spray or a tidy boxwood hedge you don't mind trimming every few months. The easy answers to problems aren't meant to deny anyone the pleasure of growing plants that need special care. The gardener gets to choose what plants are worth the extra effort, and what plants are candidates for shovel surgery. It may be high maintenance, but don't ever suggest I get rid of my contorted filbert.

Q Should I add fertilizer to the planting hole?

A Adding compost to the planting hole or as a mulch around the roots is much better than fertilizing a tree with plant food. Compost in the soil can help trees fight off fungal infections. Slow-release organic plant foods like cottonseed meal and composted manure are other good sources of tree nutrients.

PROBLEMS

Q The leaves on my cherry tree wilt and droop after the tree is done blooming. Then the foliage turns yellow and drops off. The tree grows uglier each year. What could the problem be?

A It could be one of many problems, but summer yellowing and dropping of leaves is a symptom of verticillium wilt—a fungus infection. Although a sulfur fungicide applied every seven to ten days in the spring is the traditional treatment, the easy answer is to make like George Washington and cut that cherry tree down. Trees planted with lots of organic matter in the soil have better luck at recovering from this disease.

Q My cherry tree has spots on the leaves that turn red or purple and then fall out, leaving a shot-hole look to the foliage. The tree then loses almost all its foliage and looks just terrible!

A Cherry leaf spot is the easy answer to this polka-dot plague, and again a sulfur fungicide is the common treatment, but even frequent sprayings do not guarantee a healthy tree. Clean up all the fallen diseased leaves and if it doesn't outgrow the problem next summer, give it the ax. Better that the tree goes down with some dignity than to suffer the humiliation of defoliation year after year.

Q My cherry tree is oozing a gummy residue in the spring and fall from shoots and limbs that then wilt and die by summer. I have tried cleaning up all the fallen debris and cutting out the bad branches, but each year it grows worse. I am running out of healthy branches. Please help.

A Sorry to break it to you, but the tragedy of bacterial canker has worked its way into your cherry tree and there is no easy cure. When you first notice the oozing sap and dying branches, you could try to cut them out, being sure to disinfect your pruning shears in a bleach-water solution between cuts, but this is what I consider taking heroic measures. The easy answer is to say good-bye and choose a more disease-resistant blooming tree—such as a *Cercis* (redbud)—to replace your cranky, canker-infested cherry.

Gardening Tip

"I water young trees with a screwdriver. I want the water to go down deep to the roots, so I first poke the ground with a large screwdriver and then let the water from the hose seep slowly out for a few hours near the base of the tree. Deep soakings are best for trees."

Dead Trees as Garden Accents

Instead of cutting up or pulling down a dead tree, use it as a trellis for a flowering vine such as clematis, honeysuckle, or wisteria. Or remove most of the side branches and nail a collection of whimsical and colorful birdhouses to the tree. Dead trees can also be the support system for a collection of wind chimes, weather vanes, or bird feeders. These are easy answers to avoiding the expense of tree removal, and if visitors or the neighbors inquire as to your taste, you simply raise an eyebrow and ask why they don't recognize "modern art."

Q The leaves of my pink dogwood have black spots and blotches, and the tree has dieback of twigs. I have tried spraying a fungicide on it, but the problem gets worse each year. The poor tree hasn't bloomed for three years.

A Dark spots and lesions on the foliage of a dogwood sound like signs of anthracnose, a fungal disease that kills the tree slowly. The first line of defense is to cut out infected branches and gather fallen leaves to keep the fungal spores from spreading. Sometimes healthy trees will outgrow this problem, so keep the tree well watered and fertilized. Spraying fungicides is no guarantee of a cure, but any tree that has diseased foliage all summer and hasn't bloomed for three years either needs to be seen by an arborist or is a good a candidate for ax surgery.

Q The leaves on my pink dogwood are blighted and discolored, and the twigs develop bumps and then begin to die off. Please tell us something we can do to save this tree.

A Sounds like a blight on the reputation of this much-loved landscape tree. Actually there are several different kinds of blights that cause foliage problems, but

Gardening Tip

For a happy flowering cherry tree, place it in an open area in full sun. Do not even attempt to plant a cherry tree if the soil is wet or drains poorly. Watch early in the spring for signs of curling, wilting, or eaten foliage so you can deal with the problem early. Do not prune just for the sake of pruning, as this weakens the tree. Remove only dead, diseased, and damaged branches.

none of them are easy to treat. The best you could hope for is to keep your dogwood so vigorous that it will fight off the infection without you having to resort to repeated sprayings with a copper fungicide. Water and fertilize the tree so that it can build up its resistance, and hope for a dry spell. Blights thrive in cool, moist weather.

Q **Why is sap running out of my birch tree? I park my car in the shade of the tree, and every morning sticky yellow sap is all over my clean car.**

A I hate to break it to you, but that's not sap on your hood. Manure happens, and aphids produce it just the same as cows. Many birch trees are full of aphids, and they excrete a sticky, yellow honeydew (isn't that a nice word for bug poop?). You can use an organic soap to control the aphids, but this may be impractical on a large tree. Even if you hire a spray service, the aphids will be back with a vengeance next year, especially if you use a strong pesticide that kills all the ladybugs as well as the aphids. Better to find someplace else to park the car.

Chapter Ten

Ground Covers
The easy answer to too much space, too many weeds

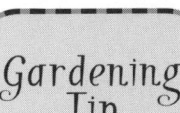

Gardening Tip

Here are my top five reasons to go with ground covers:

1. They crowd out many weeds.
2. They shade the soil in the summer and insulate it in the winter, providing trees and large shrubs with a more uniform temperature.
3. They hold back hillsides and prevent erosion.
4. They take the place of a mulch.
5. They provide more foliage and flowers with less work than does any other class of plant.

Rambling vines and rambunctious ground covers—now this is a topic fraught with controversy and passion. You either love the overgrown jungle of healthy plants competing for space, or you abhor the chaos and aim for a garden with plenty of open space between neatly trimmed and sharply controlled plant growth. ✂ *I admit to enjoying the lushness of ambitious growth, and find that a garden smothered with vines and ground covers needs less maintenance than one with lots of space between plants. Gardeners who love plants and enjoy seeing things grow are the group that enjoys solving landscaping problems with vines and ground covers. But I realize that there is a second group of gardeners who cringe at the sight of a ground cover peeking over the edge of a barrier and dipping its toes into a perfectly edged lawn. These tidy gardeners feel compelled to arm themselves with pruning shears whenever a vine scales the top of a trellis and then valiantly makes it way past any barricades to twine higher, wider, and farther than any vine before.* ✂ *If you belong to this second group of gardeners and want total control of your plants, then you may not consider vines and ground covers the low-maintenance partners that are welcomed by more free-spirited gardeners. However, if I may attempt to convert the control fiends: The advantage of gardening with ground covers is that they really do crowd out the weeds*

and offer different colors, textures, and flowers to the landscape without requiring as much feeding, weeding, and pleading as perennials, annuals, and some blooming bushes. The trick to master is knowing which ground-cover plants may grow too well and require constant trimming and pruning to keep them controlled.

SELECTING & SITING

Q What makes a plant a ground cover?

A Once again, we mere mortals keep trying to classify plants into neat little boxes, but they spill, twine, and clamor away from our strict definitions the way ivy spreads through a small garden. Ground covers are simply plants that grow low and spread to cover the ground. This means that many vines (such as clematis) can serve as ground covers if they are not trained to grow vertically. Some shrubs (such as winter creeper euonymus) can even be considered ground covers unless they are regularly pruned into hedge form, and some plants used as ground covers work well in hanging baskets or container gardens because their growth habit makes them lovely as trailing plants.

Q I've seen some plants such as lamium 'Beacon Silver' called a perennial, but it is also sold as a ground cover in the garden center.

A That is the most confusing part about ground covers. Some traditional perennial plants become ground covers when they are happy, content, and allowed to colonize an area of the garden. These plants behave differently depending on what part of the country they are growing in. So in the Pacific Northwest, lamium 'Beacon Silver' (also available as 'White Nancy'), that shade- and moisture-loving perennial, will root happily where it touches moist soil and becomes a thick ground cover. The same plant might sulk and refuse to spread in sunny southern California. Conversely, here in the Northwest, ice plants and other heat-loving spreaders are enjoyed as annuals or in container gardens, while they carpet the ground yearlong and are considered ground covers in warm climates.

Q What type of ground cover do you recommend between rhododendrons and azaleas?

A Ground covers and low-growing perennials that make good companions for rhododendrons and azaleas include lamiums, pulmonaria, ajugas (especially the less-aggressive variegated and burgundy varieties), forget-me-nots, and hardy primroses. These all like moist soil and partial shade and can get along with the rhodies and azaleas.

A Ground-Cover Quilt

Does your landscape need warmth and personality? A patchwork quilt made from ground covers is the easy answer!

Here's how to make a ground-cover quilt: Divide an area into squares using bricks or landscape timbers so that one type or color of ground cover does not ramble into another. Now use slow-growing, low ground covers such as creeping thyme, golden stonecrop, and hen and chickens (*Sempervivum*) to fill in the various squares. Trim back the ground covers once or twice a year to keep them contained within their boundaries.

These ground-cover squares can also serve as a checkerboard boundary alongside a driveway, or as a giant outdoor chessboard if you use only two different ground covers with contrasting light and dark foliage. Light-colored golden thyme and darker blue-gray woolly thyme are two contrasting ground covers that would work well for an outdoor chessboard design in a sunny location.

Q I want to avoid weeding between my rhododendrons and azaleas. Should I use a ground cover or mulch?

A Mulch first for several years with bark dust around newly planted shrubs, and then consider using a ground cover. This little wait ensures that the young shrubs build a good root system before competing with the ground covers. The years of mulching with bark dust also make the top layer of soil rich in organic matter due to the decayed bark pieces, and this is the right type of organically rich soil for happily supporting woodland ground covers that won't compete aggressively with the shrubs.

Q How close should I let the ground cover grow up around my rhododendrons, azaleas, and other shrubs?

A Once a year or so, pull any encroaching ground covers away from the stems of the shrubs, giving them a foot of breathing room in all directions. This ground-cover-free zone around the base of the shrubs provides better air circulation and lessens the competition for root space. *Warning:* Newly planted trees and shrubs do not like ground covers or mulches right up next to their stems or trunks. Give the new roots extra breathing room.

Q What ground cover do you recommend using between the stepping-stones in my very small garden?

A If the soil is dry and the area sunny, use one of the creeping thymes, such as woolly thyme or mother-of-thyme. If the area is moist and shaded, the tiny leaves of Corsican mint or blue star creeper will fill the tiny space politely—but use a barrier to control these fine-leafed ground covers, or they will hop on over into your lawn and flower beds.

Q I've noticed a low-growing juniper that hugs the ground, blocks out the weeds, and is used as a ground cover. What is the name of this ground-cover shrub?

A You must be thinking of 'Blue Rug' juniper or one of its brothers in the ground-hugging juniper family.

Dirt Cheap Tip

When I fill a pot with shade-loving impatiens and the young plants look lonely, I grab a handful of shade-loving lamiums or vinca by the roots. Poking them into potted flowers means they'll cascade over the sides of the pots in a month. I also use *Vinca minor* and variegated ivy to cascade out of tall urns, and mix sedums and thymes with sun-loving yuccas and gray-leafed licorice plants. My own private supply of ground covers automatically overwinters, and I'll never need to buy "filler" plants for my container gardens again.

Some species have the name *horizontalis* on their plant I.D. tags to specify that they like to grow horizontally across the ground. I call junipers the evergreen and ever-boring landscape shrub because they are often overused, but in many difficult sites they are the smart solutions for covering the ground.

Q **My garden has deep shade and root competition, but I want evergreen color and flowers too.**

A Ajuga, pachysandra, and *Vinca minor* and *major* are the classic shade-loving ground covers. Sweet woodruff, dwarf dogwood, and wintergreen are less aggressive but more interesting ground covers.

Dirt Cheap Tip

On a tour I visited a lovely garden that consisted mainly of trees, pathways, and ground covers. The trees were natives and some were so tall the sun-loving ground covers could bask at their base, while other trees were low and branching, providing shade for the wood-land ground covers. Nonliving garden accents like bird-baths and recycled objects used as art-work sprang from the islands of ground covers. What inspired the home owner? Lack of money. The trees came with the property and she decided ground cov-ers were less expen-sive than grass seed and topsoil.

Easy Answers

Latin Lovers Learn the Low Life

Botanical names really do serve a purpose besides just confusing the beginning gardener. Latin is the universal language of gardeners so that growers in Russia can communicate with growers in India and America and everyone knows they're all talking about the same plant. Common names change from country to country and even region to region. Go to the nursery and ask to see a 'Rose of Sharon' and you could be shown two different plants, neither of them related and neither of them roses. (One is a ground cover, *Hypericum calycinum*, and one is a shrub, *Hibiscus syriacus*.) The Latin names describe the color, form, and growth habit of a plant, so that with a bit of Latin knowledge, you can read a label and picture a plant.

If you want to grow a plant with a low growth habit that can function as a ground cover, look for these words in the botanical name: *reptans, pumila, procumbens, supina*.

Q I have a large area with hot sun and poor soil. I need colorful plants to cover uneven ground with some sloping, but want lots of flowers and some evergreen color.

A Use blooming St. Johnswort (*Hypericum*) for nearly evergreen foliage and large yellow summer flowers. It can get leggy after a few years, or die back to the roots in harsh weather, but cut it back low with a weed whacker in the spring to renew its beauty.

For more detail or as pocket garden plants grouped around large boulders, add creeping sedums and succulents such as gold moss stonecrop (*Sedum acre*).

Q I have a low, damp area in the spring garden that may dry out in the summer.

A Use forget-me-nots as a flower carpet; the blooms are beautiful in the spring but the plants are easy to rip out in the summer if you want to tidy up. I leave the tiny seedlings that will provide next spring's plants, and this habit of continuous reseeding is what gave forget-me-nots their nickname. Their Latin name is *Myosotis*.

Another lower-growing and more tidy blooming ground cover that tolerates both sun and shade, and dry and moist conditions is sweet woodruff (*Galium odoratum*). The tiny white spring flowers have a sweet smell. That's what the Latin word *odoratum* is telling you.

Q I have a steep bank suffering from erosion, with some sun and some shade. Can a ground cover help?

A For erosion control, use tough ground covers like cotoneaster 'Lowfast' or a small-leafed ivy. English ivy would be the fastest of all to stabilize and cover a bank, but remember that this is the ivy that doesn't know when to quit. Hall's honeysuckle is a ground cover/vine that also controls erosion, but its aggressive personality requires that you prune it once it reaches the bottom of the bank.

Q What should I do with a very, very steep hillside that is more like a wall or a cliff than a slope?

Gardening Tip

"I love ajuga and use it to loosen up the soil. It grows slowly in sun, but takes off in the shade and keeps the weeds down. When I think about planting in a new area, I send in the ajuga first as a scout to loosen things up. It's an easy plant to rip up and move to a new place, and comes in several different foliage colors, including a deep purple, and a green and white version. The purple spikes of flowers are a wonderful spring bonus."

A First you need to drape a jute or rope net over the area. Now plant in the squares of the net by cutting pockets into the hillside. This may be a good place for English ivy because it will survive almost anywhere. This may also be a good place to give up and give nature the hillside. We humans sometimes want to control too much.

PROBLEMS & CARE

Q What can I do to stop my ground-cover plants from growing beyond the space I planned for them? I planted (take your pick: ivy, St. Johnswort, or pachysandra) and now it is creeping into my lawn and flower beds.

A You need a strong, wide barrier. A stone wall, cement curb, or brick edging will contain the roots, but you'll always have the job of trimming back any top growth that tries to make a break for freedom. For small spaces, choose less-aggressive ground covers such as creeping thyme, Corsican mint, or the spreading Irish and Scotch mosses.

Q I moved to a garden with lots of ground covers. What type of maintenance do I need to do to keep them healthy?

A The easy answer to maintaining ground covers is to keep your shears sharpened and prune whenever things get out of control. Ground covers are not maintenance free. Trimming and ripping out ground covers that spread too much are the most common maintenance chores, but you also have to water during dry times and fertilize some ground covers if they begin to turn pale or do not grow and fill in as fast as you'd like. The first year after planting any ground cover, you need to hand-weed or mulch between the new plants. Young ground covers will not smother weeds without your help.

Q Won't ground covers choke and kill my other plants?

A Some ground covers are secret killers, getting a choke-hold on other plants so slowly that you barely notice until you hear that last gasp for life. These aggressive members of the ground-cover clan usually go after the weak and the young, and can be controlled if you know about their Mr. Hyde personality beforehand.

Gardening Tip

"I have arthritis in my hands, but I've found that metal sheep shears are the answer for easy trimming, pruning, and dead-heading of flowers and ground covers. The blades close so smoothly and spring open on their own easily, so now working in the garden is a joy again."

Is Ivy Evil or an Enduring Ground Cover?

Ivy is a dominant ruler in all forms, but the bigger-leafed varieties such as English ivy are the worst of the space hogs, and are actually banned in some communities. English ivy is the number one, "most wanted" murderer in backyard gardens, and some horticulturists even blame it for the death of full-grown native trees. Ivies grow anywhere, but are most invasive in rich organic soil that is kept moist in the summer. One way to slow it down just a bit is to never water in the summer.

Other horticulturists claim that no studies have proven it is the ivy that kills trees. I think it has its place in some gardens, especially to hold a steep bank from eroding or to grow up the trunks of old stumps or half-dead evergreen trees, but even now I can hear the protests of the "English ivy is evil" groups that fear this plant as the leader of an evil empire, out to control the gardening world. Some environmentalists point out that English ivy growing up tree trunks produces fall fruit that feeds the honeybees and hummingbirds when not much else is available. Ivy-covered trees also provide a great place for bats to roost, which could be another reason why ivy is such a controversial plant. Small-leafed green and white ivy is much more polite than its British cousin, and is lovely in hanging baskets, especially the gold-tinged or fine-textured needle-leafed varieties. These are the types I usually recommend for covering structures.

Gardening Goof

"In the first garden I ever planted, I remember planting a small sprig of ivy at the base of an archway. I also planted some roses, perennials, and an azalea or two. Then we moved from that home and I abandoned the tiny garden. Years later I returned to the old house to see what was left of my first garden. It was covered with ivy. That one tiny ivy sprig had grown to devour every other plant in the yard."

Q What other ground covers besides ivy have a tendency to take over?

A If it's malicious gossip you're after, look no further than the topic of ground covers. Many gardeners have a passionate hatred for aggressive ground covers that have caused them summers of toil and wheelbarrows of cursing. But these same ground covers are much loved by others, and I use many of them in my own garden with proper editing. Check the list in the sidebar "Overly Enthusiastic Ground Covers That Some Gardeners Love to Hate" before you invite any of these gregarious guests into your garden.

Q Help me; I didn't listen! I was warned not to plant ivy in my front yard but longed for quick cover. Now it has grown out of control and I want to get rid of it.

A There's no easy way to get rid of ivy. Most ambitious ground covers can be murdered by pulling, poisoning, or smothering. Ivy is one that often needs to be removed, but isn't so easy to eradicate. You will need to hand-pull the top growth, smother any roots, and properly dispose of the vines. (For more help, see the sidebar "Removing Ivy and Other Rambunctious Ground Covers," on page 147.)

Overly Enthusiastic Ground Covers That Some Gardeners Learn to Hate

Avoid these in small yards or if you like complete control.

CARPET BUGLE (*Ajuga*): This is one of my personal favorites, because I have so much shade in my garden and this ground cover acts as an evergreen in our mild climate. Ajuga swallows up weaker plants, so I pull it away from the crowns of rhododendrons and azaleas so it won't suck all the moisture from around these shallow-rooted shrubs. It is most suitable for large shady areas under mature trees, where it acts as a living mulch and blooms spectacularly in the spring with blue flower spikes that make bees delirious with joy. Shade, moist soil, and lots of organic matter turn ajuga into a raving maniac, but I slow its growth by using it in deep shade with rather poor, dry soil. Give it a strong border to keep it from jumping its boundaries and taking over the lawn.

CHAMELEON PLANT (*Houttuynia*): With heart-shaped, colorful leaves that remind me of the tropical prints on Hawaiian shirts, this orange and yellow ground cover works well in contained beds where the underground roots cannot spread all over the neighborhood. It does die down to nothingness in the winter, and in deep shade or hot sun without water, its galloping growth slows to a trot. I use it under a similarly loud and boldly colored variegated dogwood tree, and the young dogwood doesn't seem to mind the wild party going on at its feet. In this same area I have foxgloves, lychnis, and feverfew plants that reseed themselves and bloom despite the blanket of houttuynia spreading throughout the bed.

JAPANESE SPURGE (Pachysandra): Over time this evergreen ground cover with the whorls of rounded leaves and white flowers will drive you nuts as it spreads continually in shaded areas, but sometimes it hits the mark and fills in neatly where nothing else wants to grow. It is a rather overused ground cover in commercial landscape designs where curbs and cement sidewalks keep it in check.

PERIWINKLE OR MYRTLE (Vinca minor): Trailing branches on this shrubby but vinelike ground cover make quick cover in large areas, but the tubular blue or white spring flowers are such a delight that I think it's worth growing despite its overly enthusiastic ways. I keep a patch of the variegated variety going in the woods and rob from it every spring to add trailing delight to my hanging baskets and container gardens. A version with larger leaves and even faster growth is called *Vinca major*, and I happily put it to work on a shaded berm of rocky soil to keep down the weeds. It's been growing there for more than a decade and I rarely have to prune it back. Vinca is great under large trees, but will choke out smaller, weaker plants.

HONEYSUCKLE (Lonicera japonica): This is a climber or ground cover for steep banks. There are more than 100 species of this semi-evergreen rambler, and some have taken over and destroyed entire woodlands, so be careful about inviting this sweet-looking and (if you suck the nectar at the base of the blooms) sweet-tasting ground cover. To protect banks from erosion, climb up dead trees, or cover sheds, this is a much-loved plant, but if you ignore it for a few years, it could creep into the windows and sneak a few tendrils around your neck as you sleep—so beware. I grow honeysuckle over a lattice archway that covers a bench, but since it is in the shade and forced to grow in the poor soil of cedar trees, the plant behaves itself and I delight in its tough constitution. If you want it covered with flowers, give it full sun to partial shade, and for the greenest leaves, add lots of organic matter in the soil.

ST. JOHNSWORT (Hypericum): A great blooming ground cover for sunny sites and perfect for areas contained with cement curbs, this plant does escape by underground roots and can invade lawns, driveways, and shrub beds. It will grow to several feet tall and sport an unkempt shaggy look if not trimmed back in the spring.

Removing Ivy and Other Rambunctious Ground Covers

Many ground covers have such thick, waxy leaves that they resist herbicides like Roundup until after you remove the bulk of the plant. (Tender new growth is more susceptible to herbicides.) This is why the pull-and-smother technique becomes your best removal method for mature ground covers.

STEP ONE: Start at the end of the ground cover patch that has the newest growth, and pull or lift up the tendrils, trying to roll them into a bale as you pull and cut so they can be stuffed into a plastic garbage bag.

STEP TWO: Once you pull up and cut off all the top growth and have it safely encased in plastic, smother the area with sheets of heavy cardboard and weight this down with a gravel or bark-chip mulch at least three inches deep.

STEP THREE: Watch for new growth peeking through the seams of your cardboard or mulch; spray with an herbicide such as Roundup. The lack of light (caused by the cardboard and mulch) will starve the still-living roots of the ground cover after a year.

Q Okay, I pull up the ivy (vinca or honeysuckle) and roll the vines into a plastic bag. Why not just pile it in a wheelbarrow, let it dry up, and add it to the compost?

A Because sometimes all it takes is a tiny piece of root to get the whole colony going again in your compost pile. These aggressive ground covers have a way of lying low and looking dead, only to sprout forth when you turn your back. You could leave the works encased in the plastic garbage bag in the hot sun for a few months and then add the rotting mess to the compost, but even that idea could come back to haunt you. Tossing them out with the trash is the safest way.

Q So once you roll up and dispose of the ground cover, smother the roots with cardboard, and pile on a mulch, how long before you can plant something new?

A In a year the area should be safe to remove all the cardboard and work the mulch into the soil—unless the cardboard is rotted, and then you can work that into the soil as well. If you're impatient, shove aside the mulch, cut through the cardboard barrier, and remove the roots of the ground cover from the planting hole and pop in your new plants. Now carefully arrange the mulch back around the hole and newly planted plant to block the light and keep the old ground cover from flowing forth from the cut-out section.

Q **Can I use plastic or newspaper instead of cardboard to smother and kill ground covers?**

A Use newspaper if it is 25 to 30 pages thick, and plastic only if you will remove the plastic in a year when the ground cover is dead. Black plastic under mulches peeves me greatly because it does not allow the soil to drain or breathe, and if you poke holes in the plastic for drainage, the ground cover will find this outlet and try to escape.

Chapter Eleven

Vines

The easy answer for onward and upward growth

Vines share a tendency with ground covers to overtwine their welcome, but they also have a growing enthusiasm that is part of their charm. Many vines are loved for their showy flowers, and so wisteria, clematis, and honeysuckle are sought out by beginning gardeners. As the garden and gardener mature, then some vines are begrudgingly trimmed back as the tiny trellis provided for their support is overpowered by enthusiastic growth. ✻ Vines and ground covers also share the trait of problem-solving, which makes them both worth the extra effort to keep them under control. Like ground covers, vines grow quickly and can tolerate challenging growing sites, and thus solve a multitude of design and maintenance problems.

SELECTING & SITING

Q **Where is a good place to plant a fast-growing, aggressive perennial vine like wisteria, trumpet vine, or honeysuckle?**

A Not near your house! No matter how devoted you think you will be about pruning, a tendril may escape your shears and things could get nasty. These vines have been known to sneak an arm or two under roof shingles or poke a long leg into house vents. Give fast-growing, aggressive conquerors like these their own pergola, shed, or dead tree to colonize, and you won't have to worry about their terrorizing tendrils causing structural damage.

Gardening Tip

"I love to grow flowering vines like clematis up trees. To get the vine started, I dig a large hole about eight inches wide near the trunk of the tree and loosen the soil. Then I use a small piece of chicken wire at the base of the trunk to give the vine something to hold on to. It takes a couple of years, but then watch out as the clematis races toward the sun, climbing the tree and blooming throughout the branches."

Climbing Clematis
and Creative Supports

A clematis on a trellis is a classic garden accent, but use these blooming vines in other areas to add color in creative ways.

CLEMATIS IN CONTAINERS: Yes, pot them up and let them hang. Use a loose, quick-draining soil; offer plenty of water and fertilizer; and place the pot in partial sun. Prune back hard in late winter or early spring to a six-inch stump. Your clematis will bloom in hanging baskets or drip over the edge and ramble from patio pots for years. Train a potted clematis along the railing of a deck or over a slope or hillside. *Note:* If you cannot harden your heart to sweet new growth, then you may not be able to grow clematis in pots. It takes a good disciplinarian and a no-nonsense attitude to accomplish the severe pruning that clematis in pots needs to look good.

CLEMATIS IN TREES AND SHRUBS: Picture a deep purple clematis winding through the rich burgundy leaves of a purple smoke tree. There's no need to stake or train; the tendrils find the branches and just keep climbing up. This dynamic duo does a dandy duet in my garden, and the smoke tree doesn't complain about playing the supporting role so the clematis can be the star and shine. You can also try planting clematis at the base of lilacs, small trees, and even an evergreen hedge. *Jackmanii* spills out all over my otherwise boring screen of 'Pyramidalis' arborvitae each summer. Visitors even ask the name of the unusual evergreen hedge with the huge purple flowers.

STUMPED FOR A SUPPORT SYSTEM: Many vines love to clamber up tall stumps, and for this reason, if you need to have some trees taken down, try to leave your stumps eight to ten feet tall. Clematis seems to adore the soil full of rotting roots and decaying bark that is found at the base of old cedar stumps, and I haven't ever seen a clematis clambering up a stump that didn't look absolutely giddy and gleeful with delight. Don't try a stump support for climbing roses, however. They don't handle the root competition as well.

Q We moved into a big old house with a large country garden. I want to decorate the outdoors with garlands of flowers, so what vines would be best?

A For beautiful flowering vines, plant wisteria, honeysuckle, and clematis. Climbing roses are also favorites, but since they are not true vines, they are covered in the rose chapter.

Clematis is the best-behaved vine for growing near the house, because it has no suction cups or root-end tendrils that can cause structural damage.

Q What vines will bloom in the shade? I want to train something to grow over an archway in the woods.

A Honeysuckle seems to adapt to many light conditions, and can bloom in deep shade—although with not nearly as many flowers as it would have in a partly sunny site.

Some clematis also bloom in part shade. Three hours of sun a day is enough to get my *Clematis jackmanii* to set buds and bloom for months in the summer.

Q Can I grow wisteria in the shade?

A You can, and you'll have lots of lush growth, but it won't bloom.

Q Since hydrangea bushes grow in the shade, will a climbing hydrangea bloom in the shade?

A You'd think so, but the climbing hydrangea needs more sun than a shrub hydrangea. It also has tendrils like suction cups, so beware if you plant it near your house.

Q I have a small yard and a husband who can't stand anything overgrown. What type of vines should I grow?

A The easy answer is annual vines, which live just one year. They grow fast but die at the end of summer, unlike perennial vines that live on from year to year and start to take over. Examples of annual vines are scarlet runner beans, nasturtiums, and morning glory.

Dirt Cheap Tip

Build a frame or form for your vine structure using inexpensive rebar, the pliable but rusty-looking metal bars used to reinforce concrete. Rebar can be bent into curves for garden arches or curling garden supports for other vines. Wrap the length of rebar around a telephone pole to bend one end and make it curve for an arch. Some nurseries offer classes in how to work with rebar to make cool garden accents. Art in the garden doesn't have to be expensive sculpture.

All Decked Out for an Exciting Nightlife

Moonflower (*Ipomoea alba*) is the perfect vine for gardeners who work the late shift or enjoy the nightlife. This cousin of the morning glory has huge, fragrant white blooms that open at sunset and also on dark and cloudy days. This helps make overcast summer days more bearable. Use moonflower in a pot on your deck or patio if you enjoy sitting outdoors on summer nights. They need warm temperatures to grow and bloom, so plant the seeds in early summer or visit a greenhouse and buy vines that are already growing. Once the warm weather arrives in midsummer, these vines really take off, twining ten feet or more up strings or trellis supports. They crash and die at the first hint of frost, so they'll never invade your home or take over the garden.

Q How could you possibly recommend morning glory vine! The morning glory weed has overtaken my garden and is my worst nightmare!

A Calm down. There are two vines with the common name of morning glory. The obnoxious and noxious bindweed (*Convolvulus arvensis*), which is also called wild morning glory, is a perennial vine that is very hard to get rid of. Bindweed is not related to the real morning glory (genus *Ipomoea*), which are most often annual vines that die in the winter and do not spread by underground roots the way bindweed does. They both have large, beautiful, cuplike flowers and a twining habit, but annual morning glory vine comes in a heavenly blue as well as pink and rose-colored forms. Annual morning glory is safe to plant in the garden, while bindweed, a look-alike with white blooms, should be banished.

Q What clematis vine do you recommend if I want large flowers?

A For huge, showy blooms on a dependable vine, think of Nelly and Jack. 'Nelly Moser' is a pink and rose bicolor that does well in partial shade and blooms twice—in early and late summer. *Jackmanii* is a purple bloomer that shows off giant blooms all summer long. Clematis might sit and ponder their new home for the first year, but after that, Jack and Nelly grow fast!

Q What is the clematis that blooms in the spring and has pink fragrant flowers? It is used to cover sheds and house roofs.

A The fast and furious *Clematis montana* or the anemone clematis is very hardy and easy to grow, with small anemone-like flowers. You can prune it hard as soon as it finishes blooming to keep it under control.

Q What honeysuckle vine should I use to control erosion on a steep slope?

A The easy answer for fast and furious, dependable growth is Hall's honeysuckle, the old-fashioned, fragrant bloomer that has been used to sweeten front porch hideaways, hold back hillsides, and control erosion for generations. Sun or shade, it grows to 30 feet.

Q We are interested in attracting more birds to our garden. What is the blooming vine used to attract hummingbirds?

A Trumpet vine (*Campsis radicans*) is heralded as the late-summer resort of the hummingbird set and is a great addition to backyard bird sanctuaries. It is also a glorious bloomer with orange or yellow trumpet-shaped blooms; it needs no support or ties to scramble up a fence, arbor, trellis, or wall. There is some bad news that isn't often trumpeted about. This vine can grow out of control with enthusiasm, and the stem rootlets can dig in and cause surface damage to wooden structures. It also demands full sun and loses all its foliage in the winter.

CARE & PROBLEMS

Q I have heard that clematis like their roots in the shade and their tops in the sun. How am I supposed to manage that?

A The easy answer is to just pile a compost or bark mulch around the roots about three inches deep, but don't let any mulch touch the stem or it could cause clematis wilt, a common disease. Or plant your clematis behind a low evergreen shrub. Do not lay a flat rock on top of the roots. This will absorb heat and make the roots even warmer.

Gardening Tip

"I circle each of my clematis vines with a metal collar made from an old tuna fish can. I remove both the top and bottom of the can and snip the sides so I can surround the clematis stem with this metal barrier. It keeps mulch from rotting and pets from bruising the tender stem, and I've never had trouble with clematis wilt."

Pruning Your Clematis

A more detailed answer for clematis pruning, for those who want to maximize every potential bloom and understand these complex vines, follows. Pruning depends on what type of clematis you have; there are in general three types.

TYPE I: Blooms in spring, like *Clematis montana* or anemone clematis. Prune if necessary a month after it blooms, sometime in late spring.

TYPE II: Blooms in early summer, so for the most new growth and new flowers, prune back in March to the point of healthy buds. This encourages lots of new growth.

TYPE III: Blooms summer and fall (*Jackmanii* and 'Nelly Moser'). Prune back to 12 inches every year in March, or in late fall when blooming is done. As the plant gets older, don't prune so severely, leaving two or three feet of old growth.

Q I planted a clematis vine, it grew and bloomed, then almost overnight the vine wilted and died! I see no signs of bugs or slugs.

A Sounds like the dreaded clematis wilt. There is no cure, but there is hope. Your clematis may spring anew from the roots to surprise you—or maybe not. Such is the adventure of gardening. See the preceding clematis planting tips for ways to discourage this problem in the future.

Q How and when do I prune my clematis?

A The easy answer for gardeners who feel dazed and confused is to trim any clematis by one-third right after it is done blooming. You won't kill the plant if you prune away one-third or less, even if you do it at the "wrong time." You can thin out old, dead, and broken branches, shorten long vines growing too tall, or just make a quick cut to shorten the whole vine by several feet.

Q Is too much shade the reason my wisteria isn't blooming?

A Not necessarily. Wisteria refuses to bloom if it is too young (a three-year-old wisteria is just entering adolescence and not mature enough for the sex involved in flower production), if it doesn't get enough sun, or if it gets too much high-nitrogen fertilizer (usually from a nearby lawn where its roots have wandered). Too much nitrogen encourages leaf growth instead of flower production. Another reason you may be missing flowers is if you prune your wisteria in early spring. Remember the rule: pruning after blooming.

Q Help! My honeysuckle vine has grown out of control. When do I prune and how far back can I prune?

A The easy answer for gardeners who feel dazed and confused: Prune honeysuckle any time of the year and cut it back to a stump just one foot tall. If you don't want to sacrifice any blooms, prune honeysuckle right after it blooms in the spring; shorten some of the long branches to one foot, some to six feet, and some just shorten by a foot or less. This gives you a bushier plant with blooms from top to bottom.

Q What can I do to make my wisteria bloom?

A Assuming you have enough sun and you're not pruning your wisteria in early spring, you can give your budless wisteria the shovel-shock treatment and try to jolt it into flowering. Drive a shovel halfway around the root system of your vine about a foot away from the trunk. Now into these slits slip two or three fruit-tree fertilizer spikes. They are solid cores of fertilizer that slowly dissolve and leach bloom-inducing nutrients into the soil near the wisteria. (Do not use fertilizer spikes meant for evergreens because they are too high in nitrogen.) If after a year you still don't have blooms and the plant is mature, cut it down and get over it. Wisteria grow too fast and demand too much pruning to put up with such ungrateful behavior. Try a clematis, a honeysuckle, or a climbing rose instead.

Q What is the secret to getting my wisteria to stay in bloom all summer?

A I don't try to keep it a secret, but here's the technique that keeps my wisteria blooming from May until September. I cut off as many of the faded flowers as I can reach after the first big flush of blooms in the spring. Then I let the long growth tendrils grow about a foot, and a few weeks later I prune the new growth back to the point where the tendril is thicker and darker green in color. (This is close to the spot where it bloomed from earlier.) Now the wisteria thinks it hasn't bloomed, and has no long tendrils to sap its strength, so it buds up and blooms again. I don't get as many flowers as I did in the spring, but it just takes a few sporadic wisteria blooms every few weeks to perfume the summer air.

Gardening Tip

"If I'm working on training a vine to a frame, I store several extra twist ties for the project by attaching them to the supporting frame. Then as the plants grow and need more help following the form, I have the ties where I need them and don't have to make a special trip to the shed."

COVER-UPS

Q What should I do if I have an ugly metal or wood structure in the landscape and want to conceal the eyesore?

A Cover the building with a vine or several vines, pruning away just enough growth each year to clear the doorway. Evergreen vines such as Virginia creeper or honeysuckle need strong support because they grow quite heavy over time, but if the building is very old and not so strong, use lighter vines such as clematis. Fast-growing clematis such as the small flowering varieties (*Clematis montana*) cover any eyesore quickly, but the lack of foliage in the winter may leave a tangled mess to view.

Q My kids have grown up and moved out, leaving sturdy structures such as a basketball hoop, swing set, and jungle gym in the landscape. Any ideas for using these?

A Give some vines a place to play by putting those kid structures to work as support systems for any type of vine. Add a rafter system and some support poles to a tall swing set to form an outdoor room covered with vines. Cover the compacted soil beneath the play structure with sand or gravel and add flagstones or brick as a floor for your new room. You'll have a place to set a bench or a couple of chairs for an adult retreat inside the vine-covered alcove.

Q I want quick coverage of the tall, bare side of a building (such as barn, garage, or shed) with no windows, but there's not a wide enough space to plant trees or shrubs.

A Use a vine to clamber up the side of the blank wall. Many vines do not need more than a bed six inches wide to get a foothold as they begin their quest toward the rooftop. For two-story or taller buildings, the silver lace vine (*Polygonum aubertii*) grows up to 20 feet the first year, but does not destroy wood with suction-cup roots.

Q If I have a cement or cinder-block building, what should I use to cover the surface for yearlong interest?

A Plant a climbing hydrangea next to a masonry wall, and it will use the suction cups on its branches to cling and climb. Striking bark in the winter, white summer blooms, and rich green leaves make this an attractive vine four seasons of the year. Climbing hydrangea can also be used as a ground cover on a sunny slope or to twine up the trunk of a tree for a true marriage of convenience.

A Living Gazebo

In a shaded raised area of my garden, surrounded by variegated ground covers (they are hiding the mole holes—see Chapter Thirteen, "Pests & Weeds"), stands my living gazebo. This is a structure framed by one-inch-wide plastic piping that joins at the top in a graceful point. You would never know that such inexpensive building materials make up the walls of this outdoor "summer house" because the entire structure is covered with the green and white foliage of small-leafed ivies.

At just the four corners of this outdoor structure, I planted different varieties of ivy, including needleleaf ivy and some lovely golden-tinged types. (No large-leafed English ivy is allowed.)

The floor of the gazebo is brick set in sand with dry mortar mix swept into the cracks. Most of the gazebo is open on the sides, with the ivy covering the supporting pillars. It took just three years for the ivy sprigs to completely cover the structure. Now I just trim the ivy once a year to keep it tidy. The haircut that the ivy requires is a lot less maintenance than repainting a traditional white, lattice-and-wood gazebo.

Q I do not like the looks of or lack of privacy provided by a cyclone fence, but it is too expensive to remove and replace, and does a great job of keeping the kids and pets in place. I'd also like to cover the ten-foot-tall wire fence I've built to keep the deer out of the orchard.

A Mix a collection of vines along the fence line for an ever-changing display and always-growing privacy. Start with solid coverage all year long by planting a variegated or small-leafed ivy, and guide the new shoots horizontally by weaving them in and out of the fence openings. Five feet or so away from the nearest ivy planting, you could plant a lightweight flowering vine such as a clematis to add blooming color. Honeysuckle, akebia, and trumpet vine (*Campsis*) are other blooming vines to try along a wire or cyclone fence. Vines also work to cover a sturdy wood fence, but they make future maintenance of a wooden structure difficult.

Q There is no privacy on our second-story deck, and we're too impatient to wait for a tall hedge or trees to grow. The neighbors view the area from their kitchen window.

A Use vines in pots to make a quick living screen. A long, narrow container like a window box can be set on an upper-story deck with a section of lattice secured to the back of the container or added to the top of the deck railing. Now choose an evergreen vine such as ivy or honeysuckle, or use a flowering annual vine if you want screening only during the summer months. Vines such as clematis and vinca can also be used in hanging baskets to make a living wall when the pots are hung from a pole or rafter that extends horizontally from the house.

Chapter Twelve
Lawns & Lawn Substitutes
The easy answer for showcasing plants

Dirt Cheap Tip

"Instead of a drop spreader or whirly-bird seed spreader, I use a plastic flower pot with holes in the bottom to sprinkle grass seed. I walk at an even pace carrying the bag of grass seed in one arm and scooping seed out with my gallon-size plastic pot with the other hand. Then I just shake the pot and the seed falls out through the holes. This is especially efficient for overseeding bare spots, and I find it easier to control the seed and keep it from falling into flower beds and pathways."

Growing grass should be one of the easiest of all types of gardening. After all, grass sprouts in gravel driveways, fills in vacant lots, and spreads beyond its boundaries to cannibalize flower beds if you don't edge or corral it with a border. Grass even pops up in the sun-baked cracks of sidewalks and thrives in wet roadside ditches. So what's with all the lawn-growing problems? Many gardeners just don't realize that getting to the grass roots is the answer to a more carefree lawn. Growing a great lawn starts with great soil, which encourages a deep root system. ✿ *Instead of going to the expense of treating every individual lawn problem popping up (or dying out), enjoy a more carefree lawn by improving your soil with organic fertilizer, mowing your lawn at the proper height, and watering in a way that encourages deep instead of shallow roots. A thick, green, weed-resistant lawn will be the natural result.* ✿ *Face the fact that a great-looking lawn cannot be grown anyplace you want. Most problem areas in a lawn shouldn't have been planted with grass in the first place. Slopes, dry spots beneath trees, deep shade, wet spots—these are not natural areas for meadows and pastures, so why fight Mother Nature and insist that grass should grow where it has no business growing?*

STARTING · SEED & SOD · FERTILIZING · WATERING
MOWING · PROBLEMS · MOSS · WEEDS

STARTING NEW

Q We are putting in a new lawn from scratch with nothing but lousy, rocky soil as a base. Would you recommend we sod, hydroseed, bring in topsoil, or what? Our goal is a lawn that demands low maintenance and no chemicals.

A What a wonderful concept! Do it right at the beginning, and you'll enjoy the fruits of your labor (or lack of necessary labor) for years and years.

Start by loosening and amending that "lousy rocky soil" to a depth of six inches or more, or loosen the soil as much as you can (if you have hardpan or really heavy rocks, loosening the soil six inches will be almost impossible) and add good topsoil to a depth of six inches. (See the sidebar "Proper Soil Preparation for New Lawns: Dig Deep!" on page 161.) A seeded lawn will be superior to a sodded or hydroseeded lawn only if you buy better-quality grass seed than what the sod and hydroseed growers use. Ask your county extension agent for the most recent listing of new grass seed varieties best for your area. These change constantly as new varieties are introduced.

Q We moved to a new house and the lawn is horrible. It is full of weeds and dead grass, and it is so stiff it hurts to walk on it. Should I just poison the whole thing and start all over again?

A The easy answer is no, just hang in there and improve what you have. In almost all cases, it is quicker (and a lot less expensive) to improve the lawn you already have than to kill off an existing lawn and try to start over. Improving the soil and reseeding a new lawn directly on top of the old lawn is the easy way to renovate a lawn that is weedy, weak, and considered worthless.

Q How do I begin improving my soil and planting a new lawn if there are already grass and weeds growing in the area?

A Just ignore the old lawn and work on top of it. Early spring is the best time to do this job.

Q What can I grow in place of the perfect lawn?

A Use ground covers, trees and shrubs, more pathways, and patios—or learn to enjoy and appreciate a green and "good enough" lawn. A few weeds, some moss in the spring, some dry spots in the summer—these "problems" are part of the normal cycle for any mowed meadow, and by focusing on a grassroots campaign of improving the soil instead of treating the problems, your "good enough" lawn can be as lush, green, and healthy as that lawn on the other side of the fence that is doused with chemicals.

Proper Soil Preparation for New Lawns: Dig Deep!

Putting in a new lawn means hard work at the beginning, so you can avoid hard work for the remaining life of the lawn. The secret is all in the depth. The deeper you can loosen and amend the soil, the deeper the grass roots will grow and the more independent the lawn will be. For more details on seeding a new lawn, ask at the garden center where you purchase the seed. Local professionals are your best source of local information on where to buy good topsoil and seasonal planting tips.

- Rent a heavy-duty tiller to loosen the top six inches (or more!) of soil. Rent out the job if necessary. If you can't till the soil, add as much topsoil as you can afford.

- Apply Claybuster, an effective soil amendment sold at garden centers, to loosen hard, clay soils.

- Amend the soil with at least two inches of topsoil, composted manure, or Milorganite (sewage sludge, available at a reasonable price from many municipalities).

- Add a "starter fertilizer" made especially for newly seeded lawns. This gives the new lawn the nitrogen and other nutrients it needs to get growing.

- Now mix the soil amendments into the original subsoil by tilling again. This is the important secret that gets the roots to grow down deep. If you spread the good stuff on top of the subsoil but don't mix it in, the roots won't venture down past the soft layer of amendments on top.

- Level the soil before you seed. Low spots collect moisture and the seed you spread will puddle up and float away.

- Wait until the new lawn is established at least a month before using even organic fertilizers to keep it growing fast.

Planting a New Lawn on Top of the Old One

First aerate the soil by poking holes all over with a core aerator. You can rent this machine or hire a lawn maintenance company to do the job. (It is hard on the back!)

Next mow the old lawn as short as you can, leaving the clippings to improve the soil.

Now is the time to add a one-inch layer of sand if the lawn drains poorly. Rake this evenly on top of the lawn, filling in any dips or depressions.

Next spread an organic lawn food, then two inches of topsoil on top of the old lawn and sand base. Continue to rake and level any low spots.

Sprinkle seed directly on top of this new soil layer.

Now the most important part. Continue to use organic lawn food following package instructions (wait one month after seeding to use any fertilizer), and you'll be amazed at how quickly the earthworms return and your soil begins to loosen up, the roots head farther south, and a youthful new lawn replaces the stiff and weedy grass.

SEED & SOD

Q What type of seed do I buy for reseeding the lawn or putting in a new lawn?

A The easy answer is to buy the more expensive seed, which is a mix of seed types, not the budget brands with no variety details on the label or just one type of seed. Look for "named" varieties listed on the back of the lawn seed package, not just generic grass seed. For example, instead of just "perennial ryegrass," higher-quality seed has a variety name such as 'Pennfine' or 'Manhattan' ryegrass. Many garden centers and home center stores custom-mix their own brand of grass seed, and these are excellent choices for seeding a lawn because the named seed varieties have been tailored specifically for your part of the country.

Q Is it true that installing a sod lawn is less work because you don't have to prepare the soil as well or water as much?

A Not true! Sod lawns grow more complaints than seeded lawns because it's so tempting to take shortcuts with soil preparations. You must prepare the soil for sod and hydroseeding just as you would for seeding the traditional way. It is true that

sod lawns require less water to become established than a seeded lawn, and you will have fewer weeds to battle in the beginning (not to mention the instant gratification factor).

Q Our front yard is in the sun and the backyard is in mostly shade. Can I use sod for both?

A The easy answer is to use sod in the sun and seed in the shade. Sod is grown on farms in full sun with grass seed that likes full sun. In your shady yard, you need grass seed made and developed for the shade (see the sidebar "Lawns Made for the Shade," on page 173).

Reseeding Every Spring for Luxurious Lushness

Imitate the lushness of the finest golf courses by reseeding your old lawn each spring for fresh new growth.

The advantages of reseeding old lawns with new grass seed is that you can enjoy all the advancements and improvements in lawn seed genetics by planting the newer, more disease-resistant, slower-growing, and drought-resistant grass seed varieties. This is why the "named" varieties are more expensive but worth the money. They have to pay the scientists for these new developments in turf technology.

To encourage the new seeds to sprout, make them a soft bed by spreading compost or topsoil on top of your old lawn in a thin layer. Rake it level and sprinkle the new seeds on top, then keep it moist until the seeds sprout. Your old grass will push up vigorously, nourished by the topdressing of new soil, and grow along with the new grass seed.

Outlandish Ideas

Crave the Perfect Lawn? Relax with a Lawn Chair

If you're a "lawn ranger" on patrol for perfection, grow a "lawn chair" and have a patch of lawn small enough to control completely. Recycle an aluminum-framed patio chair by building a box or frame to fill the seating area with at least six inches of soil. Plant grass seed or lay down sod for the seat of the chair. Keep a pair of scissors handy for frequent mowing. Add a tiny golf flag or grazing toy sheep to further decorate and satirize the perfect lawn.

Q What if I already installed sod and now it is not doing so well in the shady sections of my yard?

A You can reseed right over the sod with a shade-tolerant grass seed mix. Just add an inch of topsoil to the top of the sod and sprinkle on the new seeds. Keep it moist for a few weeks until the new seeds germinate.

FERTILIZING

Q What's in the organic fertilizers I see for lawns and how do they work?

A Organic fertilizers are made from dead stuff (things that once were living) and their by-products, such as ground-up bones, chicken manure, pulverized fish bodies, and even dried blood. All this blood and gore breaks down into nitrogen and other nutrients that your lawn is starving for. It takes awhile to do this, however, and so the nitrogen is released slowly into the soil and feeds all sorts of microorganisms while it breaks down. This makes the microscopic creatures in your soil so happy that they make more of themselves, so that your soil becomes a teeming factory of living microscopic creatures, and it softens up even more as earthworms go crazy with the delight of so much company.

Q So are regular chemical (synthetic) lawn foods bad for my lawn?

A No. Chemical lawn foods are not "bad" for the lawn (in fact, they do a terrific job of turning the grass green), but they just are not good at feeding the soil microorganisms and so they are not good at improving the soil. Good soil is the secret to a carefree lawn. Most "chemical" fertilizers (more properly called synthetic fertilizers, since all fertilizers break down into chemicals) have quick-release nitrogen that is made from factory chemicals instead of organic or living things. It gets to the grass roots quickly and greens the lawn evenly, but this type of nitrogen just doesn't feed your soil. As times goes on, the lawn needs more and more nitrogen to stay green and becomes dependent on more and more fertilizer. You could logically say that your lawn develops an addiction to high-nitrogen fertilizer over time and needs more and more of the stuff to get the deep-green "high." Continued and constant use of high-nitrogen chemical fertilizer turns your lawn into a chemically dependent fertilizer addict.

Q I would like to "go organic" with our lawn care but can't convince my husband that there are any benefits. What's the big advantage of the organic fertilizers?

A Organic fertilizers encourage more life in the soil by feeding the tiny creatures that live there and help make your lawn healthy. That way, the grass roots can grow deeper into the soil, searching for their own food and water.

Q Okay, we've made the decision to conquer our lawn's addiction to synthetic chemical fertilizers. What organic fertilizer am I supposed to use and where do I find it?

A Most garden centers and large nurseries carry organic or organic-based lawn foods. There are several brands out there, including Whitney Farms, Lawn Restore, and Lily Miller organic-based lawn food. Many of the large fertilizer companies are adding organic sources of nutrients to their regular lawn fertilizers. You could also check with the city where you live for Milorganite, a by-product of municipal sewage treatment plants. (Sounds bad, works good.) *Most important:* Read the labels on all fertilizers and follow instructions.

Just Say No! Freeing the Chemically Dependent Lawn

Here are ten steps to a chemical-free lawn—and support for the codependent, enabling gardener:

1. Admit there is a problem. This may take group intervention, where neighbors can together confront the water-hogging, chemical-dumping, "perfect" lawn owner to talk frankly about the fact that his "perfect," shortly mowed lawn is making the rest of the neighborhood "good enough" lawns look bad. It is a fact that most addicted lawns have male enablers. Men seem genetically predisposed to the disease, so be gentle with them. (Others argue that the addiction is not an inherited trait or "disease," just a sign of character weakness.)

2. Write up a plan. A new fertilizing schedule with organic lawn food in the spring and fall will wean the lawn from the quick fix of nitrogen. Give yourself a year and you'll see withdrawal to the point where your lawn is independent enough to get a natural high from organics and turn away from the cheap thrills of instant green-up.

3. Start by overdosing the addicted lawn with a double shot of organic lawn food. Expect a few bad days at the beginning of the withdrawal, as the natural smell and higher price of organic lawn foods sink in.

4. Gain strength during these difficult early days by reading inspirational material. *Organic Gardening* magazine, *Silent Spring* by Rachel Carlson, or even the back of a bag of organic fertilizer will help with the painful withdrawal symptoms. You will long for the old life in the fast lane, when a sweet rush of green happiness followed a nitrogen fix. Hang in there.

5. Avoid visiting the golf course or competing mentally with the old friends still immersed in the addiction cycle. They will try to taunt you into joining them in dependency. Some may even be angry that you are breaking free of an addiction you once shared together. They may call you names (like "granola-eater") as they make fun of your lawn, pointing out weeds and slower growth. Ignore them. These pitiful users have no future. Five years from now, they will still be wasting good money on fast nitrogen, and you'll be relaxing (maybe even in Birkenstock sandals) while your organic lawn takes care of its own feeding, weeding, and watering.

6. The first summer, start raising the height of your mower blades. Gradually allow the lawn to grow taller, while removing only one-third from the top. As the weather warms in the summer, the lawn should be allowed to grow even taller, to shade the roots, conserve water, and shade out the weeds. Your goal is to be comfortable with a lawn three inches tall between mowings.

7. When you start to weaken (usually after visiting a putting green) and long for a short and scalped lawn, take off your shoes and walk barefoot on your chemical-free lawn. The blades will be soft and supple, instead of the stiff and sharp stubble of the addicted, crew-cut lawn.

8. Start watering less often but for longer periods. A deep soaking once a week is better for leading the roots down deep than is frequent watering every few days. Those grass roots may throw a fit or two during hot weather and have a meltdown temper tantrum with some summer browning, but don't give in. Make them wait for that weekly watering, and they'll learn to send their roots down deep for moisture.

9. Attack the weeds with a screwdriver, a hand tool called a "Diggit" or "Weed Hound," or more grass seed. This is not the time to backslide and reach for the chemical weed-and-feed. For real persistent weeds, you could try spot-spraying the weeds just where the grass cannot win control, but don't spread weed killer all over the lawn. Have faith that eventually your thick, deep-rooted lawn will crowd out most weeds.

10. Now don't just sit smugly and smile about your carefree and chemical-free lawn—get fired up about your conversion and spread the word to other addicted "lawn rangers." Imagine a neighborhood where everyone's grass is two to three inches tall, deep green and weed free, and no longer filling the groundwater with overdoses of nitrogen. Best of all, imagine a neighborhood that can maintain deep green lawns even during times of water rationing—lawns that stay green and healthy while using less water, less fertilizer, and less pesticides should be a goal for every neighborhood.

Gardening Tip

"We don't fertilize our playing fields in the summer because that's when the grasses go dormant. A summer feeding would be fertilizing the weeds."

Q When is the best time to fertilize the lawn?

A The easy answer is fall and spring. If you feed just one time a year, do it in the fall. To really improve a sad lawn, fertilize with an organic lawn food two or even three times a year, following the instructions on the label.

WATERING

Q We have an automatic sprinkler system for our lawn. How often should I have it come on and how long should I let it run?

A There is no easy answer here. Water until the top six inches of soil is wet. This means you have to use a shovel and actually see how far the water has soaked in so you can figure out how long you need to water. As you improve the soil, your lawn will require less frequent watering because good soil acts like a sponge to hold water for the dry times. The weather, the season, and how often you fertilize all affect the water needs of a lawn. An average lawn needs one inch of water a week.

Q My husband likes to stand outside on hot summer nights and water the lawn with the hose. Isn't this worthless?

A Although it does do wonders to relax the gardener on hot summer nights, hand-watering with the hose just wets the top inch of soil and does not encourage deep penetration of the roots. It is training the lawn to be superficial and shallow. Infrequent, deep soakings with an overhead sprinkler are best for developing a lawn with strong character and an independent nature.

Q My neighbor waters his lawn once a week in the summer, but lets the sprinkler run all night long. Isn't this wasting water?

A Maybe, maybe not. He may have the sprinklers running at a very low volume. Eight hours of slow watering may be what the soil needs to soak it to a depth of six inches. Clay soils absorb water slowly, so setting a sprinkler at low volume for a long time is the only way to get heavy soil to take in enough moisture. Sandy soils absorb water quickly and then lose it, so they need water more often for shorter periods of time.

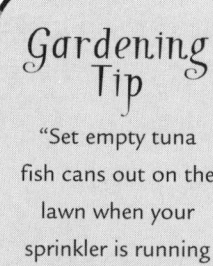

Gardening Tip

"Set empty tuna fish cans out on the lawn when your sprinkler is running so you can see how much water actually hits the lawn and how long it takes for the cans to fill with one inch of water."

Q I have sandy soil and cannot keep my lawn green in the summer unless I water every day. What can be done about this?

A The easy answer is to add organic matter to your soil to make it more spongelike and able to hold moisture. Spread compost or topsoil on top and use organic lawn foods to encourage your sandy soil to beef up. Leave your grass clippings on the lawn after mowing. They decompose and return nitrogen as well as organic matter to the soil.

Q There is a patch of lawn near the roots of a large tree that dries out and turns brown each summer. What can I do to keep it green?

A The easy answer is to grow drought-tolerant ground covers instead of grass in those areas. You could also add lots of organic matter. Or try this for a quick fix: Lay the end of the hose in the middle of the dry area and turn it on just a trickle for three or four hours, moving the hose head every so often around the dry patch. Slowly soaking the area with water every few days will bring the lawn back from dormancy, but you will need to improve the water-holding capacity of the soil with organic matter if you don't want to remain a slave to summer watering.

MOWING

Q I thought leaving the grass clippings on the lawn caused the buildup of thatch. Why do experts now recommend leaving the clippings?

A Because now we know better. Thatch is the buildup of dead stems and roots often encouraged by too much high-nitrogen fertilizer. Leaving the grass clippings on the lawn improves the soil by adding organic matter in the form of cut grass particles. A lawn fed with organic lawn food eats up thatch quickly because the soil is alive with millions of microorganisms.

Q If I don't have a mulching mower, should I still leave grass clippings on the soil?

A Yes, but you may have to mow more often. A mulching mower cuts the clippings into nice tiny pieces. These decompose and act as organic matter to feed all the good microorganisms in your soil. The more organic matter, the more good little creatures in your soil and the less you have to water and feed your lawn.

Better Mowing

The number one rule: Never remove more than one-third of the blade of grass! If your lawn is brown after mowing, you cut it too short. Shame on you.

- Make the first mowing in the spring the shortest mowing, to stimulate growth.

- Set the mower to one and a half inches.

- Gradually raise the mower so that it is at two to three inches by summer.

- Change the pattern you travel each week to avoid leaving ruts from the wheels.

- Mow often enough so that you can leave the clippings and they won't be matted clumps.

- In late fall, lower the mower to one and a half inches again to put the lawn to sleep for the winter.

Q **I want to leave the clippings on my lawn, but my wife objects because the grass clippings sit in big clumps, which turn the lawn yellow underneath and make the whole yard look messy!**

A You're right, if you wait too long between mowings. The easy answer to this problem is to mow more often. The smaller the clippings, the neater the look. But leaving the clippings saves so much time (you won't have to collect and dump the clippings) that you'll have more time to mow more often. Collect the clippings if you are overdue for a mowing and they fall in large clumps. Use them to heat up your compost pile or spread them thinly over bare soil in your beds to act as a weed-blocking mulch. It also helps to prevent grass clumping if you mow when the grass is dry.

Gardening Tip

"If I come home from vacation to a tall lawn, I just raise the mower so that I still remove only one-third of the grass blade. In a few days, I cut the lawn again a little lower. Soon I am caught up without scalping the lawn. If I am going to be gone for longer than two weeks, I stop watering and let the lawn go brown and dormant in the summer. It stops growing but returns to green in the fall when I begin watering again."

So You Still Want a Perfect Lawn? Small Is Beautiful

The less lawn you have to care for, the easier it is to hand-weed, improve the soil, water, and mow as often as necessary. "Lawn rangers" always on grass patrol with a quest for the perfect lawn should continue to find ways to have less lawn. One tiny patch of perfect green lawn in the middle of a sea of healthy plants is a lovely sight. Here are some ways to shrink the size of your lawn, so you won't have to see a shrink about your obsession.

🌿 Make your flower beds and shrub borders wider. As the plants grow, don't prune or pinch, just remove more sod from around the perimeter. Take away a foot of sod each year as your shrubs continue to spread and your lawn continues to shrink.

🌿 Add pathways, patios, decks, and structures where the grass has trouble growing. Don't fret about the compacted grass from the kids or your own steps to the garage or garden shed; put in a pathway and plant flowers along the sides, or add a sport court, deck with chairs, or patio.

🌿 Add ground covers instead of lawn. If it's too hot and dry for a lawn, plant sedums and succulents; too shady and wet, plant vinca, lamium, or ajuga. See the ground cover and vine chapters for more ideas. As the ground covers grow, don't cut them back—cut out more lawn.

🌿 Add a front courtyard with ornamental grasses and drought-tolerant shrubs for a formal look in a sunny front yard, or a woodland walk and native plant garden in a shaded front yard.

🌿 Add a circular driveway or parking pad surrounded by a raised bed of flowers in the front.

🌿 Divide your large lawn into "pasture" and lawn with a split-rail or post-and-rail fence. The small area close to the house could be lawn, while the large area behind the fence could be considered meadow or pasture and allowed to grow taller. A gate or arch leading into the meadow makes this "countrified" view even more soothing than acres of a perfect lawn.

Dirt Cheap Tip

"I keep my lawn high, above two inches in the summer, but keep my mower sharp to give the grass a crisp look. The best investment I ever made was in a blade-sharpening tool for my reel mower. I sharpen the blades myself twice a year. When you buy a mower, ask how to sharpen the blades."

Q How can you say to mow when the lawn is dry, when every spring brings weeks of wet weather and the grass still grows at a rapid rate?

A Okay, easier said than done, but if you do miss a mowing because of heavy rain, don't make up for it by cutting back or scalping the lawn real close to get caught up. Raise the mower and remove just the top third of the grass blades, mowing more often until you catch up. If you scalp the lawn or cut it all the way down to the stems or stubble, it will sulk and pout for awhile until the stems grow new leaf blades, and during this "recharging" phase, weeds can get a jump start and invade the lawn.

Q I don't like the look of a lawn growing two or three inches tall! It looks messy and shaggy, and my neighbors think I'm not taking care of my lawn!

A The easy answer is to tell them you are just a trend-setter, ahead of your time. Soon water will be such a rationed resource that all lawns will be two inches or higher to conserve moisture. Other tips are to fill in any dips or hollows and have your mower sharpened. It is the evenness of the cut that makes a lawn look neatly mowed, not the height of the blades.

PROBLEMS

Q What can I do about the brown spots in my lawn, courtesy of my neighborhood dogs?

A The not-so-easy answer is to fence out the dogs. Once the damage is done, you should dilute the urine deposits with water. Doggy deposits leave a darker green ring of grass around a brown center. The dead center is the result of too much nitrogen in the dog's urine burning the grass. The dark green ring is the result of the smaller amounts of urine fertilizing the grass.

Garden centers sell repellents to keep the dogs off the lawn, or you could plant a thorny hedge, build a

---

Gardening Tip

Let's say you're leaving on vacation or work long hours and have only one day to mow the lawn—and it rains. You can knock some of the water off the grass blades by dragging a hose across the lawn. You can also use a reel mower (a similar cutting action to the old-fashioned push mower), which cuts more of the wet grass blades than a rotary mower. A lawn fanatic with a tiny area to mow could always cover the grass with a tarp at night if rain is expected and the lawn must be mown the next day. Be sure to remove the covering in the morning before the sun heats things up. Inexpensive plastic tablecloths work well for this job.

fence, talk to the dogs' owners, or catch the piddling pooches in the act and zap them with a high-powered squirt gun.

Q **I have some light brown dead spots in my lawn, and when I look closely I can see tiny pink strings in the dying sections. This is a new lawn we put in with sod and we have been careful to keep it well watered.**

A This fungus among us is easy to diagnose as red thread because of the characteristic pink strings you describe so well. It thrives in cool, moist conditions on lawns that have lots of lush, weak growth from too much water or poor drainage. Most often it is newly sodded lawns that suffer from this and several other lawn diseases. The easy treatment for red thread and other fungal diseases is to fertilize with an organic-based but high-nitrogen fertilizer so the lawn will "grow out of it." To prevent fungal infections on your lawn, do not scalp the lawn or mow down to the stems; water less often, but deeper; don't let clumps of mowed wet grass sit on the lawn.

Q **Is there a spray or poison I can use to kill the mushrooms that pop up in my lawn?**

A No. Just kick them over to destroy their spores so they'll be less likely to reproduce, then wait for a change in the weather and they will disappear. Mushrooms are a sign of moist soil and rotting material, so aerate or loosen the soil so that it drains more quickly to help discourage these fungi. If mushrooms keep appearing in a certain spot, dig in and uncover the rotting wood or debris in the center of the mushroom patch that is causing the problem.

Lawns Made for the Shade

If you are trying to grow a lawn in the shade, always invest in lawn seed mixes made especially for the shade. These contain more perennial ryegrass and turf-type tall fescue grasses that tolerate low-light conditions.

Don't mow lawns in the shade as low as lawns in the sun—they need the extra grass-blade length for making food in low-light areas. Most shade-tolerant grass seed varieties like to grow three inches or higher.

Moss moves into shaded lawns when the soil is moist and starved for nutrients. If moss is a problem, aerate and add nutrients in the form of fertilizer to your soil.

Q My lawn keeps creeping into my flower bed and I don't want to continue edging it. What do you recommend for a border?

A What's your garden style? Brick laid on edge is good for a formal garden, landscape timbers are quick and inexpensive for a more casual landscape, and cement pavers, scalloped edging, rocks, and flexible plastic edgings work as well. The point is to control the sideways creeping of the underground grass roots by setting the edging a few inches below ground level.

Q What if I don't want to install an edging around my small front lawn? The shape of my lawn has a lot of curves and it is difficult to put a border into a curving lawn.

A Edge the lawn each month with a half-moon spade or power lawn-edging tool and forget about installing a border. A string-trimmer can also be used to cut back the creeping edge of the lawn but leaves a more ragged look.

MOSS

Q What can I do about moss in my lawn? Will using organic lawn foods get rid of the moss?

A Over time the moss will disappear if you use organic lawn foods to improve the soil. Moss is not killing your lawn, it is simply an opportunist moving into the bare patches where your grass is not growing. Moss grows instead of grass where there is poor drainage (so you must aerate the soil), poor fertility (so you need to feed the soil), or too much shade (so try to limb overhanging trees or grow a shade-tolerant ground cover instead of a lawn in deep shade).

Q I applied a moss killer to my lawn with a handheld spreader, but some speckles of the granular moss killer strayed onto my cement pathway. The resulting stains are orange speckles. How can I get rid of these stains?

A It is the iron in the moss killer that stains cement (actually turning the color of rust from moisture in the cement). If you rinse all cement surfaces immediately after using iron products, you will lessen the pain of a

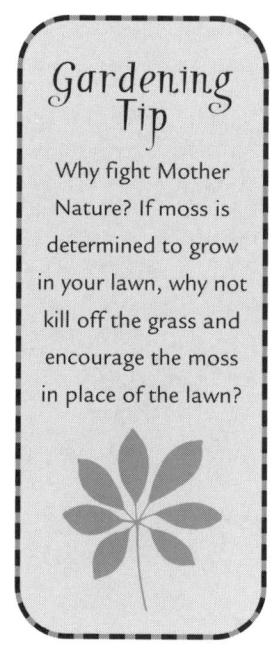

Gardening Tip

Why fight Mother Nature? If moss is determined to grow in your lawn, why not kill off the grass and encourage the moss in place of the lawn?

future stain. Otherwise, wait for time and sunlight to fade the stains. Cover your cement surfaces with a drop cloth before broadcasting moss killer, or sprinkle the product from a plastic pot with drainage holes (see the Dirt Cheap Tip on page 159) for greater control of where the product falls.

Q **What about using a moss killer on my lawn?**

A Moss control products, often mixed with spring lawn foods, work great, turning the moss an ugly black, but the moss will return if you don't change the conditions and reseed the bare patches once you get rid of the moss.

Q **What are the advantages of a moss lawn?**

A You won't have to mow. You won't have to fertilize. You won't have to water as much. Your landscape will have a mysterious, peaceful, oriental look to it, or add vine maples and rhodies for a Northwest natural look.

To encourage the moss, hand-dig the grass or smother the old lawn. Add more moss spores by gathering moss from tree trunks, rocks, and roofs. There are many different types of mosses. Collect lots to see which ones do best. Place the moss chunks that you gather into a large paper bag and shake vigorously. This breaks those chunks up into smaller pieces and releases some moss spores. Spread the broken moss chunks and debris from the bag over the ground and mist with water. Keep the new moss moist for several days as you would a newly seeded lawn. Repeat several times throughout the first year.

There's no need to fertilize or loosen the soil, because moss grows best in poor soil. Hand-pull any weeds for a year or so until the moss carpet grows thick. Add boulders and flat rocks to areas where the moss is having trouble growing or where grass keeps interrupting the velvety flow of moss.

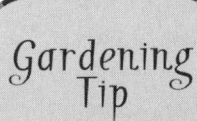

Gardening Tip

"Hand-pulling large weeds is often easier than spraying a weed killer. I keep a plastic bag of grass seed in my pocket when I garden, so every time I reach down to dig a weed from the lawn, I fill in the spot with a sprinkling of grass seed."

Taming the Moss Monster (or Not)

If your lawn seems like more moss than grass, you can take these steps to encourage lawn instead of moss—or you could stop fighting Mother Nature and let the moss grow. After all, a moss lawn is green, doesn't require mowing, and doesn't demand constant fertilizer to keep it happy. But, if a moss lawn is just too outlandish for your neighborhood, follow these steps to tame the moss monster:

STEP ONE: Aerate or poke holes all over the mossy patches using a core aerator if possible. A core aerator removes plugs of soil and can be rented—or save your back and hire this job out to a lawn care company.

STEP TWO: Use a moss control product to kill the living moss. There is no need to rake and remove the dead moss once it has been treated. This is too much work.

STEP THREE: Cover the dead moss with topsoil. Rake the topsoil so that it fills in any low spots, because this is where moisture collects and moss is most likely to thrive.

STEP FOUR: Reseed on top of the topsoil layer, using a starter fertilizer made for newly seeded lawns and lawn seed intended for the shade if low light levels have been encouraging your moss.

WEEDS

Q I have a huge lawn (more than one acre) and hand-weeding or spot-spraying the weeds is not practical. What do you recommend for organic weed control on a really large lawn?

A Change your perception. You don't have a lawn, you have a pasture, a meadow, or a field. Lower your expectations about the perfection of that much lawn, and remember that most of it is viewed from a distance; as

Gardening Tip

"When I retired, I became frustrated because my goal of the perfect lawn was ruined by grassy weeds. Finally my wise wife told me the perfect solution. She said, 'When you look at your lawn just blur your eyes, and all the wild grasses and weeds will blend together and you'll see what most visitors see—nothing but a lovely patch of green that frames our landscape.' I admit I don't take her advice too often, but this time I did, and it has made all the difference in the world—I now find lawn care fun and relaxing, instead of frustrating."

long as it's green, it will look great. As of this writing, there is much excitement about an organic lawn weed killer made from corn gluten. It should be available soon.

Q What is the easiest way to keep weeds out of the lawn?

A The easy answer (but a hard task to do) is to keep your lawn vigorous and healthy so that the thick growth of the grass crowds out the weeds.

Q I have a former pasture around my home that I would like to convert into a nice lawn. Can I just continue mowing the pasture and then use a weed-and-feed to turn it into a lawn?

A Yes. The easy answer to turning a pasture into lawn is to gradually mow the tall grass lower and lower until it is three inches tall. You never want to remove more than one-third of a blade of grass or cut it so short that only the stems are left.

A weed-and-feed product can work wonders at changing rough pasture grass into lawn. Read and follow all the instructions on the label to make sure you get the most effective treatment. Once you get most of the weeds under control, you can cover the pasture with a thin layer of topsoil and reseed right on top of the pasture grass. Do this in the fall and be sure to fertilize with an organic lawn food in fall and spring. Now wean your lawn from the weed-and-feed.

Q How can I get rid of the wild grass, creeping bent grass, or crabgrass that grows sideways and is a different color from my own green grass? It looks especially noticeable right after I mow, and weed killers don't work on these grassy weeds.

A The easy answer to this common problem is not to mow your lawn so short! If you gradually raise your mower height to two inches and as summer progresses let the lawn grow to even between three and four inches, then your lawn will shade out some of those wild grasses and lots of other sun-loving weeds.

> ## Gardening Tip
>
> "I am too lazy to get down on my hands and knees and dig out wild, sideways-growing grasses that have invaded my lawn, so I found an easier way. I chop through the very center of the wild grass clump with my shovel. Most of the time this destroys the center root and then the clump dries up. In a few days the dry clump of grass is dead and easy to remove."

The not-so-easy answer is to improve your lawn by improving your soil. A thick, deep-rooted lawn crowds out weeds—even the wild, shallow-rooted, ugly grasses that are so hard to kill with chemicals.

Q How can I get rid of clover in my lawn?

A Loosen the soil, improve the fertility, and gradually set your mower higher so the grass can shade out the clover. Or, learn to like the clover. It stays green during a drought, and fixes nitrogen from the air and adds it to your soil (clover is nature's way of making your soil more fertile). Rolling in clover and finding four-leaf clovers have always meant good things. There are also lawn fertilizers with clover control herbicides that can be applied in the spring to keep clover seeds from sprouting.

Q Why are there so many dandelions (or plantain or other broad-leaved weeds) in my lawn and how can I control them?

A Weeds are opportunists, moving in where grass won't grow or where they can muscle aside weak stands of grass. Dandelions and other deep-rooted weeds with taproots are adept at growing in hard, compacted soil, and their deep roots actually help loosen things up below ground. There is an advantage to digging out dandelions with a screwdriver, "Hound Dog," or "Diggit" weeding tool, aside from avoiding the use of herbicides. When you pull out that long root, you leave a deep channel for water and air.

Broad-leaved weeds like dandelions and plantain are also easy to kill with chemical herbicides (weed killers), but instead of spreading the poison all over your lawn or using a "weed-and-feed" over the entire lawn, spot-spray the weeds where they are growing. This uses less poison and ensures more efficient coverage of the weeds. Follow instructions as to weather conditions on the day you spray.

Gardening Tip

"I had to remove sections of sod from my lawn when I put an addition on my deck. I used these sod sections to replace some weak sections of grass in my yard. First I laid the good sod section on top of the weak stand of grass so I could outline its shape by cutting around it with an ax. Then I took out the ax-cut section of poor lawn, loosened and improved the soil below, and then fit the good sod into its place, much like switching a piece in a jigsaw puzzle."

Q I have a creeping low weed in my lawn that blooms with tiny stars of blue flowers. Weed killers don't seem to faze it. How can I get rid of it?

A The easy answer is to dry up the soil. Your weed sounds like creeping veronica, or one of the other low lawn weeds that spread by underground surface roots. The quickest way to improve drainage on a damp lawn is to aerate and then rake an inch or two of sand right on top of the lawn.

Another practical cure for low-growing weeds that do not respond to herbicides is to allow the lawn to grow gradually taller so that it is eventually three inches tall. (Yes, a taller-growing lawn seems to be a cure for lots of problems.) Most of these creeping weeds do well in soil that is acid, damp, or poorly drained. Applying dolomite lime every fall and aerating every spring are good ways to discourage moisture-loving, belly-crawling weeds.

Gardening Tip

"Don't apply fertilizer and lime to your soil on the same day. The lime can cause a chemical reaction with the fertilizer that locks up some of the nutrients. Fertilize first and water well. In a few days the fertilizer will be deep in the soil and you can spread the lime."

Murder the Weeds, Not the Grass

Everyone should try hard to use as little herbicide or chemical weed killer as possible. If you insist on using these chemicals, consider these tips:

- Cut out the bottom and top of a tin coffee can and set this cylinder over the weeds. Now just spray the herbicide into the can to keep the mist from falling on nearby lawn.

- Use a sponge paintbrush to dab the leaves of your weeds with Roundup, a soaplike weed killer.

- Hand-dig the weeds out of your lawn and immediately reseed to keep them from coming back.

- For a really bad patch of weeds in a small area, cover the area with a sheet of plastic or a plastic kiddy swimming pool weighted down with water. In a few weeks, the grass and weeds below the covering will be dead. Replace with sod or rake out the dead weeds and grass, loosen and improve the soil, and reseed the entire area.

Chapter Thirteen

Pests & Weeds

The easy answers for winning the pest and weed wars

Getting rid of pests in the garden has become a topic ripe with conflict and controversy. The truth is that pest control can bring out the worst in gardeners. Slug activists, mole lovers, and aphid fan club members, be warned: You will not like many of the ideas offered in this chapter. I am not proud of some of these rather harsh solutions to pest problems, but they do work. If you're a gardener and it comes down to the rights and sufferings of your plants versus the rights and sufferings of some sap-sucking, worm-chewing, or belly-crawling pest, the health of the plants will win out. 🌿 *Weeds are pests that can also be considered as forms of organic matter. You pull them, you hoe them, you collect them for the compost pile. Even the weeds that you leave in place and smother with newspaper and bark will return as organic matter and add nutrients to the soil.*

> ## Gardening Tip
>
> "If you find in your mole trap a mole that just looks dead, don't bury it yet! The mole might be unconscious and could wake up after you bury it safely in its home in the ground. Give it a good rap on the head and then put the carcass into a main mole runway to scare off other moles that want to take over the territory."

MOLES & RODENTS

Q **Moles are ruining my life and my lawn. What can I do?**

A I hang my head in defeat. There is no easy answer to mole control—not mothballs, chewing gum, Ex-Lax, gas bombs in the runways, pinwheels, euphorbia (gopher plant), or even an easy-to-set trap that guarantees success. Some moles learn to avoid carefully set traps.

But don't think moles can have the run of the yard. There are plenty of not-so-easy answers to the mole problem, so take your pick about what seems easiest (see the sidebar "Not-So-Easy Answers to Moles," on page 182).

Not-So-Easy Answers to Moles

MOLE TRAPS: This is the most effective and consistently successful method for actually murdering moles. The Out-O-Site scissors-type mole trap is recommended by most experts, but sometimes you'll meet a mole that has learned to avoid traps. (But then, you could always give it the ax—see the sidebar "Confessions of a (Mostly) Nonviolent Gardener," on page 183.) Some experts claim that watering the ground well after setting a trap will make the earthworms active and attract moles to the trap area.

BUILD A BARRIER: If you have a small patch of lawn you want to keep mole free, it may be practical to dig a ditch all around the perimeter and sink a barrier at least one foot deep to keep out the moles. Cement, sheet metal, and wire mesh have all been used. Moles do occasionally come aboveground, but an underground wall does a fair job of keeping them from a lawn or garden.

MOLE-MURDERING PETS: Some gardeners swear by female neutered cats as the best mole hunters, but my own female neutered cat catches more mice than moles. Others say dogs that are part terrier will dig out moles with relish, but I would think that would do more damage to the lawn than to the moles.

Q I've tried every trip and trap imaginable to rid my shaded side yards of moles, but nothing has worked. I suspect I also have mice and shrews, adding to the uneven, pockmarked surface of the lawn. It's getting downright dangerous to walk on this patch of grass, what with all the underground tunnels and passageways creating such treacherous territory. I feel like a slave to mole control.

A The easy answer is to lose the lawn, fool the eye, and free yourself from a lot of frustration. Here's what worked in a particularly mole-infested area of my own yard: I covered the lawn with a thin layer of newspaper and topped this off with a few inches of topsoil and compost. Next I planted the shade-loving evergreen ground cover lamium 'Beacon Silver', just by poking springs of an overgrown plant into the soft soil. In a few months, a sea of green and silver foliage flooded the area with lush vegetation, with not a mole mound or hole in sight. Of course, the burrows and rodents are stilll there, but since they are now camouflaged by the ground cover, I don't worry about them. Stepping stones leading through this area offer sure footing. We don't always have to fight Mother Nature. Sometimes a compromise is in order.

Confessions of a (Mostly) Nonviolent Gardener

I shall now confess my most violent deed and get it over with. First let me say that I am not the type who can stand to see anything in pain, and can't even stomach the fake wrestling on TV. I won't let my husband remove the starling nests from our roof because it might disturb the unhatched starling eggs (which I know grow into cruel, mean birds), and I can't bring myself to throw rocks at the stray cats that steal our spoiled kitty's food. So you must understand that the following episode is completely out of character—but it goes to show how crazed and deranged even nonviolent gardeners can become in their quest to protect their plants. It sometimes goes beyond pest control and turns into personal vengeance.

It was a sunny summer morning, and I wandered outside in my stocking feet and bathrobe to check on some roses near the patio. I sat on a bench in the early morning sun, pondering the roses, when what should catch my eye but the lawn—it was moving.

I looked again. Our lawn was breathing up and down like an accordion. It was a mole at work. This was the mole that had evaded my traps all summer and done considerable damage by burrowing under my newly planted roses. Now it was making its way across the lawn in the early morning light, and I could see the rise and fall of the sod as it forged its underground passageway.

The "fight or flight" response kicked in and I ran for the house. However, my normally heroic husband refused to leave his warm bed to save our yard from the attacking mole, and so in desperation I ran to the garage for a shovel. Instead I saw the ax.

What came over me next must be blamed on the heat of battle or the passion of the moment. I was temporarily insane. I grabbed that ax and ran (in my stocking feet no less) to the heaving ground, and chopped with a vengeance. The ax went down hard and came up bloody. I had chopped up a living mole with an ax! Terrified, I dropped the bloody weapon and escaped inside to double-bolt the doors. I had visions of millions

Gardening Tip

"When I plant crocus and tulip bulbs, I keep the pesky squirrels away by sprinkling the bulbs and the ground with red cayenne pepper."

of avenging moles attacking my stocking feet with their sharp, axlike teeth. How does a peaceful pursuit like gardening turn normal, level-headed people into ax-wielding monsters? And were there bloodstains on my stockings linking me to the murder?

I could not return to the scene of the crime, and left the gory mess for my husband to clean up. To this day I harbor a fear of being attacked by furious and angry moles, and will never step shoeless onto our lawn again.

The moral of the story: Moles can make you crazy. (But so can slugs and deer. And then there are those aphids . . .)

Q I never had much trouble with moles until I started to build up the soil in my perennial beds with grass clippings, compost, and manure. Now it seems like I'm attracting moles from miles around. Could this be true?

A Unfortunately, you've discovered the dirty little secret of great soil. It's soft and loose and full of earthworms—just perfect for mole feeding frenzies. The vibrations of the wiggling worms are what attract the moles.

But don't go back to hard-packed, lifeless soil. Instead, make it more difficult for moles to enter the garden beds. Outline your beds with a border of rocks, metal edging, or even fiberglass strips sunk at least six inches below the soil level. If you know that the moles (and possibly mice) are entering from woods on one side of the beds, install a sheet-metal barrier three feet deep, to force the moles to travel aboveground where they are more vulnerable to enemies. Now trap the moles already inside and your underground barriers should deter at least some of the rodents.

Q I did a good job of trapping the moles in my lawn by finding the main run, covering the trap with a bucket, and putting a mound of soft earth in the runway both in front and in back of the trap. I think the

Gardening Goof

I once had a bad habit of peeling off my gardening gloves and leaving them on the back porch. Never again. One morning I stopped at the steps to slip my hand into my gardening glove. My fingertips met a wiggling body. One peek into the glove, and my screams awoke the neighborhood. There was a slightly bloodied but still-living mouse burrowed into the finger of my glove. It must have escaped from an encounter with the cat and made a desperate break for a hiding place—finding my gardening gloves to be the perfect spot. I now hang my gloves indoors, and still look for tails each time I put them on.

moles are gone, but sections of the ground are still collapsing. I see no mounds, just dry brown strips where underground tunnels are forming. The souls of murdered moles, perhaps?

A You aren't being haunted by mole spirits in the lawn, you're just hosting new underground guests. There is a lot going on down there. Mice and voles (yes, there's a rodent called a vole) use old mole tunnels for new homes, and in dry weather you'll more easily notice the shallow tunnels. Trade the mole traps in for mouse traps, as mice are more likely to feed on bulbs and plant roots than the mostly meat-eating moles. This is where an ambitious cat would earn its keep.

Q This is a 92-year-old, very arthritic gardener writing in great haste to rescue all gardeners with moles. The simple solution is to pour a quarter cup of dolomite lime into any underground runway, using a trowel, and then to softly replace the earth without tamping it down. In all my experiences over the years, and those of my friends, this works, even in a severe case where a lawn went from 100 molehills to none. Surely you must know that lime is an excellent mole deterrent! Now why have you not spread the word to your readers?

A Mole control is an ongoing issue, and I rarely consider the unusual repellents that some gardeners think can ward off moles (including human hair in the holes, buried pop bottles, and used kitty litter). Well, I did try lime in the runways and you're right, it worked! For awhile anyway. Then the moles came back. I beg your mercy for not spreading the word sooner. Until you wrote in, I had never heard of such a thing—I guess I deserved your scolding. Experienced gardeners always know the best dirt.

Note: Some research among the scientific community suggests that when the earthworms and grubs ingest the lime, they become inactive, and it is the vibrations of these underground critters that attract the moles to the lawn in the first place. Or maybe the moles and mice hate the smell of lime in their home. Or perhaps the rodents get sick when they lick the lime off their paws. If you really don't want to mess with mole traps (or argue with feisty 92-year-old gardeners), try adding dolomite lime in the mole runways for some temporary mole relief.

Gardening Tip

"I saved the drum from inside my old washing machine and sunk it into the ground, filled it with soil, and used it as underground protection for my spring tulips. I plant the bulbs inside the steel drum, top it with chicken wire, and the mice can't even get close."

DEER

Q Our problem is deer. I do not want to harm these beautiful creatures, but they have eaten my roses down to bare stems and they leave deer droppings all over the yard. We even had a landscape designer do a plan for the yard using deer-proof plants, but in the winter the deer eat these anyway! I know we can spray the plants with a repellent, but we are gone a lot and cannot keep spraying after every rainfall. A barking dog is not an option.

A Bambi isn't as endearing in the garden as he is on the movie screen. In many parts of the country, human encroachment combined with wildlife protection laws has resulted in too many deer for the amount of wild vegetation available. The now-tame deer are thriving without their natural enemies to keep them in check, and they've developed both a taste for landscape plants (especially roses) and lack of fear of humans.

It is time to treat the deer like the pampered pets they have become. Invest in a fence. A battery-powered electric fence system five feet tall can be quite effective, and as a bonus will keep neighborhood dogs and cats away. Another less-expensive option is a fence of clear plastic mesh. You buy the mesh in four-foot-wide rolls and wrap it around the perimeter of the property using inexpensive stakes, or just hook it onto trees and shrubs to hold it in place. From a distance you can hardly tell the mesh fence is there. To keep deer from jumping, you need a fence at least eight feet tall, so that means two four-foot rolls stacked on top of each other. Some deer will jump this anyway. Another option is a solid fence six feet tall. Deer won't jump over if they can't see what's on the other side.

A deer fence around the property is no easy answer, but it is effective. A final note about deer-proof landscaping: Hungry deer will eat just about anything—including the bark from your trees. Some plants are just less desirable than others.

Q The deer leave our garden alone in the summer months as they are very shy, but in the winter they are a bit braver and sometimes venture to the outskirts of

> ## Gardening Tip
>
> "I have found that the black-tailed deer in our neighborhood do not like Shasta daisies, and so I've planted a screen of Shasta daisies across the back of the property, with Rugosa roses mixed in. They rarely bother the roses because it would mean sticking their noses down near the daisy smell they hate."

the property to feed on trees in our orchard. A fence or dog is out of the question. Any other ideas?

A Christmas lights left up all winter may work for shy deer like the type you describe. Set the lights up on a motion detector, so they come on only when the deer cross the path of the detector. A floodlight works as well, but somehow tiny twinkle lights decorating the orchard trees seem a friendlier way to discourage timid deer. Be prepared for the deer to become braver as time goes on. You may have to resort to the water method described below.

Q We have a vegetable garden that is difficult to protect from deer and raccoons. My neighbor claims dousing these pests with a strong jet of water from a hose will keep them out for good. Is it worth staying up all night and trying to spray the thieves?

A Invest in instant security with an automatic motion sensor hooked up to your hose. Any human or animal that passes in front of the sensor will be doused with a powerful jet of water. Works on dogs, cats, and forgetful gardeners as well. Many nurseries and garden supply centers sell these motion detectors, complete with hose and stand.

Another gardener plagued by friendly deer says that using "zoo doo," or manure from large predator-type animals, frightens the deer away—while helping support the local zoo.

SLUGS

Q I'm in desperate need of solutions to my slug problems, but with pets in my yard, I don't want to use poisonous baits. What nontoxic methods have been most successful?

A By far, my most highly recommended solution is a good squirt of Parsons ammonia (see the sidebar "Slugs in the Garden: Tolerance or Open Season," on page 188). Following are other ideas:

- Sinking a shallow saucer of beer in the ground seems a kinder way to kill slugs than freezing them. (Wonder why the slug activist didn't suggest beer drownings?)

🌿 Set out grapefruit half rinds in slug-infested areas. The slugs and snails are attracted to the citrus smell and hide under the rinds. You can gather them in the morning, slip them into plastic bags, and send them out with the trash.

🌿 Commercial slug baits are very effective, but to keep them away from children and pets, place the bait in a plastic margarine tub and cover with the container's lid. Then cut flaps into the sides of the tub so that slugs can crawl in, but the bait will stay covered.

🌿 There's some new less-toxic slug baits coming on the market that work well on even tiny baby slugs; they use iron phosphate as a bait. They have the advantage of poisoning the slugs a few hours after they feed and have returned to their homes, so you don't have to find slug carcasses all over the paths and beds. Look for these under the name of Sluggo and Worry-Free Slug Bait.

Q Every year, no matter what I do, the slugs chomp through my hostas and marigolds. I'm ready to surrender to the slimy beasts. Is there any hope?

A Yes. One way to win the slug war is to give up on slug-attracting plants, such as hostas and marigolds, especially in slug-infested areas where control is an ongoing process. Instead, cultivate slug-resistant plants. Some that do well in my own shaded woodland garden are *Saxifraga umbrosa* (London Pride), corydalis, candelabra and Wanda primroses, purple-leafed heuchera, ferns, and gray foliage plants such as lychnis, thyme, artemesia, and lamb's ear.

Conflict & Controversy

Slugs in the Garden: Tolerance or Open Season

I would vote the slug, that slimy, plant-eating belly crawler, as garden enemy number one in our moist climate, and surely the most destructive pest in my own mostly shaded landscape. I'm always looking for new slug control methods, and am thankful to the gardener who shared this safe and inexpensive home-made slug spray:

Mix one part ammonia and two parts water in a trigger spray bottle. (Parsons ammonia, the brand your grandmother cleaned the bathroom with, is still found in the cleaning supplies aisle at any grocery store—and it's cheap!)

Aim and fire on small slugs. It skins them alive!

This solution dissolves those hard-to-get tiny baby slugs that hide in the crown of newly emerging daylily shoots and at the base of hostas. Large slugs may be able to survive the ammonia spray by shedding their skin. The ammonia spray that hits the plants converts to nitrogen, so you are feeding the plants while ridding them of slugs. You can adjust the trigger spray to reach the bigger slugs crawling just out of reach. You can even load the squirt guns with the ammonia solution and send your youngsters outdoors after a rainstorm or with flashlights at night. Although the ammonia-and-water mix may damage the leaves of some tender ferns and plants, it is still safer than many slug baits or salt.

This slug-melting ammonia spray solution is not welcomed by all, however. There are those who find it unacceptable to harm any creature, even a slimy slug. When I insisted that slug control is necessary in some situations, a tender-hearted slug lover suggested that the kindest way to dispose of slugs is to gather them gently, place them in plastic bags, and put them in the freezer—where they presumably fall into a deep sleep in the deep freeze and die a painless death. Sorry to say, I do not practice this pain-free slug euthanizing. I figure any frozen slugs in my freezer could be mistaken for mushrooms and might end up in the spaghetti sauce. However, I am trying not to be so gleeful about killing slugs.

INSECTS & OTHER PESTS

Q When should I spray for the European craneflies that are flying all over my lawn? These large mosquito-like creatures show up every fall, then live in my soil as larvae in the spring and eat my lawn.

A Cranefly adults do indeed mate and lay eggs in the lawn and flower beds in the fall, but it is not effective to spray these insects at that time. The larvae are wormlike, tough-skinned creatures called leather jackets that may damage but rarely destroy lawns unless they are newly planted. Treat lawns infested with cranefly by fertilizing in the spring, and the grass can grow through the damage. Ignore cranefly larvae you find in your flower beds—they don't seem to harm plants.

Q How can I get rid of the shiny black beetles that I find hiding under rocks in my garden?

A There's no need to worry. Don't rid the yard of beetles; rejoice instead. The large black ground beetles do not eat plants, but feed on slug eggs and other insect pests.

The Solution to Most Pest Problems? Just Ignore the Damage

Not every pest needs to be controlled. Some, like the spittle bug, are seasonal and go away on their own. Others, such as the whitefly, do just a tiny bit of damage when the population is small, and it isn't worth the bother of treating the pest unless the numbers multiply and cause some serious damage. If you wait long enough, nature often takes care of the problem on her own as natural predators and a change in the weather move in to wipe out the problem.

Q **Will the spiders making webs under the eaves of my house harm my camellias?**

A Spiders may not look as cute as ladybugs, but they are just as beneficial. Appreciate the beauty of their webs and pest-eating ways, and then ignore them.

Q **There are wads of spit on my lavender plants, and inside I find a small green bug. Do I need to spray the plants?**

A Using a jet of water to remove the spittle is the easy answer, but doing nothing at all is easier still! Spittle bugs build spit homes in late spring, but they soon mature and leave the scene, doing very little damage to healthy plants.

Q **I notice small white flies that flit about my rhododendrons when the shrubs are disturbed. Each summer these insects show up, but I haven't yet noticed any damage to the plants. Should I be doing something about this problem?**

A Not really. Whiteflies cause damage in large numbers, but a full-grown shrub can usually survive some whitefly infestation with no visible damage. You can hit the plant with a strong jet of water to dislodge them, or use a homemade sticky yellow trap to lure them to their death. Paint a tin can yellow or wrap yellow paper around a can. Now slip a clear plastic bag over the can and coat the bag with petroleum jelly. Turn the yellow can upside down and set it on a stake near the infested plants. The whitefly will be attracted to the yellow can

Gardening Tip

"I use a zinc strip sold for roofs called Z-strip around the edge of my raised-bed vegetable garden, and it works for me to keep the slugs out."

A good rule to remember when you see an insect: If it moves fast, leave it alone (spiders, beetles, ladybugs, butterflies). It is the slow-moving creatures that tend to feed on plants (slugs, larvae, aphids, cutworms).

and become stuck in the petroleum jelly coating. Remove and replace the plastic bag every few days as it becomes coated with dead flies.

Thwarting Cats and Dogs: Spice Up Your Garden

The most sane approach to pet control is to retrain the habits of the offending animal over a two-week period. Squirt the visitors with water from a high-powered squirt gun or sprinkle their favorite digging spot with red or black pepper every few days.

As with deer, a good fence solves the wandering pet problem. If your own pets are doing the damage, here are some ways that gardeners and their pets can live in peace:

✍ Put your flowers in tubs or pots. Then cats won't dig and dogs won't step on them.

✍ Use thorny plants like barberry and roses to make a protective hedge around more fragile plants.

✍ Keep a long-range squirt gun by the door and try to catch your pets in an undesirable act. Use the water to redirect them.

✍ Potty train your pet. Both dogs and cats can be trained to relieve themselves in a certain area of the garden that you wish to leave wild. Start training the animals when they are young by bringing them to the same area to relieve themselves every time they need a potty break.

Q Starlings and crows are making a mess of my patio and ruining my peaceful garden. They are also bullly birds that scare off the smaller birds I want to welcome. Any nonlethal ways to discourage these noisy birds?

A Try Tanglefoot, a black goo that you spread where the birds are nesting or roosting. It bothers their feet and in many cases makes them irritated enough to move on.

Snakes and Lizards: Creative Answers for Unwanted Reptiles

Years ago most people solved their large pest problems with a shotgun or hound dog, but in these times there need to be kinder, gentler ways to tackle the problem—at least at first. The most creative pest-control method sent to me by a fellow gardener involved snake control.

An elderly woman wrote that she could no longer enjoy her garden because of the large and multiplying number of snakes that would bask in her flower beds and sleep on her porch and patio. (Yes, she knew how beneficial snakes are with slug and insect control, but they gave her the creeps anyway.) She did not wish to kill or ignore the critters, but catching them was almost impossible. I appealed to my always-inventive readers for ideas, and one gentleman sent in this solution, which had worked in his own snake-infested garden:

"Lay a large plastic garbage can on its side in the yard. Into it place a heating pad, using an extension cord if necessary. Plug in the heating pad at night, and after a few days you'll find a congregation of snakes that gather on the warm pad each morning. Tiptoe out, quickly pull the garbage can upright, and secure the lid. Set the can of snakes into the back of a truck and drive to the country. It is easy to pour the snakes into the woods without having to actually handle them—or look at them too closely."

Gardening Tip

"I have a solution for the lady who was terrified to garden because of all the lizards in her yard. Get two or three neighborhood children and pay them if necessary for each lizard they capture. My husband had to capture some lizards for a project in Mexico one time, and he couldn't come close to grabbing one. Finally he offered to pay the local children a bounty, and in no time he had more than enough unharmed lizards."

WEEDS

Q What's the easy answer to weeding if I have weeds coming up in my mulch?

A It's time for a sunny hoedown! Choose a sunny morning, a sharp hoe such as a sharply pointed "Winged Weeder," and a radio station with lively music. Now dance about the area, slicing all the weeds off at ground level and stomping on them as you feel the urge. There's no need to bend over and collect the weed carnage, and no need to pull each individual weed. Retreat indoors before the day heats up. The sun will do its part to dry up the sliced-off weed tops and suck all the moisture out of the newly decapitated stems, helping to kill off the roots. After a few days, when you're sure the weeds are dry and dead, spread your organic matter or, for maximum weed blockage, your newspaper layer and then your organic matter, on top of the soil. If the weeds are really vigorous, such as blackberries or thistles, use cardboard instead of newspaper to smother the cut weeds, and pile wood chips on top at least three inches deep.

Q How do I kill the weeds without working up a sweat?

A The easy answer to weed control is to smother them. Tiny weeds can be smothered by the covering of organic matter you spread on top of the soil. But first, you may need to suffocate any juvenile-sized weeds with newspaper. The bigger, more vigorous the weeds, the more layers of newspaper you need: five pages deep for low weeds, fifteen or twenty pages deep (or use cardboard) for weeds higher than your ankles.

Q How do I keep the weeds from coming back?

A Don't invite them. Weeds look for naked soil that has no protective mulch, or soil that is freshly dug and disturbed. Lazy gardeners tend to avoid digging around and disturbing the soil, and this is good. There is no need to continually cultivate or dig your beds. Now concentrate on using a mulch as a weed deterrent.

> ## Gardening Tip
>
> "After I seed anything in the garden, I spread chicken wire over the soft soil. This keeps my cats from digging up the seeds and using the garden as their litter box."

Landscape with Your Weeds—Just Call Them Wild Flowers

Sometimes all that's needed to improve a weed problem is a change in attitude. At one point I had a rather unkempt bed of perennials and pass-along plants, and needed to tidy the spot up quickly for a garden tour. This was when the English Cottage Garden Look was in full rage, and I much admired the picket fences, watering cans, and straw hats that set the mood for this cozy garden style.

It took me just a few minutes to lean a prepainted section of white picket fence up against the back of the weedy perennial garden to give it some enclosure, add a weathered bench with stepping-stones leading to the center of the plant mess, and then, the ultimate Cottage Garden accent, a beribboned straw hat, was laid casually upon the bench.

This was a lot more fun than picking out every weed. I did pull the weeds near the front of the bed and close to the stepping-stones, but the really tall weeds I just called wildflowers. A cottage garden is just a mishmash of colorful, casual country flowers, and the blooming weeds fit right in. When this little pocket garden was given a white background for the flowers to bloom against, a strong focal point in the form of a bench, and a bit of charm with the straw hat and stepping-stones, it was transformed from messy to magical.

Plant Diseases: Good Air Circulation Is the Preventive Medicine

Most of the diseases that bother plants are from the mold and fungus family; these culprits love still, damp air. Often a change in the weather is all that is needed to dry up the problem. Here are some tips to keep you from reaching for that fungicide sprayer:

- Don't crowd your plants. The free flow of air around plants discourages disease.

- Be careful not to overwater. Waterlogged soil stresses a plant and makes it more susceptible to disease.

- Prune off any leaves or stems that start to turn yellow or show signs of problems. This includes faded flowers. A clean garden is less likely to harbor pests.

- Do not water your plants at night; the cool air, combined with wet foliage, invites unwelcome disease spores.

Gardening Tip

"I use vinegar as a weed killer that kills on contact. I just use white vinegar and spray it from a trigger spray bottle right on the weeds in the cracks of my sidewalk and along the edge of my patio. You can also add a squirt of Ivory soap to the vinegar to make it stick on the surface of the weeds. Vinegar as weed killer works best on a sunny day."

Q Help! My garden beds are being taken over by a small weed with clover-shaped reddish leaves and yellow flowers. The seed pods from this weed explode when I try to pull them from the soil.

A Sounds like oxalis, an invasive weed that has cousins sold as ornamentals with pink instead of yellow flowers. This weed is best controlled by smothering it with newspaper and mulch, because trying to cut or pull the plants spills more seeds about the garden, as you have discovered.

Persistent Weeds: Don't Yank Out Your Horsetails and Morning Glory!

Dreaded morning glory (or bindweed) and horrible horsetail are the two weeds that gardeners find most persistent. Unfortunately, the only cure for them, other than moving to a new home, are hard work and persistence (more persistence than they have). These obnoxious weeds come back stronger if you try to pull them from the ground and in the process break off sections of the root. Instead, you should cut them off at ground level with scissors. They'll be back, but be ready to cut them again, and again. Three cuttings should starve out those roots. Use a weed whacker or string trimmer to cut back large patches. Keep at it by mowing the weeding area if you have to.

Both of these determined weeds are difficult to kill with glysophate herbicides like Roundup, so before you reach for the really toxic poisons, put your energy into cutting and recutting until they give up.

Gardening Tip

Vinegar, boiling water, and even soapy water will kill some weeds where they grow. But be careful not to over-use these methods—you could sterilize your soil or damage nearby plants.

Walk the Garden and Nip Pests and Weeds in the Bud

Gardening Tip

"When I am done with an old shower curtain, plastic table-cloth, or piece of carpet, I use these items for weed control. They make great weed barriers in pathways covered with wood chips, or as slow but sure vegetation killers when laid atop a weedy patch of ground."

Next to a lichen-covered bench in my garden, I have my grandfather's old leather boots filled with soil and planted with sedums. The boots had been resoled several times, worn thin by a man who took care of other people's gardens and then came home each night to work in his own greenhouse and tend his immaculate vegetable plot.

His boots are a reminder of the old gardener's saying, "The best fertilizer for any garden is the footsteps of its owner." So get out there and walk your garden often. You'll see what's happening as the story unfolds and be able to enjoy the wonder of an unfurling rosebud, as well as pinch the start of a growing insect problem and destroy young weeds before they have a chance to go to seed.

Index

A

Ajuga (carpet bugle), 56, 138, 141, 142, 145, 171
Alchemilla mollis (lady's-mantle), 79
Alfalfa pellets, 4
Annual plants
    caring for, 41–44, 48–49
    characteristics of, 37–38
    deadheading, 44
    fertilizer burn on, 43
    fertilizing, 41, 43
    fragrant, 48
    as ground covers, 138
    growing your own, 39
    hardening off, 48–49
    mixing with perennials, 66
    in narrow beds, 44
    for patios, 47
    pinching, 44
    preventing damage from cold nights, 48–49
    as privacy screens, 47
    protecting against slugs and snails, 49
    on retaining walls, 44
    selecting, 40, 44, 46–48
    siting, 40
    in specially shaped beds, 45
    for tropical resort looks, 46
    vines, 151
    vs. perennials, 37–40, 65–66
Anthracnose, 134
Antirrhinum (snapdragons), 24, 48
Ants, 86
Aphids, 106, 107–8, 135
Asters, 73, 77, 81, 82
Astilbe, 71, 73
Aurinia (basket-of-gold), 82
Azaleas, 15, 112, 115, 118, 138, 140

B

Bacterial canker, 133
Bark chips/dust, 6
Basket-of-gold *(Aurinia)*, 82
Bearded iris, 84–85
Bedding plants. *See* Annual plants
Beetles, 189
Begonias, tuberous, 15, 24
Bigleaf hydrangeas *(Hydrangea macrophylla)*, 110, 112
Birch trees, 135
Black spot, 105
Bleeding heart *(Dicentra spectabilis)*, 73, 77
Bloodmeal, 5
Blue fescue, 74
Bonemeal, 5
Botrytis blight, 86
Buddleia davidii (summer lilac), 114
Bugs. *See* Pests
Bulb flies, 59
Bulb mites, 58, 59
Bulbs, tubers, and corms
    advantages of, 51
    buying bargain bulbs, 52–53
    caring for, 58–62
    in containers, 56–58
    diagnosing problems
        daffodils, 59
        dahlias, 60–61
        gladiolus, 60
        tulips, 58
    Easter lilies, 62
    easy-to-grow tulips, 53, 54
    fertilizing, 62
    for lazy gardeners, 55
    lilies, 54, 56, 62
    under low shrub branches, 55
    mixing annuals and bulbs in pots, 56–58
    planting bulbs deep enough, 61
    protecting from rodents, 58–59, 60, 185

protecting tender bulbs, 64
replanting in diseased spots, 62
in shady spots, 54, 55
for snowbirds, 55
spring *vs.* summer blooming, 54
storing, 64
using full-size bulbs, 52–53
Buxus microphylla (little leaf boxwood), 115

C

Calcium, 9
Camellia *(Camillia)*, 2, 113, 118, 190
Campsis radicans (trumpet vine), 153
Candelabra primroses *(Primula japonica)*, 86
Candy tuft *(Iberis)*, 77
Cardboard, as mulch, 7, 147
Caring for plants
annuals, 41–44, 48–49
bulbs, tubers, and corms, 58–62
ground covers, 143–48
ensuring good air flow, 195
perennials, 75–78, 80–86
roses, 98–108
shrubs, 116–22
trees, 129–35
vines, 153–58
Carpet bugle *(Ajuga)*, 56, 138, 141, 142,
145, 171
Catnip, 73
Cats, 191, 193
Cedar Grove compost, 4, 32
Chaenomeles (flowering quince), 110
Chameleon plant *(Houttuynia)*, 145–46
Chemical fertilizers. *See* Fertilizer
'Cherish' roses, 88
Cherry trees, 133, 134
Chinese dogwood trees *(Cornus kousa)*, 127
Chrysanthemum parthenium (feverfew),
67–68
Chrysanthemums, 67-68, 82
Clay soils, 1, 2, 5
Claybuster, 5, 161

Clematis, 149, 150, 152–53, 153–54
Clematis wilt, 154
Climber roses, 92
Clover, 178
Cold, damage from, 48–49
Columbine leaf miner, 82
Columbines, 82
Compost
adding dead ground covers to, 147
adding to potting soil, 32–33
compost-bucket stew, 10
making and using, 3
as a mulch, 7
mushroom, 4
spot composting, 5
in tree planting holes, 132
weed seeds in, 76
See also Fertilizer
Conflict & Controversy
difficult delphiniums, 84
disease-prone flowering cherry trees,
125–26
high maintenance contorted filbert
trees, 132
invasive ivies, 144
killing moles, 183–84
killing slugs, 188–89
organic *vs.* synthetic fertilizers, 42
returning tulips, 63
roses as "royalty," 101–3
Container gardens
adding compost to potting soil,
32–33
alternative pots, 25, 28
as an alternative to using poor soil, 6
bulbs, tubers, and corms in, 56–58
chairs as containers, 26
choosing color combinations, 21, 22
choosing potting soil, 31–32
ground covers in, 140
grouping pots, 28
making your own potting soil, 32

matching containers with
  architectural styles, 27
matching plants with containers, 21
mixing herbs and vegetables in, 23
perennial plants in, 74–75
pots inside of pots, 28
recycling broken pots, 30–31
reusing old pots, 28
selecting plants for, 19–24
selecting pots, 24
in shady spots, 22
stacking pots, 29–30
in sunny spots, 22, 23
teacup gardens, 20
using garden soil for, 31
using large pots, 36
using potting soil, 31–33, 36
Coreopsis grandiflora (tickseed), 79
Corms. *See* Bulbs, tubers, and corms
Cornus kousa (Chinese or Korean dogwood
  trees), 127
Cornus stolonifera (redtwig dogwood), 110
Corydalis, 79
Craneflies, 189
Creeping phlox, 77
Creeping veronica, 179
'Crimson pygmy' barberry, 115
Crows, 191

Daffodils, 59, 61
Dahlias, 60–61, 64
Dandelions, 178
Daphne, 114
Daylilies *(Hemerocallis)*, 68–69, 83
Deadheading annuals, 44
Deer, 186–87
Delphiniums, 78, 83, 84
Dianthus barbatus (Sweet William), 48, 79
Dirt Cheap Tips
  alternatives for pots, 28
  building frames for vines, 151

finding money to buy plants, 66
getting catalogs, 13
getting expert help on trees, 135
ground covers as grass
  substitutes, 141
ground covers in container
  gardens, 140
homemade grass seed spreaders, 159
making your own seed tape, 38
purchasing bulbs inexpensively, 52
sharpening mower blades, 171
using Christmas tree branches, 7
using coffee grounds, 6
using organic lawn foods, 165
Dogs, 172, 191
Dogwood trees, 127, 129, 134–35
'Dora amateis' rhododendrons, 116
Dusty Miller, 45, 47
Dwarf Chinese holly *(Ilex cornuta)*, 115
Dwarf dogwood, 141
'Dwarf licorice', 47
Dwarf nandina, 115

Easter lilies, 62
Easy Answers
  adding a jungle look to your patio, 46
  adding non-living objects, 121
  avoiding watering worries, 15
  carefree rhododendrons, 116
  caring for rhododendrons and
    azaleas, 118
  chemical-free lawns, 166
  choosing roses, 91, 92–93
  color combinations for container
    gardens, 22
  disease-resistant dogwoods, 127
  fragrant annuals, 48
  fragrant shrubs, 114
  growing your own annuals, 39
  ignoring pests, 190
  imitating professional plantings, 111

insuring air flow around plants, 195

low maintenance hedges, 119

mowing lawn, 170

perennials for shady or sunny
    spots, 73

plants for narrow, shady beds, 70

primroses for garden paths, 86

pruning trees, 130

replanting perennial divisions, 78

selecting annuals, 40

selecting ground covers, 141

shrubs close to your house, 115

shrubs for fall color, 112

siting trees, 131

staggering perennial bloom times, 82

tolerating rose diseases, 107

trees as gifts, 124

tulips that thrive in poor soil, 53

using raised beds to avoid digging, 8

using reseeding perennials, 67–68

walking your garden, 197

weed control for perennials, 76

weedless garden paths, 7

Eggs, water from boiling, 10

English lavender *(Lavandula angustifolia)*, 23

Etera perennials, 71

Euphorbia, 73

F

Fences, 158, 186

Ferns, 70, 73, 76

Fertilizer

for annuals in the ground, 43

applying, 11

avoiding overuse, 11

for bulbs, tubers, and corms, 62

choosing not to fertilize, 9

determining the need for, 2–3, 8

fertilizer burn, 11, 43

household sources of, 10

labels, 9

for lawns, 164–68, 179

mixing your own, 104

nutrients in, 9

organic *vs.* synthetic, 42, 164–65

for potted annuals, 41, 43

for roses, 104, 105

for trees, 131, 132

types of, 9–11

See also Compost

Feverfew *(Chrysanthemum parthenium)*,
    67–68

Fire, 59

Floribunda roses, 92

Flowering cherry trees, 125–26

Flowering quince *(Chaenomeles)*, 110

Flowering tobacco *(Nicotiana alata)*, 24

Forget-me-not *(Myosotis)*, 79

Foxgloves, 73, 83

Fragrant plants

annuals, 48

roses, 95

shrubs, 114

siting, 22

Fragrant snowball *(Viburnum carlcephalum)*,
    114

Frost burn, 48–49

Fuchsia magellanica (shrub fuchsia), 112

G

Gardenias *(Gardenia jasminoides)*, 24

Gardening Goofs

choosing big, already-blooming
    annuals, 37

doing nothing, 1

fertilizing roses too late, 105

mixing sod and seed, 163

not changing potting soil, 34

not checking inside gardening
    gloves, 184

not staking Shasta daisies, 81

planting invasive ivies, 144

planting too early, 48

using Styrofoam peanuts, 35

weed seeds in manure, 4
Gardening in pots. *See* Container gardens
Gardening Tips
    advantages of ground covers, 137
    avoiding lily pollen stains, 60
    caring for cherry trees, 134
    catching lizards, 192
    choosing carefree roses, 87
    chopping out wild grasses, 177
    cleaning up dead rhododendron
        flowers, 119
    composting systems, 3
    controlling aggressive herbs, 19
    controlling slugs, 190
    curtain rods as stakes, 83
    duplicating others' successes, 14
    fertilizing lawns, 167, 169
    gathering up leaves, 130
    getting rid of rocks, 2
    hand-pulling weeds, 175
    harmful *vs.* beneficial insects, 191
    homemade rose fungicide sprays,
        106, 108
    killing moles, 181
    letting children help with bulbs, 63
    lining pots with plastic, 27
    matching flower and paint colors, 21
    mixing your own fertilizer, 104
    mixing your own potting soil, 32, 33
    moisture meters for roses, 102
    moss instead of lawn, 174
    moving heavy soil amendments, 5
    mowing tall lawns, 170
    mowing wet lawns, 172
    mushrooms, 9
    naming your trees, 125
    nasturtiums as carefree plants, 41
    planting gladiolus bulbs with Shasta
        daisies, 51
    protecting annuals from cold, 49
    protecting clematis stems, 153
    pruning hedges, 120, 122
    pruning roses, 98

putting lime on lawns, 179
repelling deer, 186, 187
repelling squirrels, 183
rooting hydrangeas, 117
rooting sedum cuttings, 77
"seeing" your perfect lawn, 176
siting fragrant plants, 22
splitting root masses, 16
starting vines up trees, 149
storing tender bulbs, 64
storing twist ties, 155
transplanting sod, 178
trees and septic systems, 124
using ajuga to loosen soil, 142
using chicken wire to deter cats, 193
using cosmos, 46
using newspapers, 10
using rebar as stakes, 61
using sheep shears, 143
using tomato cages for topiary, 30
using vinegar to kill weeds, 195, 196
using washing machine drums to
    deter rodents, 185
using weed barriers, 197
watering
    lawns, 168
    roses, 103
    young trees, 133
Gazebos, 157
General Gardening Internet Site, 71
Geraniums, 14, 21, 22, 40, 72
Ginkgo biloba, 127
Gladiolus, 60
Grandiflora roses, 92
Grass. *See* Lawns
Ground covers
    advantages of, 137–38
    as an alternative to grass, 141
    annuals and perennials as, 138
    around rhododendrons and azaleas,
        138, 140
    at the base of roses, 97
    botanical names identifying, 141

caring for, 143–48
characteristics of, 138
in container gardens, 140
controlling, 143–46
disposing of, 147
between garden stepping-stones, 140
invasive, 143–46
junipers as, 140–41
killing, 147–48
making "quilts" of, 139
pruning, 143
selecting, 138–43
for shady spots, 141
siting, 138–43
on steep banks and hillsides, 142–43
for sunny spots, 142
using Roundup to kill, 147
vs. mulches, 140
as a way to hide mole tunnels, 182
for wet spots, 142
See also Lawns
Guano, bat, 4
Gypsum, 5

Hardy roses, 105
Hedge roses, 95
Hedges, 118–19, 120–21, 122
Helichrysum petiolare (licorice), 47
Hemerocallis (daylilies), 68–69, 83
Hen and chickens (*Sempervivum*), 29,
    83, 139
Herbaceous perennials, 66
Heuchera, 71, 74, 80, 181
Hollyhocks, 84
Honeysuckle *(Lonicera japonica)*, 146, 151,
    153, 155
'Honor' roses, 88
Horsetail, 196
Hostas, 15, 69, 70, 72, 73, 80
Houttuynia (chameleon plant), 145–46
Hybrid tea roses, 88, 89–90, 92, 100

Hydrangea macrophylla (bigleaf hydrangeas),
    110, 112
Hydrangeas, 15, 110, 112, 116–17, 151
Hypericum (St. Johnswort), 142, 143, 146

Ilex cornuta (dwarf Chinese holly), 115
Impatiens, 22, 40, 45, 49
Insects. *See* Pests
Ipomoea alba (moonflower), 152
Ipomoea batatas ('Terrace Lime' sweet
    potato vine), 46
Iron, 9
Ivies, 144–45, 147

Jacob's ladder *(Polemonium caeruleum)*, 81
Japanese spurge *(Pachysandra)*, 146
Junipers, 140–41

K. *See* Potassium (K)
Kelp extract, 5
Korean dogwood trees *(Cornus kousa)*, 127
Kurume azaleas, 115

Lady's-mantle *(Alchemilla mollis)*, 79
Lamium, 72, 73, 74, 138, 140, 171, 182
Landscaping roses, 95
Lavandula angustifolia (English lavender), 23,
    73
Lawn Restore (lawn food), 165
Lawns
    alternatives to, 141, 160, 174, 175
    brown spots in, 172–73
    buying seed, 162
    chemical-free, 166–67

chemical weed control, 179
converting pasture to lawn, 177
decreasing lawn size, 171
fertilizing, 164–68, 179
getting rid of weeds
    clover, 178
    creeping veronica, 179
    dandelions, 178
    wild grasses, 177
hand-pulling weeds, 175
homemade seed spreaders, 159
installing edging around, 174
keeping dogs off of, 172–73
killing moss, 174–75, 176
killing mushrooms, 173
leaving clippings on your lawn,
    169–70
mixing sod and seed, 163
moss in, 174–76
mowing, 169–70, 172
organic *vs.* synthetic fertilizers,
    164–65
organic weed control, 176–77
perfect, 160, 164, 171, 176
preparing soil for, 161
putting in new lawns, 160, 161–62
putting new lawns over old, 62, 160
reseeding old, 163
reviving dried-out patches, 169
for shady spots, 163, 164, 173
sharpening mower blades, 171
sod *vs.* seed, 162–63
spreading lime on, 179
tall, 170, 172
transplanting sod, 178
using Roundup on, 179
using sprinklers effectively, 168
watering, 168–69
weed control, 176–79
when to fertilize, 167, 168, 179
See also Ground covers
Leaf blight, 81
Leaf rollers, 120

Leaf spot, 59, 121, 133
'Lemon Licorice', 47
Leucothoe fontanesiana (rainbow bush), 110
Licorice *(Helichrysum petiolare)*, 47
'Licorice Splash', 47
'Lilac Wonder' tulips, 53
Lilacs, 117, 119–20
Lilies, 23, 54, 56–57, 62
Lily-of-the-valley shrub *(Pieris japonica)*,
    113, 114–15
Lime, 5, 185
Little leaf boxwood *(Buxus microphylla)*, 115
Lizards, 192
Loam, 1
Lobelia, 15, 22, 40, 49
Lobularia maritima (sweet alyssum),
    23–24, 48
Lonicera japonica (honeysuckle), 146, 151,
    153, 155
Lotus berthelotti ('Parrot's Beak' lotus vine), 46
'Love' roses, 88
Lychnis coronaria (rose campion), 67
Lysimachia congestiflora ('Outback
    Sunset'), 46

Ⓜ

Madonna lily, 23
Magnolia trees, 128
Manure, 4
Manure tea, 10
Marigolds, 21, 25, 40, 45
Mice, 184–85
Milorganite, 6, 165
Miniature roses, 93
Mock orange *(Philadelphus virginalis)*, 114
Moles, controlling
    building barriers, 182, 184
    making sure they're dead, 181
    planting ground covers, 182
    using lime, 185
    using pets, 182
    using traps, 182

Moonflower *(Ipomoea alba)*, 152
Morning glory, 152, 196
Motion detectors, 187
Mowing lawns, 169–70, 171, 172
Mulch
    around newly planted shrubs, 140
    benefits of using, 6
    definition of, 6
    on garden pathways, 7
    types of, 6–7
    using newspapers under, 6
    vs. ground covers, 140
    for weed control in perennials, 76
    weeds in, 193
Multiflora roses, 91
Mushroom compost, 4
Mushrooms, 9, 173
Myosotis (forget-me-not), 79
Myrtle *(Vinca minor)*, 146

chairs as plant containers, 26
cookie cutter annual beds, 45
dead trees as garden accents, 134
evergreen shrub topiaries, 113
ground cover "quilts," 139
growing a "lawn chair," 164
landscaping with weeds, 194
making free fertilizers, 10
mixing bulbs and annuals in pots,
    56–57
paint cans as pots, 25
stacking pots, 29–30
teacup gardens, 20
using a nightstand for garden
    storage, 34–35
using pot shards, 31
vines as living gazebos, 157
Overwatering, 18
Oxalis, 195

N. *See* Nitrogen (N)
Nematodes, bulb and stem, 59
Newspaper, 6, 10, 148
Nicotiana alata (flowering tobacco), 24
Nitrogen (N)
    on fertilizer labels, 9
    testing for, 2–3
Northwest Gardener's Resource Directory, 71

P. *See* Phosphorus (P)
Pachysandra (Japanese spurge), 141, 146
Paeonia (peonies), 69, 85–86
'Parrot's Beak' lotus vine *(Lotus*
    berthelotti), 46
Paths, weedless, 7
'Peace' roses, 88
Peat moss, 4
Peonies *(Paeonia),* 69, 85–86
Perennial plants
    allowing young plants to mature,
      80–81
    alongside driveways, 73
    bloom-less daylilies, 83
    bloom-less foxgloves, 83
    brittle delphinium stems, 83
    carefree, 68–69
    caring for, 75–78, 80–86
    challenges of delphiniums, 84
    as companions to roses, 97
    in containers, 74–75

Old-fashioned roses, 90–91, 99–100
Old garden roses, 92–93
Organic fertilizers. *See* Fertilizer
Oriental lilies, 23
Osier (osier or pussy willows), 110
Osier willows *(Osier),* 110
'Outback sunset' *(Lysimachia congestiflora),* 46
Outlandish Ideas
    bedstead rose gardens, 94
    cement culverts as planters, 74

controlling weeds, 76
cutting fern fronds, 76
dead hen and chickens, 83
diagnosing problems
    asters, 81
    bearded irises, 84–85
    peonies, 85–86
diseased hollyhocks, 84
dividing, 77, 80
dividing primroses, 77
extending the blooming season, 78
as ground covers, 138
herbaceous, 66
infected columbine leaves, 82
insuring easy maintenance, 75
leggy chrysanthemums, 82
longer-blooming, 79
for low damp spots, 71
mixing with annuals, 66
non-dividable, 77
planting in groups, 72
for poor soil, 70
preparing for winter, 75
pruning creeping phlox, 77
purchasing very specific varieties,
    68, 71
relieving overcrowding, 77–78
replanting divisions, 78, 80
selecting, 66–73
self-seeding, 67–68, 79
in shady spots, 70, 72, 73
shrubs and trees as, 65
siting, 69–73
for small gardens, 72
staggering bloom times, 82
staking Shasta daisies, 81
in sunny spots, 70, 72, 73
supporting Jacob's ladder plants, 81
unhealthy basket-of-gold plants, 82
unhealthy oriental poppies, 85
vs. annuals, 37–40, 65–66
Periwinkle (Vinca minor), 146
Perlite, 32

Pests
    ants, 86
    aphids, 106, 107–8, 135
    beetles, 189
    bulb and stem nematodes, 59
    bulb flies, 59
    bulb mites, 58, 59
    cats, 191, 193
    columbine leaf miner, 82
    craneflies, 189
    crows, 191
    debugging potting soil, 33
    deer, 186–87
    dogs, 172, 191
    ignoring, 190, 191
    leaf rollers, 120
    lizards, 192
    mice, 184–85
    moles, 181–85
    raccoons, 187
    rodents, 58–59, 60, 63, 181–85
    root weevils, 121–22
    slugs, 49, 61, 187–89
    snails, 49
    snakes, 192
    spiders, 190
    spittle bugs, 190
    squirrels, 60, 63, 183
    starlings, 191
    thrips, 60
    voles, 184–85
    whiteflies, 190
Petunias, purple, 48
pH levels, 2
Philadelphus virginalis (mock orange), 114
Phlox, 77, 78
Phosphorus (P)
    on fertilizer labels, 9
    testing for, 2–3
Pieris japonica (lily-of-the-valley shrub), 113,
    114–15
Pinching annuals, 44
Pine trees, 131

'Pink Peace' roses, 88
'PJM' rhododendrons, 116
Plant care. *See* Caring for plants
Plant locations. *See* Siting plants
Plant problems. *See* Caring for plants
Plant selection. *See* Selecting plants
Planting
 determining proper spacing, 17
 digging holes for new plants, 17
 releasing root balls, 18
 testing soil before, 2
 watering after, 18
Plastic tablecloths, as mulch, 197
Polemonium caeruleum (Jacob's ladder), 81
Potassium (K)
 on fertilizer labels, 9
 testing for, 2–3
Pots, gardening in. *See* Container gardens
Potting soil
 adding compost to, 32–33
 changing, 34
 choosing, 31–32
 debugging, 33
 in large pots, 36
 making your own, 32, 33
 perlite in, 32
 reusing, 32
Powdery mildew, 120
Primroses, 73, 77, 86
Primula japonica (candelabra primroses), 86
Primula juliae (Wanda), 86
Primula veris (yellow cowslips), 86
Privacy screens, 47, 158
Pruning
 clematis, 154
 creeping phlox, 77
 ground covers, 143
 hedges, 118, 120, 122
 honeysuckle vine, 155
 hydrangeas, 116–17
 lilacs, 117
 rhododendrons, 117
 roses, 89, 98, 100

 trees, 128, 129, 130
 using sheep shears for, 143
Pussy willows *(Osier)*, 110

Q

'Queen Elizabeth' roses, 88

R

Raccoons, 187
Rainbow bush *(Leucothoe fontanesiana)*, 110
Raised beds
 as an alternative to using poor soil, 6
 making, 7, 8
Rebar, 61, 151
'Red Riding Hood' tulips, 53
Red thread, 173
Redtwig dogwood *(Cornus stolonifera)*, 110
Rhododendrons, 2, 15, 112, 116, 117–18,
 121–22, 138, 140
Rodents, 58–59, 60, 63, 181–85
Root balls, 18
Root weevils, 121–22
Rosa rugosa, 91
Rose campion *(Lychnis coronaria)*, 67
Rose crown gall, 106–7
Rose mosaic virus, 106
Roses
 alongside driveways and patios, 96
 alongside picket fences, 96–97
 aphids on, 106, 107
 caring for, 98–108
 climber, 92
 demanding nature of, 101–3
 diagnosing diseases, 105–8
 disease-resistant, 87–88, 91, 93, 95
 diseased leaves, 105–6, 107
 easy-to-grow, 87–88, 91, 93
 fertilizing, 104, 105
 floribunda, 92
 fragrant, 95
 getting starts, 98, 99–100

grafted, 90
grandiflora, 92
ground cover underneath, 97
growths at the base of, 106–7
hardy, 105
hedge, 95
homemade fungicides for, 106, 108
hybrid tea, 88, 89–90, 92, 100
landscaping, 95
on low walls, 96
miniature, 93
moisture meters for, 102
multiflora, 91
old-fashioned, 90–91, 99–100
old garden, 92–93
perennials as companions to, 97
pruning, 89, 98, 100
purchasing, 93, 95
selecting, 87–93
in shady spots, 97
shrub, 90–91, 92, 95, 100
siting, 96–97
on slopes, 96
species, 93
suckers, 100
tree, 93
on trellises, 97
understanding rose labels, 90
watering, 103
wild, 91
winter protection for, 105
Roundup, 147, 179
Rugs, as mulch, 7, 197
Rust, 84

S

St. Johnswort (*Hypericum*), 142, 143, 146
Sandy soils, 1, 2, 5
Sarcococca, 114
Sawdust, 7
Scabiosa, 79
Scarlet runner beans, 47

Scorch, 59
Seaweed, 5
Sedums, 14, 15, 70, 73, 74, 77
Seed tape, 38
Selecting plants, 66–73
    analyzing your conditions, 13
    annuals, 40, 44, 46–48
    bulbs, tubers, and corms, 52–55
    for container gardens, 19–24
    finding drought-resistant plants, 14
    ground covers, 138–43
    for hot, dry sites, 14
    lawn seed, 162, 163, 164, 173
    observing neighbors, 14
    roses, 87–93
    for shady spots
        annual plants, 40
        bulbs, tubers, and corms, 54, 55
        container gardens, 22
        ground covers, 141, 142
        lawn seed, 163, 164, 173
        perennial plants, 70, 72, 73
        roses, 97
        shrubs, 111, 112–13, 114–15
        trees, 124
        types of plants to use, 14–15, 17
        vines, 151
    shrubs, 109–16
    for sunny spots
        annual plants, 40
        container gardens, 22, 23
        ground covers, 142
        perennial plants, 70, 72, 73
        shrubs, 110, 112
        trees, 123–24
        types of plants to use, 14–15
    trees, 123–28
    vines, 149–53
    visiting local nurseries, 13–14
Sempervivum (hen and chickens), 29, 83, 139
Shady spots, selecting plants for
    annual plants, 40
    bulbs, tubers, and corms, 54, 55

container gardens, 22
ground covers, 141, 142
lawn seed, 163, 164, 173
perennial plants, 70, 72, 73
roses, 97
shrubs, 111, 112–13, 114–15
trees, 124
types of plants to use, 14–15, 17
vines, 151
Shasta daisy, 73, 81
Sheep shears, 143
Shower curtains, as mulch, 197
Shrub fuchsia *(Fuchsia magellanica)*, 112
Shrub roses, 90–91, 92, 95, 100
Shrubs
adding non-living objects, 121
around house foundations, 111
carefree rhododendrons, 116
caring for, 116–22
close to your house, 109–10, 115
in dark, protected areas, 111
diagnosing hedge problems, 120–21
diagnosing lilac problems, 119–20
on dry, sunny hillsides, 110, 112
fragrant, 114
low maintenance hedges, 119
notched rhododendron leaves,
121–22
in poorly drained soil, 110
pruning
hedges, 118, 120, 122
hydrangeas, 116–17
lilacs, 117
rhododendrons, 117
selecting, 109–16
in shady spots, 111, 112–13, 114–15
siting, 109–16
topiary, 113
transplanting rhododendrons, 118
Siting plants
annuals, 40
ground covers, 138–43
perennials, 69–73

roses, 96–97
shrubs, 109–16
trees, 123–29, 131
vines, 149–53
Siting your garden
finding convenient spaces, 16
moving leggy plants, 17
moving sunburned plants, 17
moving unhealthy plants, 16
throwing away plants, 16
Slugs, 49, 61, 187–89
Snails, 49
Snakes, 192
Snapdragons *(Antirrhinum)*, 24, 48
Sod. *See* Lawns
Soil
acidic, 2
alkaline, 2
checking for quality, 1
clay, 1, 2, 5
color, 1
for container gardens, 31–33, 36
drainage, 1, 5
fertility, 1–2
improving
adding soil amendments, 4, 5
with compost, 3, 4, 5, 7
layering organic matter, 3, 4
loam, 1
sandy, 1, 2, 5
texture, 1–2
using existing soil, 3–4
Soil, potting. *See* Potting soil
Soil testing
to determine pH level, 2
to measure nutrient levels, 3
before planting, 2
Species roses, 93
Spiders, 190
Spittle bugs, 190
Spot composting, 5
Squirrels, 60, 63, 183
St. Johnswort *(Hypericum)*, 142, 143, 146

Stakes, 61, 129
Starlings, 191
Streambeds, dry rock, 2
Summer lilac *(Buddleia davidii),* 114
Summer lilies, 23
Sunburn, on plants, 17
Sunny spots, selecting plants for
    annual plants, 40
    container gardens, 22, 23
    ground covers, 142
    perennial plants, 70, 72, 73
    shrubs, 110, 112
    trees, 123–24
    types of plants to use, 14–15
Sweet alyssum *(Lobularia maritima),* 23–24,
    40, 48
Sweet box, 114
Sweet William *(Dianthus barbatus),* 48, 79
Sweet woodruff, 141
Synthetic fertilizers. *See* Fertilizer

T

Tanglefoot, 191
'Tarda' tulips, 53
'Terrace lime' sweet potato vine *(Ipomoea
    batatas),* 46
Thrips, 60
Thymes, 14, 73, 74
Tickseed *(Coreopsis grandiflora),* 79
Tree roses, 93
Trees
    alongside driveways and
      sidewalks, 126
    aphids on birch trees, 135
    caring for, 129–35
    colorful accent, 128
    contorted filberts, 132
    diagnosing cherry tree problems, 133
    diagnosing dogwood tree problems,
      134–35
    disease-resistant dogwoods, 127, 129
    fertilizing, 131, 132

flowering cherry trees, 125–26
foolproof, 127
as gifts, 124
keeping pine trees compact, 131
under large firs, 124
magnolia trees, 128
naming, 125
for poorly drained soil, 128
pruning, 128, 129, 130
selecting, 123–28
and septic systems, 124
for shady spots, 124
sight-obscuring, 126
siting, 123–29, 131
staking newly planted trees, 129
for sunny spots, 123–24
with surface roots, 126
using dead trees, 134
watering young trees, 133
Trumpet vine *(Campsis radicans),* 153
Tubers. *See* Bulbs, tubers, and corms
'Tulip Toronto' tulips, 53
Tulips, 53, 58, 63

V

Vegetables, water from boiling, 10
Verticillium wilt, 133
Viburnum carlcephalum (fragrant
    snowball), 114
Vinca minor (myrtle or periwinkle), 74, 140,
    141, 146, 171
Vinca major, 141, 146, 171
Vinegar, 195, 196
Vines
    aggressive, fast-growing, 149
    annual, 151
    building frames for, 151
    caring for, 153–58
    clematis, 149, 150, 152–53, 153–54
    covering buildings with, 156
    as fence covers, 158
    flowering, 151

getting wisteria to bloom, 151,
   154, 155
honeysuckle, 151, 153, 155
hydrangeas, 151
kid structures as supports for, 156
as living gazebos, 157
moonflower, 152
morning glory, 152
as privacy screens, 158
pruning clematis, 154
pruning honeysuckle, 155
selecting, 149–53
for shady spots, 151
siting, 149–53
starting clematis up trees, 149
supports for clematis, 150
as a way to attract
   hummingbirds, 153
Voles, 184–85

Wanda *(Primula juliae)*, 86
Watering
   adding organic matter to reduce, 15
   after planting, 18
   droopy leaves and, 18
   general guide for, 103
   grouping plants, 15
   lawns, 168–69
   overwatering, 18
   roses, 103
   selecting drought-resistant plants, 14
   using mulch to reduce, 15
   young trees, 133
Weeds
   horsetail, 196
   landscaping with, 194
   from manure, 4
   morning glory, 196
   in mulch, 193
   oxalis, 195
   smothering, 193

   using weed barriers, 197
   vinegar as a weed killer, 195, 196
   See also Lawns
Whiteflies, 190
White Flower Farm, 71
Whitney Farms, 4, 32, 165
Winged Weeder, 193
Wintergreen, 141
Winter protection
   bulbs, tubers, and corms, 64
   perennials, 75
   roses, 105
Wisteria, 151, 154, 155

Yak rhododendrons, 116
Yellow cowslips *(Primula veris)*, 86

Zinc, 9
"Zoo doo," 4